A Photographic Guide to the

BIRDS

OF INDONESIA

Morten Strange

CHRISTOPHER HELM
LONDON

NATUNAS

KALIMANTAN

1

2

3

8

4

9

5

SUMATERA

6

10

11

7

I N D O N

13

JAVA

BALI

S

LOMBOK

LIST OF SMALLER ISLANDS :

01 : SIMEULEUWE	16 : WETAR
02 : BANYAK/TAPAH	17 : LETI
03 : NIAS	18 : MOA
04 : BATU/PINI	19 : BABAR
05 : SIBERUT/SIPURA	20 : KAI
06 : NORTH/SOUTH PAGAI	21 : SANGIHE
07 : ENGGANO	22 : TALAUD
08 : RIAU	23 : BANGGAI
09 : LINGGA	24 : SULA
10 : BANGKA	25 : BACAN
11 : BELITUNG	26 : OBI
12 : BAWEAN	27 : MISOOL
13 : KANGEAN	28 : WAIGEO
14 : ALOR	29 : BIAK
15 : ROTI	30 : YAPEN

Published 2002 by Christopher Helm, an imprint of A&C Black Publishers Ltd., 37 Soho Square, London W1D 3QZ

ISBN 0-7136-6404-5

A CIP catalogue record for this book is available from the British Library.

A & C Black uses paper produced with elemental chlorine-free pulp, harvested from managed sustainable forests.

Printed in Singapore

10 9 8 7 6 5 4 3 2 1

CONTENTS

CONTENTS

Acknowledgements

My close association with Indonesia over 20 years has enriched my life in many ways. Here I have met some of the finest, most hard-working, honest and gentle people imaginable, and my sincere hope for the country is that these are the people who will prevail, to see this great nation successfully through the years ahead.

First, I would like to thank Eric Oey and the staff at Periplus Editions for making this book possible. The publisher's ambitious task of producing a comprehensive photographic coverage of the birds of Southeast Asia and Indonesia in two volumes has been completed. *A Photographic Guide to the Birds of Southeast Asia, including the Philippines and Borneo* and this volume feature all of the significant bird species from south China to the island of New Guinea, many of which have been shown in photographs for the first time. Most have been recorded on location in the field. While researching this book in 1998, it soon became obvious that some photographs would be very difficult to come by. Many Indonesian species had never been photographed, especially those found only in Nusa Tenggara and West Papua. The only way to obtain photos of these birds was to travel to those locations, which I did later that year. This trip was coordinated through BirdLife International and supported financially by the Loke Wan Tho Memorial Foundation.

A female Hooded Cuckoo-shrike *Coracina longicauda* at nest in New Guinea.

Loke Wan Tho

Loke Wan Tho

Friendly Fantail (see page 301) at nest.

The works of the late Loke Wan Tho, businessman and bird photographer, have been a great inspiration to me. The two stunning photographs on pages 7 and 8, taken on a visit to New Guinea, demonstrate his exceptional technical ability and a remarkable affinity and respect for his subjects. I would like to thank his family for their support, especially that of his charming sister, Lady Yuen-Peng McNeice.

I would like to single out the garrison captain at Wamena, in West Papua, for special mention. He overruled the decision of the police and allowed me to do a very productive hike from Lake Habbema to Ibele in the Snow Mountains (with two bodyguards in tow, armed with Indonesian-made M16 rifles, see page 21). Also, the Chief of Security with the police in Manokwari (West Papua) deserves thanks. His assistance in obtaining travel permits for the Arfak Mountains was crucial to the success of my venture. Many people guided and assisted me in West Papua, but I would especially like to thank Ebanus Wenda in Wamena, who worked from dawn to dusk to find spectacular species, and who turned out to be a gourmet cook! Countless other helpful persons assisted with the trip, far too many to mention here.

Paul Jepson was carrying out a survey of the Bali Starling in the Bali Barat National Park together with Dr. Bas van Balen when I met him some ten years ago. He was just a young kid, fresh out of school, struggling to learn

Bahasa Indonesia and dreaming about establishing a branch of BirdLife International in Indonesia. When I later visited him in 1994, his vision had materialised—he was behind a desk at BirdLife International's office in Bogor. Paul is now one of the world's experts on Indonesian birds and the principal author of *Birding Indonesia* (Periplus Editions 1997). I would like to congratulate Paul on his success and thank him for his support.

Dr. Richard Grimmett, who has now taken over Paul Jepson's position, did much to help with the 1998 project, and Dwi Lesmana and Raf Drijvers worked tirelessly to find appropriate birds for me to photograph in the field. And just two months before this book's deadline, my long-time bird-watching friend, Lim Kim Chuah took me to a superb location and helped photograph four important Sunda subregion species, the Black-and-yellow Broadbill, the Black-and-red Broadbill, the Malaysian Blue Flycatcher and the Crested Jay—all in one day!

Many have offered advice and assistance in the preparation and production of this book, too many to mention here by name, but their efforts were very much appreciated all the same. I would, however, particularly like to thank Dr. Bas van Balen, Dr. Elizabeth Fox, Kelly Hague, Kelvin Lim, Lim Kim Keang, Lim Kim Seng, Ng Bee Choo, Shelagh Tonkyn and Colin Trainor.

Not least I would like to acknowledge the photographers who assisted with additional images. They in fact made this book possible, since photographs from these outside sources make up twenty-one per cent of the systematic coverage. The photo credits speak for themselves, but I would especially like to thank Bernard van Elegem, Alan OwYong, Dr. Margaret Kinnaird, Jon Hornbuckle and Filip Verbelen.

The energetic and resourceful Ong Kiem Sian put her best photos at my disposal as usual. Dawn and Clifford Frith, Brian Coates and Alain Compost are all professional photographers and I would like to thank them especially for allowing me access to the very rare and significant frames selected for this book.

And, finally, many thanks to those photographers who provided one or a few images–these were a vital contribution as well. Every image is important and every photograph helped make this coverage by far the most comprehensive documentation of Indonesian birdlife that has been produced to date.

INTRODUCTION

Birding Indonesia, edited by Paul Jepson and Rosie Ounsted (Periplus Editions, 1997), provides an excellent introduction to this volume. This guidebook includes a list and descriptions of all bird families found in Indonesia and provides comprehensive preparation for any visitor or local wishing to enjoy Indonesia's diverse birdlife.

Birdwatchers in Indonesia are fortunate because so many islands and areas are still relatively unexplored and many bird studies still need to be done. Every year, new and exciting information surfaces. In 1997 a new species was recorded for Indonesia when two tourists spotted a Sooty Oystercatcher, *Haematopus fuliginosus*, on a Bali beach, most likely a vagrant from Australia.

In 1996 even more important discoveries were made on the small islands of Talaud and Sangihe north of Sulawesi, when three species new to world science were found. Although scientists had visited these remote islands previously, some in the last century, they had overlooked these more elusive birds. This truly astonishing development shows just how much research remains to be done in this country.

Birding Techniques

Birdwatching can be enjoyed without much equipment, but a good pair of binoculars definitely helps. Since binoculars have few mechanical components, a pair should last you a long time—probably a lifetime, unless you lose them, since the top brands give a 30-year guarantee. So you might as well select the best pair you can possibly afford, then you won't waste money upgrading later. Selecting the appropriate pair can be difficult because there are so many brands and types available on the market. Consult an experienced birdwatcher or a dealer that you trust.

There are vast differences in optical quality. Good resolution, clarity and colour reproduction are vital and you usually get what you pay for. Binoculars are described with two numbers; the first is the magnification and the second is the front lens diameter in millimetres. Using a 10x40 pair, a bird ten metres away would look as if it were one metre away, and the 4 cm lenses should give a reasonably bright image. A 7x42 pair will produce a smaller but significantly brighter image.

Many experienced birdwatchers also carry a telescope, although it is slower to operate, since a tripod is required to keep it steady. The eye-piece is interchangeable and allows for different magnifications. Quality telescopes have fixed magnifications in the range of 20–30 times and some zoom to 60x, but then the image is not as clear. A 'scope' is useful in open country and at remote mudflats, and can be used to pick out stationary forest birds. It is especially handy in a group because more people can take turns watching, once the bird is in the frame.

Birdwatching is a social exercise. The BirdLife International Indonesia Programme has established a network of bird clubs in Java, Sumatra and Maluku that conduct training courses and publish the newsletter *Warta IBA*. In October, each year, these groups participate in the World Bird Count. If you are a beginner, try to attend these and other outings, since you will be introduced to the best locations in your area. If you go bird-watching alone, bring a small notepad and take notes on any bird you cannot recognise right away. Look for diagnostic features such as bill and tail shape and distinct colour bands around head and/or wings, and write down what you see. You can always consult your field guide later, once the bird has flown off.

As you become more experienced you will find that bird identifica-tion is often done quickly, using the so-called 'jizz' of the bird. This slang expression that birders use is derived from 'gis', which stands for General Impression and Shape in US Air Force terminology. The jizz of that small grey garden bird hopping through the bushes lets you know right away that it is a warbler of some kind. Then, as you examine it more closely, you will find that the two distinct white bars in the wing indicate that it is a Bar-winged Prinia, which is only found in Indonesia.

Some birdwatchers keep databases of all their observations, and most importantly, a world list of all the species seen. Before you know it, adding to this list becomes a compulsive urge, and a so-called 'twitcher' (a birdwatcher who travels the globe in relentless pursuit of new bird species) is born.

Other birdwatchers carry tape recorders and collect bird calls. Many scientists in Indonesia are very good at this and deposit their new recordings with the British Library of Wildlife Sounds (BLOWS) in London. In the dense forest habitat of the tropics, doing surveys by call greatly improves your efficiency. You can tell exactly what species are out there, far from the trails and high in the canopies, without having to look for them.

Photographing Birds

Photographing birds is difficult and expensive, but it can be done, and if you produce worthwhile results, you can recover your expenses from picture sales.

To get the best pictures, do not move around too much. Find a location where the bird density seems promising and where the birds come into the open for good views. Then wait or hide at a fruiting or flowering tree, a forest clearing, a pool of water, a nest or some other place that will attract one or more birds. It is better to cover two species with perfect quality shots than to cover twenty species with mediocre photos.

Photographed birds appear without the artificial background or artistic inaccuracies in proportion and colour that are sometimes present in illustrations, and usually look just as they would when encountered in the field. Photographs are an invaluable reference, especially when attempting to identify groups with many similar species, such as shorebirds, bulbuls, babblers, whistlers, white-eyes and honeyeaters.

Documentation

Apart from binoculars, a birdwatcher must have a field guide to successfully pursue his/her hobby. This guide should identify all the birds in the area and these should be illustrated in colour. Fortunately, Indonesia is well provided with field guides.

Exotic Borneo and West Papua were the first areas to be covered with complete field guides. Beehler, Pratt and Zimmerman's *Birds of New Guinea* (1986) is still the most appropriate for West Papua. Until recently, any traveller to Sumatra had to identify his sightings from Marle & Voous (1988), which is just a checklist with no illustrations or descriptions. For populated Java even this rudimentary tool was not available. When MacKinnon and Phillipps' *A Field Guide to the Birds of Borneo, Sumatra, Java and Bali* (1993) was published, this problem was solved. And in 1997 when Coates and Bishop's *Birds of Wallacea* was released, the whole of the Indonesian archipelago was finally covered. Now you can travel the 5,000 kilometres from west to east with just these three guide books in your luggage.

This volume is an important supplement to these three major field guides, since the nation is treated as an entity. The photographs will take you from the swamps of Sumatra, across the remote islands of Tanimbar and Biak, to the tree limit in the Snow Mountains of West Papua. The maps will help illustrate the way the fauna is distributed within the regions and the subregions.

Several new, smaller regional guides published by Oxford University Press and New Holland provide limited additional information based on drawings or photographs. Paul Andrew's *The Birds of Indonesia: A Checklist (Peters' sequence)* (1992), an overall view of all Indonesian species, was a major breakthrough when it came out.

Habitats

One of the most fascinating aspects of birdwatching is how the birdlife changes with habitat. However, habitats often alter gradually, and some birds can occur in several different habitat types. For instance birds such as the Oriental White-eye can be found in mangroves, gardens and in montane rainforest.

Even the definition of a habitat is sometimes ambiguous. Because of the many types of lowland forest in this country, a forest bird in wet and lush Sumatra has different requirements than a forest bird in arid Timor. However, knowing approximately which birds to expect within each habitat type makes the identification of many species much easier.

Four main habitat categories apply for Indonesia—the Coast, Disturbed Habitats, Lowland Forest and Montane Forest. The **Coast** is a relatively well-defined area. The birds found here are mostly from the 'primitive' non-passerine groups and depend largely on food from the sea and mudflats. A rich mix of light mud and nutrients is generated where a freshwater source joins the tidal sea, creating extremely fertile habitats. The enormous expanse of tidal mudflats off southeastern Sumatra is one such habitat, but there are several around Java, Sulawesi, Kalimantan and in many other areas.

Extensive mangrove forests grow along such sheltered shores, but this terrain is extremely difficult to traverse and to survey. Often it is best to approach by sea to observe the mudflats and mangrove forests.

Resident herons feed in this habitat in large numbers, and in remote areas possibly the stenotopic specialists such as storks, pelicans and the Beach Thick-knee as well. Rails often venture out onto mudflat edges and kingfishers perch nearby. However, mostly migrant birds, especially shorebirds, are found in this particular habitat. Over fifty different members of the Charadriidae and Scolopacidae families (plovers, sandpipers, etc.) occur in Indonesia, and almost all are visitors from the huge landmasses in temperate and arctic East Asia, where they breed during the short, northern summer. In fact, they spend more time in their winter quarters in Indonesia than they do at their nesting grounds.

Since Indonesia is a nation of islands, there are plenty of sea birds, although there are some indications that they might be in decline. You might be disappointed if you look for gulls, however. I have spent much time on oil rigs in the Java Sea and on ferries and small boats around many islands, yet I have never seen a gull in Indonesia. There are four on the checklist, but they are all rare or vagrant and none breed here, a surprising difference compared with nearby Australia or East Asia.

However, terns are everywhere and usually frigatebirds as well—the Lesser Frigatebird will even fly across land near the coast. If you are lucky you may spot a tropicbird, a booby or a migratory shearwater. Many terns and frigatebirds are mainly pelagic; tropicbirds and boobies are even more so. They are rarely seen near the coast, except when they come in to breed on remote islets far from the main islands and people. Raptors like the White-bellied Sea-eagle and Brahminy Kite often fish in the sea near the coast in spectacular fashion.

Where there are people, there are **Disturbed Habitats**. These include gardens, parks and cultivated areas, from cities to villages. Open country and wet freshwater areas, which blend into other disturbed rural environs in Indonesia, are also included in this category.

The gardens and parks of western Indonesia are dominated by the Yellow-vented Bulbul, Sooty-headed Bulbul, Coppersmith Barbet, Common Iora, Pied Fantail, Magpie Robin, Olive-backed Sunbird, and some tailorbirds, flowerpeckers and kingfishers. Those that have adapted well to more open areas include the Spotted Dove, the Zitting and Golden-headed Cisticola, Dollarbird, Lesser Coucal, Long-tailed Shrike and many munias and bee-eaters; swallows and swifts. The White-breasted Waterhen and Cinnamon Bittern are always found near wet areas, where weavers and warblers often inhabit the grasses. Most other rails and ducks require extensive marshes with plenty of vegetation cover and a fairly large water surface. Some of these species extend into eastern Indonesia, but many new ones also appear, specific to these regions, such as the Black Sunbird and many pigeons, cuckoo-shrikes, white-eyes and honeyeaters. The Spotted Kestrel and Black-winged Kite are typical open country raptors in much of Indonesia.

Disturbed habitats and open countryside attract numerous migrants, typically from temperate or subtropical regions, so these species shy away from dense rainforest and settle in more open places, often near the coastlines they follow on their travels. Watch for the Fork-tailed Swift, Rainbow Bee-eater, Barn Swallow, Brown Shrike and some wagtails and flycatchers, but these are only found during certain months of the year.

Wooded cultivated areas are also disturbed habitats. Here the bird mix is different and more arboreal birds occur. In fact, forest birds often turn up in mature plantations bordering forest. The plantations cannot sustain them permanently, but commercial trees provide some morning feeding opportunities. In Western Indonesia, some pigeons, barbets, woodpeckers and other groups venture out into forest edges and nearby cultivation to feed. In Wallacea, parrots often fly into coconut trees and other crops and ornamental trees, to chew on flowers and fruits. In West Papua, the Lesser, the Greater and the Superb Bird of Paradise feed in fruiting trees near villages. These birds will retreat back into the nearby forest later in the day to rest, and mostly depend on primary forest for breeding sites.

The **Lowland Forests** provide the richest habitat of all in Indonesia. More birds can be found here than in any other environment and most are sedentary residents that can be found all year. A great number of these birds are endemic to one or a few islands within the country. Please see the next chapter for a brief definition of the main forest types.

Birdwatching in the forest is the most difficult birdwatching there is. In rainforest, the trees grow to 30 metres or more in height and the foliage is massive. Less than two percent of sunlight reaches the forest floor, so the light is dim at ground level. The birds here are shy and difficult even to spot, so good views are few and far between. But then again, birding in this habitat is also the most rewarding. So many different species are found here, but most of them are scarce, which means that you are likely to see different species on each trip into the forest.

Pheasants, hornbills, barbets, woodpeckers, broadbills, bulbuls, leafbirds and babblers are some of the families that dominate the rainforest in the west. Very few of these cross Wallace's Line. In the east the forest is dominated by cuckoo-shrikes, monarchs, fantails, whistlers, white-eyes and honeyeaters, and, in West Papua, by bowerbirds and birds of paradise as well. Pigeons, owls, thrushes, flycatchers, flowerpeckers, drongos and crows are well represented in both regions.

As you travel higher, the avifauna changes. At 900 metres you enter the **Montane Forest** and with that comes a totally different set of birds. This astonishing transformation is one of the highlights of birdwatching in Indonesia. In West Papua, it is possible to travel almost continuously along the north coast, from the lowland rainforest at sea level to the summit of Gunung Trikora at 4,743 metres, where snow falls. The trip takes a week or so, but can be compared to travelling from the Equator to the arctic. It is interesting that Gunung Trikora had a permanent ice-cap until quite recently, the last of it disappearing only 50 years ago. Gunung Jaya further west at 5,030 metres still has a glacier.

All subregions in Indonesia and almost all islands have elevated areas that support different habitats. Within the so-called 'ring of fire' (in Sumatra, Java, Nusa Tenggara, Flores, and in northern Sulawesi and Maluku), mountain peaks are mainly actively volcanic. In Kalimantan and West Papua, the mountains are older, uplifted sediment formations.

Insect life is abundant at montane elevations, especially in the lower montane forest from 900 to 1,800 metres, and in the tall moss forest at higher elevations as well. Insectivorous bird families (babblers in the west, white-eyes in the east, warblers and flycatchers) are especially well represented, but almost all the other forest bird families (bulbuls, broadbills in the West, honeyeaters, whistlers and birds of paradise in the East, cuckoo-shrikes, thrushes, fantails, pigeons and flowerpeckers) have one or a few representatives in the mountains.

Some of the most accessible mountains and the highest peaks on the major islands are shown in the table on the opposite page. The higher reaches of the upper montane habitat, above 2,400 metres, is dominat-

Island/Area	Peak	Elevation (metres a.s.l.)
Sumatra	Gunung Leuser	3,140
	Gunung Kerinci	3,800
Kalimantan	Gunung Niyut	1,701
	Gunung Liangpran	2,240
	Gunung Raya	2,278
	Gunung Guguang	2,467
Java	Gunung Gede	2,958
	Gunung Pangrango	3,019
	Gunung Bromo	2,329
	Gunung Semeru	3,676
Bali	Gunung Batur	1,717
	Gunung Agung	3,142
Lombok	Gunung Rinjani	3,726
Sumbawa	Gunung Tambora	2,851
Flores	Gunung Ranaka	2,140
	Keli Mutu	1,640
	Poco Mandasawu	2,350
Timor (West)	Gunung Mutis	2,427
Timor (East)	Gunung Mau Lau	2,963
Sumba	Wanggameti	1,225
Sulawesi	Gunung Malino	2,443
	Gunung Tumpu	2,400
	Gunung Baleasi	3,016
	Gunung Rantemario	3,478
Halmahera	Gunung Saolat	1,508
West Papua	Arfak Mountains	2,970
	Gunung Trikora	4,743
	Gunung Jaya	5,030

ed by smaller and lower trees, which become gradually more stunted as you travel higher. There are obviously fewer bird species here. However, those birds that do occur at higher altitudes, are only found there. Many have developed endemic forms, and, since they face less competition, they are often locally numerous. The vegetation is more open and the birds are active most of the day and sometimes quite confiding. The climate is pleasant, so the mountains can be an exciting place to birdwatch.

The vegetation that occurs above 3,000 metres is mainly bushes, with small trees in sheltered places. The air is bitterly cold at night and walking uphill in the thin air is a struggle. Above 3,200 metres the habitat is alpine and above 3,600 there are only low bushes, grasses and rocks. Few birds venture above this height, but in New Guinea the Alpine Pipit has been recorded to 4,500 metres. Climbing enthusiasts can look out for the

Elevation (m)	Sumatra	Sulawesi	New Guinea
500	78	n/a	n/a
600	n/a	70	n/a
1,000	60	n/a	138
1,500	54	n/a	137
1,600	n/a	50	n/a
2,000	25	n/a	n/a
2,200	n/a	30	n/a
2,500	22	n/a	80
3,000	13	n/a	n/a
3,500	6	n/a	26

Indonesian endemic Snow Mountain Robin, *Petroica archboldi*, restricted to the zone between 3,850 and 4,150 metres on the two highest peaks, but few people have seen this bird and it is not illustrated in this volume.

The table above, which shows the number of bird species at certain elevations, was compiled from our three main references. The numbers refer to the approximate number of species recorded. Here Sulawesi is represented by Lore Lindu National Park and New Guinea refers to the eastern part of the island that is not West Papua.

The Bird Year

Seasonal variations occur, even in tropical Indonesia, and the birdlife is not the same year round. During the northern winter, migrants from the north pass through or settle to spend the season, especially in coastal areas. These visitors appear mainly from September to April, although some migrants can turn up at any month of the year. To a lesser extent, southern parts of West Papua and Wallacea attract some Australian residents during the southern winter (July–August), but these are much more sporadic in number, and very few make it into western Indonesia.

Most resident birds in Indonesia are sedentary. A few species such as sea birds shift away from the breeding grounds, in nomadic movements during the non-breeding season, but in general, the resident birds do not move out of the country. In fact, they probably don't move far at all. Some small stenotopic rainforest birds never transfer out of a small home territory within a certain section and level of the forest.

In Equatorial areas, rainfall and temperature are remarkably even throughout the year, although there is typically a somewhat wetter season during the northeast monsoon (November–March). In the Sunda subregion, most insectivorous birds breed toward the end of the wet season, at the beginning of the year (March–May). Water birds prefer the wet conditions early in the year, while fruit eaters breed slightly later, and open country species and seed eaters such as the munias breed toward the end of the dry season. Little breeding goes on in November and December.

In the area of the monsoon belt that is affected by the Australian rain shadow (see Figure 6, page 33) there is a distinct dry season from April to September. Here breeding patterns have been little studied, as is the case throughout the Wallacea subregion. However studies from Flores indicate a peak of breeding activity at the end of the wet season (April–May) and little activity during December and January, much as in the Sunda subregion.

In West Papua, weather patterns are highly localised depending on the contours of the terrain. Breeding can occur during any month of the year, but often seems to occur just prior to the rainy season.

Nests are difficult to find in the tropics, since many birds build high in remote forest areas and within dense foliage. Even so, the breeding season can be an interesting time for the birdwatcher, because males tend to defend their territory more aggressively and call more often. The birds are also somewhat bolder and easier to observe at this time. Toward the end of the breeding season, juveniles appear and add to the activity. Passerines typically feed their young for some time after they fledge, and many nesting and breeding records have been established by observing the feeding. Otherwise, the nests would be nearly impossible to locate.

Although vast local variations occur, November through February (and especially the month of December) seems to be the period with the highest rainfall throughout Indonesia. Avoid planning too much fieldwork and camping during the month of December, as the conditions are simply too difficult and the birds are at their most elusive. Go out early in the year, once the rains have come to an end. The resident birds breed then, are vocal and active, and some migrants are passing through. Alternatively, plan your trip toward the end of the dry season (September–October), before the heavy rains, just when the northern migrants arrive.

Places to Go

Indonesia is the world's largest archipelago—from the capital of Jakarta to the provincial capital of West Papua (formerly known as Irian Jaya), Jayapura, it is a staggering 3,500 kilometres. Flying to Jayapura from Jakarta, with stop-overs, takes most of a day and is equivalent to flying from Singapore to Bombay, from London to Bagdad or from New York to Bogota, Colombia.

Of the 17,000 islands that make up the archipelago, only 600 are inhabited. Eighty per cent of Indonesia's 210 million people live in the western half—115 million on Java, 40 million on Sumatra, 11 million on Kalimantan and 3 million on Bali. In the east, Maluku and West Papua have only 2 million inhabitants each. Although the population density is 850 persons per square kilometre on Java, the population density is just five persons per square kilometre in West Papua.

Most of Indonesia's endemic bird species occur in the east. Some major zoogeographical subdivisions exist within the country, as explained in the next chapter. The table below, which has been extracted from Andrew (1992), Mason & Jarvis (1989) and Periplus Editions (1998), lists all major Indonesian islands and territories, and the number of bird species that can be found there. Major sites refer briefly to protected areas most visited and studied; see Jepson & Ounsted (1997) for more details. Endemics refer to species found only in this country, not species shared with neighbouring East Malaysia or Papua New Guinea.

Territory	Size(sq km)	Species	Endemics	Major sites
Indonesia	1,948,700	1,531	381	(see regions)
Sumatra	473,481	600	37	Gunung Leuser in the north, Kerinci for montane birds and Way Kambas for lowland birds.
Kalimantan	549,032	479	5	Tanjung Puting for forest birds.
Java	135,000	498	59	Ujung Kulon (west) and Baluran (east), Gunung Gede-Pangrango for montane birds.
Bali	5,600	313	28	Bali Barat National Park and Bedugul.
Sulawesi	227,000	380	115	Lore Lindu, Tangkoko and Bogani Nani Wartabone National Park for endemics.
Maluku	85,100	344	96	Halmahera and Manusela National Park on Seram.
Nusa Tenggara	173,000	398	104	Sumba, Flores and Timor for endemics.
West Papua	421,981	647	52	Arfak Mountains and Wamena for montane birds, Lake Sentani and Wasur National Park for lowland birds.

The author and his guides, porters and bodyguards near Lake Habbema, West Papua.

However, some country endemics will obviously be shared between islands. Of Bali's 28 Indonesian endemics, only one (the Bali Starling) is restricted to that island. The other 27 are shared with Java and/or Nusa Tenggara.

Conservation

For an expert evaluation of the status of bird conservation in Indonesia see Jepson & Ounsted (1997). There is really not much to add, except that conservation in this country seems to be directed in two distinct directions—toward the common birds and toward the rare birds.

The 'common' birds are not doing very well in Indonesia. In fact, few species are as common as they could or should be, and this opinion is held by many observers who visit this country. "Birds in the Javan countryside are depressingly scarce in both numbers and diversity", writes John MacKinnon, a veteran expert on Southeast Asian environmental matters, in MacKinnon & Phillipps (1993). Judging from most reports, 'Javan' could be replaced with 'Indonesian'. An expert ornithologist, the late Derek Holmes, saw just one Spotted Kestrel and not a single Black-winged Kite during 18 days of survey in prime habitat of West Java, where these birds should be abundant. During a six-day visit to Kaliman-tan, covering 200 kilometres, he saw no hornbills except for two Asian Pied Hornbills, which are known to be tolerant to habitat disturbance (*Kukila*, Volume 8, p. 1–2). Dr. Bas van Balen laments the almost complete disappearance of the Brahminy Kite from Java (*Forktail*, No. 8, p. 83–88).

In *Birds of Bali*, Victor Mason writes, "So many visitors to Bali have remarked to me on the paucity of birds in general", and he goes on to describe a rapid decline of common birds since he started observing in 1974. While Mason attributes the decline to air-gun hunting and capture for the bird trade, Holmes thinks that excessive use of pesticides in cul-tivated areas is to blame.

However, there are some indications that the decline can be reversed. Adaptable birds near disturbed and cultivated areas have the capacity to recover, although in the tropics where broods are small and often preyed upon, they recover slowly. After air-gun hunting was banned on Bali in 1993, the common garden birds seem to have recovered moderately. I found birds in better densities and generally more approachable when I visited the island in 1997, and Victor Mason agrees.

This anecdotal evidence needs to be supported by thorough surveys of species and habitats. BirdLife International Indonesia Programmes have established a network of volunteer groups to survey all important bird areas. This could be extended into a full atlas survey, mapping all resident birds nationwide, as has been accomplished in many developed countries.

The other aspect of bird conservation is preserving the rare, endemic and globally threatened species for which Indonesia has a special inter-national responsibility. Indonesia is home to 17 percent of the earth's bird species, even though it makes up only 1.3 percent of the earth's land area. No country in the world has more national endemic birds— Indonesian has 381 and Australia is number two with 351. However, no country has more globally threatened species—Indonesia has 104 and Brazil has 103. Near-threatened and data deficient Indonesian species total 286, 18.7 percent of all Indonesian birds. Of the 381 endemics, 170 are also at risk. In visual terms, the birds population of Indonesia could be presented as shown in the figure on page 23.

Even though this book mainly features the easy-to-see species, no less than 127 of these are Indonesian endemics. Thirty of these birds are

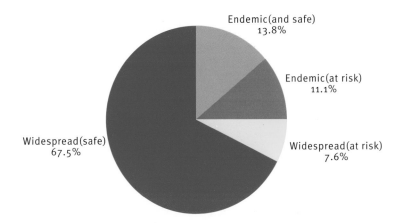

Endemic(and safe)
13.8%

Endemic(at risk)
11.1%

Widespread(at risk)
7.6%

Widespread(safe)
67.5%

globally threatened and a further thirty-five fall into the near-threatened category, which is nine percent of the species covered.

The conservation of the earth's biodiversity is an international concern and its protection should be an international effort. Fortunately, Indonesia is willing to work with outside agencies, accepting funding and technical expertise to carry out surveys and document the results. This work is carried out in cooperation with the Directorate General of Forest Protection and Nature Conservation, PKA (formerly known as PHPA), which has offices all over the country.

The selection of the 104 species considered to be globally threatened with extinction and the selection of an additional 152 species to be categorised as near-threatened, as a result of the 1994 BirdLife International survey, was a fairly delicate exercise. Please see *Birds to Watch* 2 (1994) by Nigel Collar et al., and Derek Holmes' subsequent review in *Kukila*, Volume 8, p. 161–164 (1996). More data on most of Indonesia's elusive endemic and endangered birds is desperately needed.

BirdLife International has made the decision to target a few important species for special conservation projects: the Bali Starling, Javan Hawk-eagle, Yellow-crested Cockatoo, Java Sparrow and Straw-headed Bulbul, but many more species should be investigated and assisted. A Red Data Book for all of Asia is due out in the year 2001, which will include updated information for Indonesia, which will help in setting priorities.

HOW TO USE THIS BOOK

Area Covered

In this section of the book, we have adopted the generally accepted system of dividing the world into 6 zoogeographical or faunal regions. Modified from Viney, Phillipps and Lam (1994), and as with Strange (2000), the regions are shown on the map below.

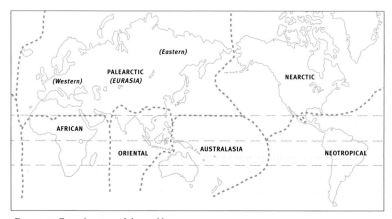

Figure 1: *Faunal regions of the world*

Regions	Subregions
Australasian	Australia, New Zealand, New Guinea and Oceanic Islands
African	Africa and Madagascar
Neotropical	Central and South America
Nearctic	North American and Greenland
Oriental	South and Southeast Asia
Palearctic	Europe, North Africa and temperate Asia

Figure 2 shows that Indonesia straddles two very different faunal regions. The term western Indonesia is used here to refer to those parts of Indonesia that are included in the Sunda subregion, often referred to by some authors as the Greater Sunda (whereas the Lesser Sunda is the area labelled Nusa Tenggara). These two areas are separated from each other by Wallace's Line.

Figure 2: *The demarcation between western and eastern Indonesia*

When the major faunal regions are divided into subregions, western Indonesia becomes part of the Sunda subregion. This subregion extends into the Malay Peninsula and includes southern Thailand and the extreme southern part of Myanmar, south of the 11th parallel. To the east lies another well-defined subregion, the Wallacea (Figure 3), which is a transitional zone with a mix of Oriental region and Australasian region bird species and a high degree of endemism.

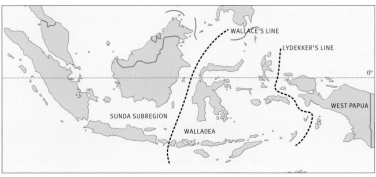

Figure 3: *The subregion of Wallacea*

Wallacea may or may not be regarded as part of the Oriental region, but in previous years the tendency has been to include it. The Oriental Bird Club regards it as part of its study area and the species found here are included in its detailed checklist, see Inskipp et al. (1996). East of the Lydekker's Line, West Papua and the adjacent islands are part of the Australasian region proper.

The Wallacea subregion includes three distinctly different areas: Sulawesi, Maluku and Nusa Tenggara. The term 'Maluku' has been adopted for compatibility with Jepson & Ounsted (1997), although Coates et al (1997) retain the English term 'the Moluccas' to describe the slightly smaller biogeographical (not political) entity. This creates discrepancies for some species. For instance, the Hooded Butcherbird occurs only on New Guinea and the Aru Islands, so it is listed by Jepson & Ounsted (1997) as occurring in Maluku, but it is not described in Coates et al (1997) because it is not in the Moluccas!

Split up this way, the birdlife of Indonesia can best be described using these seven different areas as defined by Andrew (1992) and adopted by Jepson & Ounsted (1997) as illustrated in Figure 4.

When describing the distribution of species within Indonesia, the map on pages 2–3 is used, showing all major islands and some smaller ones.

Nomenclature, Taxonomy and Sequence

Abbreviations of references have been shortened further, to conserve space, so that:

- Andrew, P. (1992), *The Birds of Indonesia: A Checklist (Peter's Sequence)* is Andrew (1992)
- Jepson, P. & Ounsted, R. (1997), *Birding Indonesia* is J&O (1997)
- MacKinnon, J. & Phillipps, K. (1993), *A Field Guide to the Birds of Borneo, Sumatra, Java and Bali* is M&P (1993)
- Sibley, C.G. & Monroe, B.L. (1990), *Distribution and Taxonomy of Birds of the World* is S&M (1990).

For nomenclature, taxonomy and sequence, our main reference was Andrew (1992). This checklist was produced by the Indonesian Ornithological Society and is used by most birdwatchers in the country. It has been reprinted almost unchanged in Jepson & Ounsted (1997).

However, to make our book compatible with the three main field guides of Indonesia (see previous chapter) we have included a few of the latest taxonomic changes here. Therefore the Osprey, Barn Owl, Oriental Darter and fantails are placed in separate families. However, Andrew's sequence—the order in which the birds are listed—has not been changed, and for convenience we have also adopted his treatment

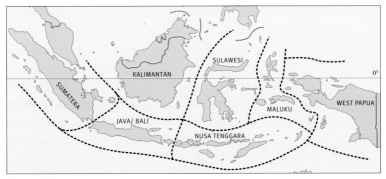

Figure 4: *The seven major bird areas of Indonesia*

of the families Estrildidae (to include munias) and Irenidae (to include the Asian Fairy Bluebird).

We have also followed Andrew (1992) and placed all ducks, cuckoos, kingfishers and warblers in Anatidae, Cuculidae, Alcedinidae and Sylviidae respectively. Coates et al. (1997) has a separate family for some genera in each of these four families. Likewise the frogmouth family is called Podargidae, while many Oriental region reference books (including Strange (2000)) uses Batrachostomidae.

Andrew (1992) uses the so-called crows-last sequence, where ducks are placed before hawks and sunbirds, flowerpeckers and white-eyes are placed before starlings, orioles and drongos. Since this sequence is used here, this book differs somewhat from the twin volume Strange (2000) which uses the buntings-last sequence in order to be compatible with most Oriental region field guides. In Indonesia both MacKinnon & Phillipps (1993) and Coates et al. (1997) use the buntings-last sequence, while Beehler et al (1986) uses crows-last. It's a nuisance, but that's the situation.

Nomenclature closely follows Andrew (1992) except where names used in popular field guides are judged to be more commonly used among field birdwatchers. On this basis, the names Brown Cuckoo-dove and Barred-necked Cuckoo-dove have been preferred to Slender-billed Cuckoo-dove and Dusky Cuckoo-dove respectively.

In those cases where we or any of our main sources use a different name than Andrew (1992) uses, the alternatives are mentioned in the text. Obvious spelling discrepancies like Pinon's Imperial Pigeon

(Andrew 1992) vs Pinyon Imperial Pigeon (Sibley & Monroe 1990) have been omitted, and names in use only in East Asia or Australia have also been excluded. However, occasional reference is made to *Handbook of the Birds of the World* by del Hoyo et al.

Currently, ornithologists under the World Conservation Monitoring Centre are making an effort to produce a new checklist for Indonesia based on Sibley & Monroe (1990). The list can be accessed by a hyperlink from http://www.orientalbirdclub.org/flyway.

Ben King in King et al. (1975) tried to standardise rules regarding the spelling of names and especially the use of the hyphen, but he didn't succeed. Paul Andrew (Appendix 2 in Andrew (1992)) has a different set of rules, but they are not always followed consistently and even when they are, can result in contradictions such as:

> bee-eater—honeyeater,
> sand-plover—sandpiper,
> bush-lark—waterhen,
> thick-knee—broadbill,
> sparrow-hawk—goshawk,
> brush-turkey—scrubfowl,
> leaf-warbler—leafbird,
> white-eye—darkeye,
> fruit-dove—ground pigeon,
> tiger-parrot—pygmy parrot,
> Javan Munia—Java Sparrow.

However, we follow Andrew (1992) in all these cases. This is also why in this volume the Greater Paintedsnipe in Strange (2000) is Greater Painted Snipe and the Collared Scops-owl is spelled Collared Scopsowl.

We are aware of the much more radical taxonomic changes inspired by new DNA-based research, which has led to the publishing of a very different taxonomic system in Sibley & Monroe (1990), adopted by Inskipp et al. (1996). However, both the sequence and the family groupings of species in this new system have been much criticised by other scholars, so, until the experts agree, we will follow the established system.

Family and Genus

The letter F stands for family and the Latin family name follows this symbol. The family name of the bird has been included because it is an important piece of information for the field observer. Otherwise it might not be clear to the reader that Paradise Crow is in fact not a crow (F: Corvidae) at all, but a bird of paradise (F: Paradisaeidae) Similarly, the Little Shrike-thrush is not related to thrushes (F: Turdidae), but to the whistlers (F: Pachycephalidae). The Latin and Greek-based family names may sound a bit awkward to use in everyday language, but if you look through the list on the contents pages, these family names (which all end in 'idae') are actually fairly easy to memorise.

Notice how the figbirds are part of the Oriolidae family named after orioles; these two groups are in fact closely related. The Asian Brown Flycatcher, Asian Paradise-flycatcher and Canary Flycatcher are all called flycatchers and yet they belong to three different families (Muscicapidae, Monarchidae and Petroicidae respectively). In fact, the Canary Flycatcher is closely related to the White-winged Robin (F: Petroicidae), which in turn has little in common with the Oriental Magpie-robin (F: Turdidae). The family label will help clarify these relationships.

Within the family, each bird is placed in a genus. This subdivision is the first of the bird's two Latin names, which is often called the bird's scientific name. Only a few birds such as the myzomelas (F: Meliphagidae) and parotias (F: Paradisaeidae) use their genus name as their common name as well: *Myzomela rosenbergii* is the Red-collared Myzomela and *Parotia sefilata* is the Western Parotia.

Some birds are unique, with no close relatives. They are monotypic and in some instances form their own genus. This will usually be mentioned in the description of the bird. Very few birds are monotypic to the family level (only the Osprey in this book), while others such as the Oriental Darter, Australian Bustard and Papuan Treecreeper are sole country representatives of very small families.

The second half of the Latin name describes the species. Many birds occur in distinct forms and are divided by taxonomists into separate subspecies or races that are designated by a third addition to the Latin name. Closely related allospecies that replace each other geographically are said to form a superspecies.

When birds are classified, the class Aves that contains all birds is grouped into orders and suborders, which are then split into families and subfamilies. However discussion of this fascinating topic is outside the scope of this book. This subject is thoroughly covered in some of the works listed in the Selected Bibliography. For the information of the reader, we have marked the beginning of the order Passeriformes–by far the largest order containing all the passerine (perching birds) families. This is regarded as the fastest evolving group of birds. While some non-passerines have remained unchanged for millions of years, dating back almost to the dinosaurs, the passerines are constantly developing. The passerines are generally strong fliers, many males have bright colors or complex voices, the young all stay in the nest for longer, and so these birds are regarded as evolutionarily more advanced.

The length of the species in centimeters follows each bird name. If there are slight discrepancies between this length and Strange (2000), it is because reference information varies. This may be due to inaccuracies in the measurements or because real differences exist between regional populations and subspecies. Within some species, notably many raptors in the Accipitridae family, the females are considerably larger than males, but for brevity only an average size has been included for comparison. Only within Phasianidae, where the male pheasant can sometimes be more than double the size of the female, have two numbers been included. Where extremely elongated tail feathers distort measurements, this has also been mentioned.

Photographs

Each species is illustrated with a photograph, sometimes two. If the sex of the bird is not mentioned, the photograph shows an adult bird that cannot be identified as to sex. When sexes differ, this is mentioned in the description. The term 'sexes similar' is only used on occasions where most other species within the family are sexually dimorphic.

Unless otherwise mentioned, resident birds are shown in breeding plumage and migrants are shown in non-breeding plumage. An additional photograph might show the other sex of the species or a flying bird.

Most photographs are taken on location in Indonesia or Southeast Asia and show free-living individuals. Where no authentic photograph was available, one showing a captive bird might be used, but in that case it is mentioned in the description. We have done this consistently as we felt it was important for the reader to know that habitat, perch and surroundings might not appear as they would in the field.

Photographs by the author were produced using Nikon equipment with lenses 500 mm F 4.0 ED (47% of total), 400 mm F 5.6 ED (42%) and 300 mm F 4.5 ED (11%). The film used was Kodachrome 64 and 200 and Fujichrome 100 ASA.

Description, Bird Topography

The description has been kept to a minimum. We have preferred to let the photograph do the talking and have only described what is not obvious, such as parts of the bird not visible in that particular position or the appearance of the opposite sex.

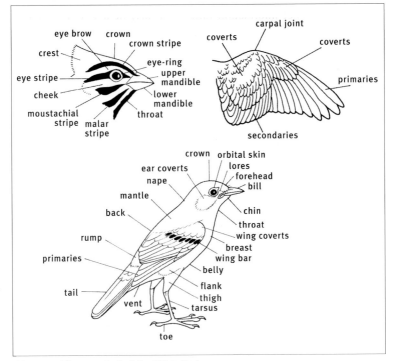

Figure 5: *The parts of a bird (by Kelvin Lim)*

Efforts have been made, however, to point out the so-called diagnostic features where appropriate. In the field, there is often a single feature that distinguishes one species from all others. The Rainbow Bee-eater has a narrow black stripe below the throat—once you spot that, all your worries are over! This technique helps to quickly identify most species and leaves more time to concentrate on the really difficult groups with no (or very faint) diagnostic features.

Some species have no relatives that resemble them closely. They are very easy to identify on all occasions and have been labelled 'unmistakable'. Please keep in mind that this term and the diagnostic label refer only to the distribution area within Indonesia. Thus the Little Minivet can be labelled 'unmistakable' within its range, which includes Sumbawa, but should a male turn up on neighbouring Lombok, where the Scarlet Minivet has also been known to occur, it can only be safely identified by its white (not red) lower belly. So use this label as a guideline only.

The parts of the bird are mentioned in the text, using standard labels which have been slightly modified for this purpose as shown in Figure 5. The upper surface of the entire body, including the mantle, wings, back and rump, is often referred to as 'the upperparts', and likewise the entire under surface of the bird, including the throat, breast, belly, flanks and vent, is labelled 'the underparts'.

Taxonomic variations and similar species that have not been illustrated in the book are also covered in this section.

Voice

Calls follow our main references: Coates et al. (1997) for the Wallacea subregion species; Beehler et al. (1986) for the West Papuan birds; and MacKinnon & Phillipps (1993) supplemented with Lekagul & Round (1991) and Lim & Gardner (1997) for the Sunda subregion species. Only in a few instances, such as the Orange-cheeked Honeyeater, are the call descriptions modified slightly in accordance with our experiences.

Even using these authoritative sources for reference, verbalisation of birds' whistling and hooting voices is a tricky business. In spite of this, we felt it was important to include a voice description. Combining the call with observations can sometimes be crucial for locating and identifying elusive forest birds. The Thick-billed Darkeye, endemic to Sumbawa and

Flores, is not an easy bird to see unless you are aware that it has a loud, trilling whistle unlike other members of the white-eye family (Zosteropidae), which have weaker, chipping calls.

However, it is our experience that calls cannot be learned from a book. Audio tapes, which might help, are available for most of Indonesia, but the best method is to find the bird making the call, often time and time again, until the connection sticks in your mind.

Habits

This section begins with an account of where the bird can be found and ends by describing how it is likely to behave. Terms describing habitat are usually self-explanatory, except for those describing the habitat of forest birds. Since the exact distribution of forest types in this vast country is a very complex subject, we have made a simple distinction between evergreen tropical rainforest and drought deciduous forests.

Tropical rainforest, comprised mainly of tall hardwood trees, is the predominant original vegetation type in Sumatra, Kalimantan, parts of Sulawesi, Maluku, and northern West Papua close to the Equator. Rainfall is generally heavy all year, in some places over 5,000 millimetres per annum, and even during dry spells the forest is saturated and green.

However, from eastern Java, through Nusa Tenggara, southern Sulawesi and into the Trans-Fly region of southern West Papua, the climate is much drier, with a dry season during the middle of the year, usually from April into November. At the end of the dry season, the open spaces are scorched and yellow, and the trees are virtually leafless. The

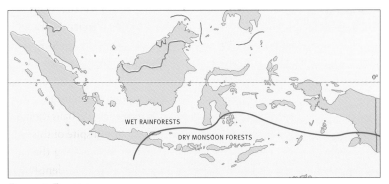

Figure 6: *Forest types*

forest here is labelled monsoon forest or drought deciduous forest. In some lowland areas with very little precipitation (less than 1,000 millimetres per annum) and few trees, the vegetation is described as coastal savanna. Adapted from Stone (1994), this terminology is illustrated in Figure 6 on the previous page.

The terms primary forest and secondary forest have been used as defined in the Glossary. Secondary forest varies from low regrowth with few large trees remaining, to areas selectively logged decades back with many large trees remaining or regrown and labelled here as mature secondary growth. Where canopies meet and form a continuous cover, even though some disturbance might have taken place, the term closed forest is sometimes applied. At the other end of the scale, where no large trees are left standing, the habitat is labelled scrub. Other habitat terms such as mangrove forests and cultivated areas are generally understood.

Very few birds occur across the whole altitudinal range; in fact most birds occur in the lowland forest. A few are restricted to the extreme lowlands below 300 metres, but many also move into the foothills or submontane elevations. At 900 metres the birdlife changes significantly, and many species can only be found in the lower and upper montane elevations. A few occur only in alpine habitats near the tree limit, between 3,200 and 3,800 metres in Indonesia, depending on local conditions.

Therefore the altitudinal range of the bird is an important piece of information. Where numbers are given, these have been taken from our main references, sometimes rounded off to the nearest 100 metres. For an explanation of the vocabulary used, please refer to Figure 7.

Within the enormous area covered by this book we have not found it appropriate to indicate where a particular species can best be found. Please refer to Jepson & Ounsted (1997), Wheatley (1996) and others for this information. We have mentioned a few special places for species that, in our experience, are mainly found in certain often-visited, protected areas such as Way Kampas National Park in Sumatra, Gede-Pangrango National Park in Java, Bali Barat National Park in west Bali and a few others.

After habitat and preferred elevation information, there follows a brief description of where within the habitat the bird is likely to be spotted.

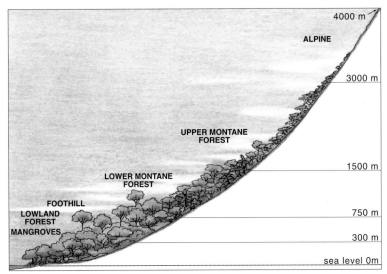

Figure 7: *The tropical rainforest at various altitudes (by Kelvin Lim)*

Especially in the lowland tropical rainforest, birds are usually specialists and occupy narrow niches within the forest. A few families like flower-peckers and honeyeaters might have members that frequently move across all levels of the forest, but this is the exception. It is true to say that an oriole will never be found on the ground or a scrubfowl in the top of a tree. Following Strange (2000), we have used terms describing the levels of the forest as illustrated in Figure 8 on page 37.

Notes on feeding and breeding behaviour that might be relevant follow at the end of the description paragraph, but for many of the resident species in remote parts of Indonesia this information is not available.

Distribution and Status

The distribution paragraph gives the extralimital range of the bird using the terms defined under 'Area covered' in this chapter. Only a few species occur worldwide; some are widespread within the Oriental and/or the Australasian regions; many are restricted to a smaller area, notably the Sunda subregion, Borneo or the island of New Guinea; and a number are endemic to Indonesia.

A few do not fit into the faunal regions as defined here. For instance, the Mountain White-eye is widespread through much of Indonesia, but can be found only in the Philippines outside the country and not in the rest of the Oriental region. Anomalies like these are noted in the text.

Indonesia is the southern limit for many Oriental region birds, so it will generally be useful to consult Strange (2000) as well, to get the full picture of these species' extralimital range. That book includes a few Oriental species that might occur rarely in small areas of Indonesia, but which have not been included in this volume.

Most resident birds are sedentary, so if nothing is mentioned on the subject in this section, assume that the bird is sedentary. Within some groups (shorebirds, raptors and warblers) there are many migratory species. Their sedentary status is sometimes mentioned for clarification and to emphasise that the species is an exception to the rule. Large families like bulbuls, whistlers, white-eyes and birds of paradise have no migratory members at all, but the status of a migratory species is always explained. The term 'nomadic' refers to a species that moves outside its breeding range when not breeding, but not in a predictable north-south route the way a migratory bird moves.

If the bird is found in no other country, the term 'Indonesian endemic' is applied. In that case, the distribution map shows the whole world range of that particular species. Please note that while only one Borneo endemic species is endemic to Indonesia (the rest are all shared with East Malaysia), a few species restricted to New Guinea do only occur in the western half, West Papua, and are thus Indonesian endemics.

After the first sentence, this paragraph covers the bird's distribution and status in Indonesia. In general, the wording is only meant as a supplement to the maps, which should be self-explanatory. Only some migrants and a few residents such as the Collared Kingfisher and Olive-backed Sunbird can be found throughout the archipelago. The vast majority are restricted to just one or two of the subregions in Figure 3 on page 25.

The maps are drawn using our three main references for source material, but these have been updated in a few instances according to the latest information published in *Kukila* up to and including Volume 10.

Where our main reference for western Indonesia, MacKinnon & Phillipps (1993), differs from *Kukila*, we have chosen to follow the information published in the latter. That especially applies to the birds of the

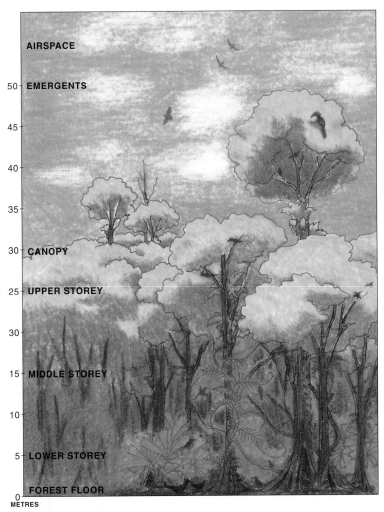

AIRSPACE

50 ─ EMERGENTS

45 ─

40 ─

35 ─

30 ─ CANOPY

25 ─ UPPER STOREY

30 ─

15 ─ MIDDLE STOREY

10 ─

5 ─ LOWER STOREY

0 ─ FOREST FLOOR

METRES

Figure 8: *Vertical levels of the rainforest (by Kelvin Lim)*

West Sumatra islands where our maps correspond to the study published in Volume 7, No. 1 (October 1994). Bird distribution on the Riau Islands has been updated according to Volume 8 (August 1996); for Sangihe and Talaud, we follow the study in Volume 9 (October 1997); and for Flores, Sumba and Tanimbar, the survey results in Volume 10 (February 1999).

A simple color-code has been applied to the maps:

- ■■■ blue indicating migratory/non-breeding visitor status only,
- ■■■ red indicating breeding range.

The text explains when breeding populations are augmented by migratory birds for part of the year. In Western Indonesia and much of Wallacea, migrants are mainly northern winter visitors. Winter here refers to the Northern Hemisphere winter months of December, January and February. For most birds the migratory season lasts from September to April, and a few northern migrants can, in fact, be found in winter quarters almost all months of the year.

Most of these migrants in Indonesia arrive on the so-called East Asian Flyway following either the Malay Peninsula or the Philippine archipelago south, as illustrated in Figure 9 after Strange (2000). In southern Wallacea and the Trans-Fly region of West Papua, a smaller number of Australian migrants visit during winter on the southern continent.

Since the maps are quite small, it will be difficult to pick out endemic species with a very small world range such as the Bali Starling, Biak Paradise-kingfisher, Tanimbar Corella and others. In those cases the size of the island might be exaggerated.

Some endemic species occur on one large and some adjacent smaller islands, notably within Wallacea. The Plain Gerygone, for instance, is on Timor and three smaller islands, and they have all been named here, although only two of the smaller adjacent islands can be located on the map. In other cases, it was impractical to name all islands, so please refer to our main reference sources for details.

For those species restricted to montane elevations, the limited range has been indicated for the larger areas such as Sumatra, Kalimantan, Java and West Papua. For smaller islands with steep mountains near the coast, such as Lombok and Flores, this has not been possible, so the text will explain details. In general it has not been feasible to draw the Sumatra maps with accuracy down to provincial level, but for a few species restricted exclusively to the south or the southwest of the island, this has been indicated. Please see Marle & Voous (1988) and *Kukila*, Volume 8, for further details.

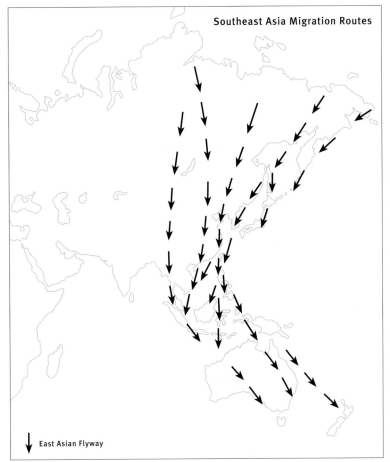

Figure 9: *Southeast Asia migration routes*

For montane New Guinea species, the term 'central mountains of West Papua' has been used for species found from west to east in the Weyland, Snow and Star Mountains, but not on the Vogelkop Peninsula. If the species is restricted to the largest and tallest of these ranges, the Snow Mountains, this is stated.

Abundance

We have tried to provide the reader with some idea of how common the bird is in Indonesia and how likely it is to be found in the field. However,

A group of birdwatchers inside Bali Barat National Park.

this is a highly subjective exercise and the codes attached can only serve as a rough guideline.

For western Indonesia, our main references either do not provide this information at all or they are not very reliable for this purpose. Note that MacKinnon & Phillipps (1993) describe the Short-tailed Starling, Asian Glossy Starling, Asian Pied Starling and White-vented Myna as 'a frequent bird', 'a common bird', 'a common bird' and 'the commonest starling' respectively.

The fact is that any starling or myna today is difficult to find on populated Java and Bali. You can easily spend your vacation on Bali and never see a single Sturnid! A visitor from Singapore (where mynas are everywhere) will notice the absence right away. Prominent Indonesian ornithologist, the late Derek Holmes, asked, in his editorial for *Kukila*, Volume 7, No. 2, "Has anyone else noted an apparent decline in the Asian Glossy Starling?". In view of this and other evidence, we have labelled all western Indonesia resident starlings as either uncommon or rare.

Often, official documentation does not seem to reflect the actual state of affairs. MacKinnon & Phillipps (1993) describes the Black-and-red Broadbill as 'Common...on Sumatra', although Derek Holmes in *Kukila*, Volume 8, reports an 'apparent scarcity' of this species on the

The author in wetland habitat.

island. The same guidebook says of the Large Woodshrike: 'In Sumatra and Borneo this is a frequent bird of lowland forests'. Yet it is absent from both the Sumatra Bird Report (*Kukila*, Volume 8) and the Kalimantan Bird Report (*Kukila*, Volume 9), and this bird is included in few recent field surveys from these areas. This species has been listed as rare on the checklist for the Way Kampas National Park, so it is listed as rare in this volume.

For eastern Indonesia, Coates et al. (1997) provides well-documented information on abundance in Wallacea, although we disagree with some descriptions. For instance, the Moluccan Owlet-nightjar is categorised as 'common...relatively easy to see'. We have spent weeks trying in vain to view a shy and elusive individual, calling deep inside prime habitat, an experience that has been shared by others. Also, the photograph included in this book is one of just a few in existence, so this description may not be accurate.

Beehler et al. (1986) covers all of New Guinea (not just West Papua) and does not provide much information on abundance. Therefore, we have relied mainly on trip reports and our own limited experience for this area. The codes in this book should always be viewed as an imprecise indication only.

Some terms used:

Abundant is very numerous, indicating that a species occurs in very large numbers, sometimes in dense flocks.

Local is the antonym for widespread and is used where a species is restricted to a special habitat within a small geographical area.

Scarce indicates that the bird occurs in low numbers (while an uncommon bird, although uncommonly encountered, could be locally and seasonally numerous or might be numerous elsewhere in its extralimital range).

Numerous is the antonym for scarce, and indicates that a species occurs in large numbers.

Widespread means that the bird occurs over a wide geographical area and in a variety of habitat types.

Abundance Code

Following Strange (2000), we have used the following color codes to indicate abundance:

●   Common. Encountered with at least 90% certainty in preferred habitat.

◉   Fairly common. Encountered with between 50% and 90% certainty in preferred habitat.

⊙   Uncommon. Encountered with less than 50% certainty in preferred habitat.

○   Rare. Encountered once a year or less in preferred habitat.

Globally Threatened Status

We have included the following codes to indicate globally threatened status. It follows the important BirdLife International study that was published in Collar et al. (1994). Please see this book for more detailed information. Briefly, this survey operated with four main categories that have been adopted unchanged here:

● Critically endangered. 50% chance of becoming extinct in 5 years.

◉ Endangered. 20% chance of becoming extinct in 20 years.

⊙ Vulnerable. 10% chance of becoming extinct in 100 years.

○ Near-threatened. Close to qualifying for the categories above.

SOUTHERN CASSOWARY

Casuarius casuarius 150 cm F: Casuariidae

Description: Distinguished from the two other members of this family by its very tall casque and long, divided neck wattle. Captive photo.

Voice: Low, booming grunts.

Habits: A lowland rainforest bird, usually found below 500 m in tall forest, often in swampy areas or along riverbanks. A shy, flightless bird, rarely seen. Walks on the forest floor searching for fallen fruits. Nests on the ground. The male is smaller than the female and tends to the brood.

Morten Strange

Distribution: New Guinea and northern Australia. Uncommon resident in parts of West Papua, Aru Islands and Seram where probably released.

NORTHERN CASSOWARY

Casuarius unappendiculatus 135 cm F: Casuariidae

Description: Distinguished from the previous species by its single wattle and orange-reddish neck. The third sympatric member of this small family. The Dwarf Cassowary, *C. bennetti*, has a small casque, a black feathered neck and is partly montane. Captive photo.

Voice: Resembles that of the previous species.

Habits: Similar to the previous species. Found only in primary lowland rainforest below 500 m, often in low-lying wet areas. Extremely shy and rarely seen, but possibly fairly numerous in remote areas of prime habitat.

C. & D. Frith: Frithfoto

Distribution: New Guinea. Uncommon resident in northern parts of West Papua and on a few smaller nearby islands.

WEDGE-TAILED SHEARWATER

Puffinus pacificus 45 cm F: Procellariidae

Description: Distinguished from other dark-coloured seabirds by its characteristic wedged tail, shown clearly in photo of dark morph. Light morph has white underparts.

Voice: Quiet at sea.

Habits: Probably the most widespread and numerous of the 10 members of this pelagic family that are sometimes seen offshore in Indonesia, although none breed here. During peak migration, frequently seen close to shore, often in the company of terns, boobies and other seabirds. Dips into surface waters for fish and other aquatic prey.

Howard Nicholls/Windrush Photos

Distribution: Breeds in tropical and subtropical Indian and Pacific oceanic areas; sometimes migrates. Generally an uncommon non-breeding visitor in offshore Indonesian waters; recorded off all major provinces except Kalimantan.

RED-THROATED LITTLE GREBE (Little Grebe)

Tachybaptus ruficollis 25 cm F: Podicipedidae

Description: Unmistakable, apart from Black-throated Little Grebe, *T. novaehollandiae*, which overlaps in range on Java and parts of Wallacea. The Black-throated Little Grebe is only numerous in southern West Papua and has a black (not chestnut) neck and throat.

Voice: A sharp *ke-ke-ke-ke*.

Habits: The only widespread member of this small, specialised, aquatic family in Indonesia. Occurs around freshwater lakes and ponds with plenty of reeds, often in resident pairs and sometimes in small colonies. Found from the lowlands to montane elevations. Dives for fish and aquatic invertebrates.

Morten Strange

Distribution: Africa, Eurasia, Oriental region east into Northern New Guinea. Rare resident Java and Bali; locally fairly common in parts of Wallacea; vagrant Sumatra and Kalimantan.

RED-TAILED TROPICBIRD

Phaethon rubricauda 46 cm + tail F: Phaethontidae

Description: Distinguished from the following species by its red tail, red (not orange) bill and all-white wings. The immature bird of both species has black barring on its back and wings.

Voice: Usually silent at sea. Sometimes screams and croaks at its breeding site.

Habits: A handsome bird that flies like a large tern with slow wing-beats. Usually seen far out at sea, where it feeds by diving into the surface water, mainly after flying fish and squid. Breeds on remote cliffs facing the sea.

Distribution: Breeds in tropical and subtropical Indian and Pacific oceanic areas; sometimes migrates. Generally an uncommon non-breeding visitor in offshore Indonesian waters; recorded off all major provinces except Kalimantan.

WHITE-TAILED TROPICBIRD

Phaethon lepturus 41 cm + tail F: Phaethontidae

Description: Note diagnostic white tail, orange bill and black markings on wing upperparts.

Voice: Similar to that of the previous species.

Habits: This species can often be seen along the majestic vertical cliffs of Nusa Penida, off Bali, and sometimes at Ulu Watu, on Bali itself. It flies in from the sea with slow, elastic wing-beats and lands on the inaccessible cliff-face. Nesting remains unconfirmed. Otherwise mainly an offshore wanderer and usually solitary. Habits similar to previous species.

Distribution: Tropical oceans worldwide; roams as far as 1,000 km outside breeding season. Resident and presumed breeding at a few locations off south Java and Bali, possibly also Wallacea; otherwise a rare offshore visitor.

GREAT FRIGATEBIRD
Fregata minor 94 cm F: Fregatidae

Description: Female (photo) distinguished with difficulty from the female of the following species by its white throat. Male is all black. The male of both species inflates its red throat pouch during breeding displays.

Voice: Silent; clappering noises when breeding.

Habits: Seems to occur in smaller numbers than the following species. However some large breeding colonies have been reported on Gunungapi, Manuk and other remote islands in Wallacea, where nesting occurs from February to September. Sometimes seen soaring high on thermals near the coastline. Roosts in dense flocks on offshore islets or in mangroves.

Martin Hale

Distribution: Tropical oceans worldwide; roams widely outside breeding season. Resident on islands in Flores and Banda seas; otherwise widespread, but uncommon, non-breeding visitor throughout coastal Indonesia.

LESSER FRIGATEBIRD
Fregata ariel 76 cm F: Fregatidae

Description: Female (photo) distinguished with difficulty from female of previous species by its black throat and white chest that extends onto wings. Male has narrow white spot at base of wing only.

Voice: Silent; clappering noices when breeding.

Habits: Generally a pelagic bird, but sometimes flies across land. The most common frigatebird in Indonesian waters, often observed during boat trips or along the coast. Usually seen in small groups, occasionally in large. Roosts on kelong poles or in trees on remote islands. This elegant flier catches fish and squid from the surface waters. They (mainly the females) also chase terns and take their fish.

Morten Strange

Distribution: Tropical oceans worldwide; roams widely outside breeding season. A fairly common non-breeding visitor throughout Indonesian seas; possibly resident on islands in the Banda Sea.

CHRISTMAS ISLAND FRIGATEBIRD

Fregata andrewsi 95 cm F: Fregatidae

Description: Note the diagnostic white lower belly of this female. Male has diagnostic full white breast and belly.

Voice: Silent at sea.

Habits: Much like the two previous species. A pelagic visitor that stays well offshore. Within Indonesia, usually observed alone or in small groups, often with other frigatebirds. This localised seabird may only number 1,600 breeding pairs in total and is regarded as vulnerable to global extinction.

Alan OwYong

Distribution: Breeds only on Christmas Island (Australia), south of Java; outside breeding season, disperses to the north, reaching Southeast Asia. Fairly common non-breeding visitor offshore Java; rarer off Sumatra and Borneo; vagrant Bali and Wallacea.

GREAT CORMORANT

Phalacrocorax carbo 81 cm F: Phalacrocoracidae

Description: Large size is diagnostic; also note whitish cheeks and throat. All cormorants belong to the same genus.

Voice: Usually silent. Grunts and groans at breeding sites.

Habits: Found around freshwater lakes, along tidal estuaries and in coastal areas. Always in small groups and is best seen as it flies strongly from site to site. Swims low in the water and dives for fish when feeding. Often sits on a low perch, spreading its wings to dry between dives.

Morten Strange

Distribution: Worldwide. Formerly a numerous resident at large lakes in Sumatra, now only a rare visitor to this island and parts of eastern Indonesia.

LITTLE BLACK CORMORANT
Phalacrocorax sulcicostris 61 cm F: Phalacrocoracidae

Description: Distinguished with great difficulty from the Little Cormorant by its slightly longer bill and blue-grey facial skin. Captive photo.

Voice: Usually silent; guttural calls near nest.

Habits: A freshwater bird found near lakes, marshes and adjacent flooded fields. Seen less often at saline estuaries and tidal mangroves. On west Java (e.g. Pulau Dua) and some islands in Wallacea, dense breeding colonies exist, however this bird is usually observed singly, or in small groups. It is often seen perching prominently near or flying low across the water, in a strong, direct flight.

Distribution: Australasia west into parts of Indonesia. Resident and locally fairly common in Java and parts of Wallacea; mainly a non-breeding visitor in West Papua, rare in Bali, and vagrant in Kalimantan.

LITTLE PIED CORMORANT
Phalacrocorax melanoleucus 60 cm F: Phalacrocoracidae

Description: Unmistakable; the only cormorant in the country with white underparts; white usually covers the entire belly.

Voice: Usually silent; guttural calls near nest.

Habits: Found near freshwater lakes and marshes, as well as tidal estuaries, brackish wetlands and mangroves. Occasionally seen along exposed coastal areas and offshore islands. Swims low in the water and dives for fish. Usually seen singly or in small groups, flying or perched near the water. Nests in small colonies.

Distribution: Australasia. Resident and locally fairly common in Wallacea and West Papua; vagrant in east Java.

LITTLE CORMORANT

Phalacrocorax niger 56 cm F: Phalacrocoracidae

Ray Tipper

Description: Note diagnostic short, compact bill. Possible to confuse with the Little Black Cormorant, where their ranges overlap.

Voice: Usually silent; guttural calls near nest.

Habits: Found near water, mainly lowland freshwater lakes and marshes. Often seen in flooded fields, estuaries and mangroves. Habits are much like those of the two previous species. Has possibly declined in numbers in Java. Visitors on northern Sumatra may be stragglers from continental Southeast Asia.

Distribution: Oriental region. An uncommon resident on Java; a rare non-breeding visitor on Sumatra and possibly Kalimantan. Status compared with Little Black Cormorant uncertain.

DARTER

Anhinga melanogaster 91 cm F: Anhingidae

Tim Loseby

Description: Unmistakable; note long, thin neck and silvery streaks in wings. The Australasian sub-species, *A. m. novaehollandiae,* which occurs in eastern Indonesia, is treated as a full species by Andrew (1992).

Voice: Usually silent.

Habits: Found in swampy areas, from tidal mangroves, brackish wetlands and freshwater lakes to overgrown rivers far inland at 1,000 m. Prefers wooded surroundings and often perches in the open to dry off. Swims low with its long neck out of the water, hence its nickname the 'snakebird'. Dives for fish and other aquatic prey.

Distribution: Africa, Oriental region, Australasia. A widespread but generally scarce resident and non-breeding visitor throughout much of Indonesia; locally common only on south Sulawesi.

MASKED BOOBY

Sula dactylatra 85 cm F: Sulidae

Description: A large bird with diagnostic black mask. Black primaries show prominently in flight.

Voice: Quiet except for honks and whistles near nest.

Habits: A pelagic bird. May forage over 1,000 km from nearest land. Flies across the sea with low, shallow wing-beats. Dives from a great height to catch fish up to 40 cm long. Feeding flocks congregate over shoals of fish. Breeds on small, remote offshore islands. Gunungapi in the Banda Sea is the only known nesting site in Indonesia.

Distribution: Worldwide tropical oceans. Breeds in Wallacea and roams widely during the non-breeding season; a generally uncommon but locally numerous visitor throughout the Indonesian seas, mostly in the east.

Colin Poole

RED-FOOTED BOOBY

Sula sula 71 cm F: Sulidae

Description: Best distinguished from the preceding species in flight, by its white (not black) tail. Also note red feet, lack of mask and smaller size.

Voice: Quiet at sea. Noisy honks and whistles near nest.

Habits: A strictly pelagic bird, rarely seen near the coast. Substantial colonies exist on Kakabia, Gunungapi, Manuk and other remote islands in offshore Wallacea. Breeding takes place from June to September and possibly longer. Otherwise wanders over the ocean alone or in small groups, diving for fish.

A&E Morris/Windrush Photos

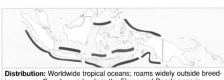

Distribution: Worldwide tropical oceans; roams widely outside breeding season. Breeds on islands in the Flores and Banda seas in Wallacea; a non-breeding visitor offshore, in most parts of Indonesia.

BROWN BOOBY

Sula leucogaster 72 cm F: Sulidae

Description: Diagnostic chocolate-brown upperparts, contrasting with white belly.

Voice: Silent, except for quacking calls near nest.

Habits: The most likely member of this family to be seen in Indonesia. Although pelagic, this booby often flies near the coast. Can be observed during ferry crossings between islands and from the beach. Flies low, diving for fish. Breeds on remote offshore islets. Its breeding population has possibly declined in recent years.

Distribution: Worldwide tropical oceans. Resident in the Flores Sea, Banda Sea, Malacca Strait and possibly elsewhere; a widespread and fairly common visitor throughout inland seas.

SPOT-BILLED PELICAN

Pelecanus philippensis 140 cm F: Pelecanidae

Description: Distinguished from the Great White Pelican, *P. onocrotalus* (a vagrant to northwest Java) by its smaller size, spots on a pinkish (not bright yellow) bill and brownish back of neck.

Voice: Usually quiet.

Habits: Found in a variety of wetlands. In Sumatra, occurs mainly in the vast mangroves of the Selatan province, where it swims and fishes in the shallow sea and in brackish coastal backwaters. Also observed in freshwater marshes. Sometimes perches on branches and kelong structures. Possibly breeds in large trees near water, in colonies with other water birds, but its nest has been not been found here.

Distribution: Oriental region. An uncommon non-breeding visitor to Sumatra; juveniles have been observed, so possibly a resident of south-east Sumatra; vagrant in Java. Vulnerable to global extinction.

AUSTRALIAN PELICAN

Pelecanus conspicillatus 150 cm F: Pelecanidae

Description: Distinguished from the previous species by its 'clean' bill and black lower back.

Voice: Usually quiet.

Habits: Frequents large wetlands, including fresh-water lakes, marshes, coastal estuaries and ponds, even coral reefs, where it feeds almost exclusively on fish. Often fishes together in flocks—300 of this species have been reported in one group. A good swimmer and a strong flier that sometimes soars high in the air. The Wasur National Park in West Papua is the best location in Indonesia to observe this species, especially during the dry season from June to December, but it could turn up almost anywhere in the east.

C. & D. Frith; Frithfoto

Distribution: Australasia. A locally common, non-breeding visitor mainly to the Trans-Fly region of West Papua; an uncommon visitor to inland West Papua and to the Wallacea and Bali, further west; vagrant in Java and possibly Sumatra.

GREY HERON

Ardea cinerea 95cm F: Ardeidae

Description: White neck and head, in combination with grey upperparts, are diagnostic. Note how its neck is bent back during flight.

Voice: Deep guttural honks in flight or at breeding site.

Habits: Usually found near the coast in saline marshes, estuaries and tidal wetlands. During the breeding season can be observed around inland lakes and swamps. Stalks prey by walking slowly along in shallow water, using its massive bill as a spear. Flies with elaborate wing-beats, high across feeding grounds. Roosts in trees.

Morten Strange

Distribution: Africa and Eurasia; northern populations migrate. An uncommon resident in Sumatra and Java; a non-breeding visitor on Bali; vagrant in Sumbawa and Sumba; a single sighting in Kalimantan.

GREAT-BILLED HERON

Ardea sumatrana 115 cm F: Ardeidae

Description: A huge bird. Note its uniformly dark grey plumage and massive bill.

Voice: Sometimes a harsh *croak*.

Habits: A coastal heron usually sighted near large expanses of mangroves on offshore islands, exposed beaches, and on coral reefs. On larger islands, it also ventures for some distance up tidal river mouths. At high tide it usually roosts in a mangrove tree. Good views are rare of this solitary, shy bird, and few nesting records exist.

Distribution: SE Asia south to northern Australia; sedentary. A widespread but scarce resident throughout the Indonesian archipelago. Near-threatened with global extinction.

PURPLE HERON

Ardea purpurea 90 cm F: Ardeidae

Description: The purple upperparts and rufous streaks on neck are diagnostic (left photo). Like other herons, it pulls its head back to its body during flight (right photo).

Voice: A harsh croak during take-off or at nest.

Habits: Mainly a freshwater wetlands bird found in extensive swamps and adjacent, flooded paddy fields. Less often seen around mangroves and tidal estuaries. Hunts alone by walking very slowly through reeds or shallow water. In prime habitat it will congregate in colonies at breeding sites, in low trees near water, often with other water birds.

Distribution: Africa and Eurasia. A generally uncommon but locally very numerous resident throughout the Greater Sundas and east into parts of Wallacea.

GREAT EGRET

Casamerodius albus 90 cm F: Ardeidae

Description: Note huge size, strong bill (top photo) and long neck pulled back in flight (bottom photo). Bill is yellow during non-breeding season; during breeding season, its bill is black and legs are reddish.

Voice: Sometimes a low, crow-like *kraa-a* when taking off.

Habits: Usually found around sheltered coastal wetlands such as mangroves, estuaries and tidal lagoons, and sometimes in freshwater swamps. Walks slowly or stands passively watching for aquatic prey, alone or in small groups. Less numerous than some white egrets.

Morten Strange

Distribution: Worldwide, in warm climates; partly migratory. A confirmed resident on Java, Sumatra and Sulawesi; generally a scarce non-breeding visitor and possible resident throughout the other major islands.

INTERMEDIATE EGRET

Egretta intermedia 70 cm F: Ardeidae

Description: A medium egret. Note the S-shaped neck. The fairly short yellow bill is its best diagnostic feature.

Voice: Silent except for croaking calls near nest.

Habits: Found mainly in freshwater marshes and paddy fields, and sometimes at tidal mudflats and estuaries. Often seen with other egrets and water birds. Moves slowly, stalking aquatic prey. Breeds in colonies in low trees, mixing with other herons.

Morten Strange

Distribution: Africa, the Oriental region and Australasia; partly migratory. Resident on Sumatra, Java, Bali and north Sulawesi; a locally fairly common non-breeding visitor on other islands.

WHITE-FACED HERON

Egretta novaehollandiae 68 cm F: Ardeidae

Description: Unmistakable; look for purple-grey neck and white face.

Voice: Usually silent; sometimes a croaking call on take-off.

Habits: Found in a variety of wetlands, from tidal estuaries and coastal areas to marshes and wet fields far inland at lower montane altitudes. Usually observed singly or in pairs; does not feed or breed in dense flocks like some other herons. Usually stands quietly near the water, but sometimes runs forward to stir up small fish and other aquatic prey.

Morten Strange

Distribution: Australasia; partly migratory. Resident on Sumba, Flores and probably Lombok; a locally fairly common visitor on other islands in east Indonesia; vagrant on Sulawesi.

LITTLE EGRET

Egretta garzetta 60 cm F: Ardeidae

Description: A small, slender egret. Look for diagnostic thin, black bill. Migrant visitor race has yellow toes, resident race has black toes.

Voice: Usually silent; croaking calls near nest.

Habits: A successful egret found in a variety of climate zones and wetland habitats. Prefers coastal estuaries, mangroves, freshwater marshes and paddy fields. Often seen near the coast, but sometimes far inland. This quick, elegant bird feeds by walking briskly along, sometimes running to catch aquatic prey. Breeds in trees near the feeding grounds, in colonies with other water birds.

Morten Strange

Distribution: Africa, Eurasia and Australasia. Resident in Sumatra, Java, Bali and Sulawesi; a widespread and locally fairly common non-breeding visitor on all major islands.

CHINESE EGRET
Egretta eulophotes 68 cm F: Ardeidae

Description: Photo shows breeding plumage. The long crest and bright yellow bill and toes are diagnostic; orbital skin is blue. In winter, only its longer legs and narrow bill distinguish it from the following species.

Voice: Silent during migration.

Habits: It is an active and energetic feeder. During winter, from October to March, great care should be taken with field identification, since this species occupies a narrow niche of tidal mudflats near estuaries where it could overlap with the resident Reef Egret. The Chinese Egret never occurs inland or on rocky shorelines.

Distribution: Breeds in a few known locations in China and Korea; winters in Southeast Asia. A rare winter visitor in east Kalimantan and north Sulawesi; single sightings from Sumatra and Java.

PACIFIC REEF-EGRET (Eastern Reef-egret)
Egretta sacra 58 cm F: Ardeidae

Description: Note its dull, yellow bill with a dark tip. Legs are pale greenish. Some individuals belong to a dark morph which has a uniformly slaty-black plumage.

Voice: Sometimes a harsh *arrk* when disturbed.

Habits: A strictly coastal egret, found on exposed sandy shores and coral reefs, on offshore islands, and on sheltered mudflats. Usually solitary or in resident pairs. Does not flock, but at prime locations a few birds may feed near each other. Catches small fish in shallow waters during low tide and roosts during high tide. Nests on the ground on remote coastal outcrops.

Distribution: East Asia into Australasia; sedentary. A widespread and fairly common resident along coasts of all major Indonesian islands and most small islets.

CATTLE EGRET

Bubulcus ibis 50 cm F: Ardeidae

Description: Distinguished from other egrets by its small, stocky shape (top photo) and rapid wing-beats in flight (bottom photo). Note strong yellow bill. During breeding has an orange wash on head, chest and back. A monotypic genus.

Voice: Silent except for croaking at nest.

Habits: Frequents open country, especially large grassy lowlands and flooded fields. Not found on tidal mudflats and beaches. Often follows cattle around, catching insects, frogs and lizards that the animals stir up as they graze. These egrets spread out when feeding, but congregate in dense flocks in low trees at communal roosts and in breeding colonies.

Morten Strange

Distribution: Worldwide warm climates; nomadic. Resident on Sumatra, Java, Bali and Sulawesi; generally common and locally abundant throughout Sunda and Wallacea; vagrant in West Papua.

CHINESE POND-HERON

Ardeola bacchus 45 cm F: Ardeidae

Morten Strange

Description: In non-breeding plumage (see photo), this bird is regarded as indistinguishable from the following species. During the breeding season, look for a much darker chocolate-brown head. In both species, the wings are white in flight .

Voice: Silent during migration.

Habits: Usually found around overgrown ponds, marshes and paddy fields, where it walks slow-ly, looking for aquatic prey. Sometimes seen on tidal mudflats and around mangroves.

Distribution: China and SE Asia; partly migratory. An uncommon winter visitor to northern parts of Sumatra and Kalimantan.

JAVAN POND-HERON
Ardeola speciosa 45 cm F: Ardeidae

Description: Unmistakable, except in non-breeding plumage, when it looks like the previous species. Note the diagnostic pale, cream-coloured head of this bird in breeding plumage.

Voice: Usually silent except for croaking calls near nest.

Habits: Found in freshwater marshes, paddy fields, prawn pond areas, tidal mudflats and along mangrove edges. Never seen on exposed beaches. Locally abundant and forms loose flocks in prime habitat. Walks slowly forward, stalking aquatic prey. Makes short flights on bright white wings. Breeds in low trees near water, often in colonies with other water birds.

Morten Strange

Distribution: SE Asia and Indonesia; mainly sedentary. A common resident and non-breeding visitor in parts of the Sunda and Wallacea subregions.

STRIATED HERON (Little Heron)
Butorides striatus 45 cm F: Ardeidae

Description: Unmistakable; note its stocky build and crouching stance. The immature bird is brown with pale streaks. A monotypic genus.

Voice: A noisy *kweak ... kee-kee-kee-kee* when disturbed.

Habits: This adaptable and successful heron is usually found on tidal mudflats, in mangroves, on coral reefs and exposed beaches, but can also turn up far inland around lakes and large rivers. Migrants from Asia augment resident populations during the northern winter. Usually seen alone or in pairs when feeding or breeding. Stalks fish, crustaceans and insects near the water's edge.

Distribution: Tropics worldwide; partly migratory. A widespread and common resident throughout Indonesia.

Morten Strange

BLACK-CROWNED NIGHT-HERON

Nycticorax nycticorax 61 cm F: Ardeidae

Description: Unmistakable. Its legs are red during the breeding season; the immature bird is brown with streaked underparts and its wings are dotted with white.

Voice: A penetrating, deep *wo-ok* when taking off.

Habits: Nocturnal and crepuscular. During the day small groups roost in low trees above the water, in mangroves or swamps. Flocks disperse in early evening, flying like large bats high in the sky, to feed in freshwater ponds and marshes during the night. Breeds in colonies with other water birds.

Distribution: Worldwide except Australasia; partly migratory. A generally uncommon resident on Sumatra, Java, Bali, south Kalimantan and Sulawesi; vagrant on Flores.

RUFOUS NIGHT-HERON

Nycticorax caledonicus 59 cm F: Ardeidae

Description: Distinguished from the previous species by its rufous upperparts and paler rufous underparts. Immature bird (photo) is dark brown with plain wings and pale streaks on breast.

Voice: Similar to that of previous species.

Habits: Found in lowland freshwater swamps, brackish coastal lagoons and mangroves. Breeds with other water birds in colonies. A secretive bird, mainly crepuscular and nocturnal. Feeds at the water's edge, on a variety of aquatic animals such as fish, frogs, crustaceans and young sea turtles, as well as mice, insects and young birds. Not easy to observe, although possibly locally numerous.

Distribution: Australasia north into the Philippines; somewhat nomadic. A generally uncommon resident and non-breeding visitor throughout most of Wallacea and West Papua; rare east of Java; vagrant on Bali.

YELLOW BITTERN

Ixobrychus sinensis 38 cm F: Ardeidae

Description: Note its slender build and pale plumage. Has diagnostic black wingtips that are visible in flight. The immature bird is streaked with brown.

Voice: A short *kakak-kakak* when taking off.

Habits: Usually found in large expanses of overgrown freshwater swamplands, often near the coast. Sometimes seen in tidal mangroves, and less often in short paddy fields. Prefers tall, dense marsh and riverside vegetation, where it stalks aquatic invertebrates and tiny fish. This secretive and crepuscular bird is best observed when it ventures out of the vegetation on brief flights.

Distribution: Oriental region east into Australasia; partly migratory. Resident on Sumatra; a locally common winter visitor and possibly resident throughout much of Indonesia.

SCHRENCK'S BITTERN

Ixobrychus eurhythmus 38 cm F: Ardeidae

Description: Photo shows female. Male has uniformly pale brown underparts, contrasting with dark brown upperparts.

Voice: Low *squaks* in flight.

Habits: During migration frequents grassy freshwater swamps and river banks. Thrives in thick vegetation, but sometimes emerges into open areas. May be somewhat crepuscular. Little studied and not often observed.

Distribution: Breeds in northern East Asia; winters in Southeast Asia. A rare winter visitor in the Sunda subregion and on Sulawesi. Near-threatened with global extinction.

CINNAMON BITTERN

Ixobrychus cinnamomeus 41 cm F: Ardeidae

Description: Note uniformly rufous plumage with paler under-parts. In flight, distinguished from other bitterns by its uniformly rufous wings.

Voice: Sometimes a low *croak* in flight.

Habits: The most common bittern throughout western Indonesia. Although secretive and skulking, it is often seen making short flights across freshwater wetland areas. This adaptable species moves readily into wet paddy fields and flooded grasslands. Seen less often in brackish or tidal areas. Feeds by stalking small aquatic prey among the vegetation. Sometimes emerges near the water's edge as shown in the photo.

Distribution: Oriental region east into Wallacea; partly migratory. A common resident and a possible winter visitor throughout the Sunda subregion and on Sulawesi; uncommon in parts of Nusa Tengggara.

BLACK BITTERN

Ixobrychus flavicollis 54 cm F: Ardeidae

Description: Upperparts are slaty black; breast is brown with distinct creamy streaks. Appears to be completely black in flight.

Voice: Sometimes a deep *croak* on take-off; also a booming call during breeding.

Habits: A wetland species with a preference for wooded wetlands and flooded forest. This photo was taken in disturbed lowland rainforest in West Papua. Often observed near the coast, but rarely in tidal areas. Sometimes perches in the open, and often makes low flights across the reeds. Feeds on aquatic prey while walking along the water's edge, often during poor light conditions.

Distribution: Oriental region and Australasia; partly migratory. A widespread, but generally scarce, non-breeding visitor and presumed resident throughout Indonesia; confirmed breeding on Sumatra and West Papua; status in other areas is uncertain.

MILKY STORK

Mycteria cinerea 92 cm F: Ciconiidae

Description: White underparts and underwing coverts, together with yellow bill and red face, are diagnostic. Also note neck stretched out in flight.

Voice: Silent.

Habits: Usually seen feeding during low tide on remote expanses of tidal mudflats and mangroves. Sometimes flies inland to feed in freshwater marshes and paddy fields. Often soars high on late morning thermals. Nests in small colonies in mangrove trees with other water birds.

Morten Strange

Distribution: SE Asia; sedentary but forages widely. An uncommon resident in east Sumatra, west Java and probably Sulawesi; a rare visitor on Bali and Sumbawa. Vulnerable to global extinction.

WOOLLY-NECKED STORK

Ciconia episcopus 86 cm F: Ciconiidae

Description: Note diagnostic white neck. Captive photo.

Voice: Silent.

Habits: Occurs in a variety of wetland habitats, from freshwater marshes and paddy fields to coastal estuaries and mangroves. Not numerous anywhere. Rarely observed and possibly declining in numbers. Feeds by walking slowly through the vegetation, catching insects and small vertebrates. Perches in tall trees. Breeds in single pairs.

Morten Strange

Distribution: Africa and the Oriental region; mainly sedentary. A resident on Sulawesi, Flores and possibly Sumatra and Java; a rare visitor on other islands.

STORM'S STORK

Ciconia stormi 80 cm F: Ciconiidae

Description: Previously considered conspecific to the Woolly-necked Stork. Distinguished from that species by its black neck, yellow facial skin, red bill and feet.

Voice: Silent.

Habits: Found mainly in primary lowland swamp forest and river-flooded forest. Also seen around rivers and ponds at the edge of partly logged or burnt forest. Most of the world's estimated 300 individuals are found in Indonesia, possibly 150 of these in Sumatra. World range includes parts of Peninsular Malaysia, Borneo and possibly south Thailand. This low-density species feeds on fish and other aquatic prey in shallow water. Only two nesting records of this species exist, one from Sumatra.

Distribution: Sunda subregion. A rare resident in parts of Sumatra and Kalimantan. Endangered with global extinction.

LESSER ADJUTANT

Leptoptilos javanicus 114 cm F: Ciconiidae

Description: A large stork with a massive build. Note its diagnostic orange neck and dark under-wings.

Voice: Silent.

Habits: Found along extensive mangrove areas. Small flocks gather in prime habitat on remote shorelines. Feeds on exposed mudflats at low tide and sometimes in the fields behind. A shy bird seen clearly when flying to and from its feeding grounds. Occasionally soars high like an eagle. Nests in trees near water, usually in small colonies with other water birds.

Distribution: Oriental region; sedentary. An uncommon and low-density resident in Sumatra, Kalimantan, Java and Bali. Vulnerable to global extinction.

GLOSSY IBIS

Plegadis falcinellus 64 cm F: Threskiornithidae

Description: Unmistakable; note its fairly small size and glossy greenish-black plumage.

Voice: Silent.

Habits: Can turn up in any marshy area. Prefers extensive freshwater shallows, cultivated grasslands and paddy fields. Often seen in brackish ponds just be-hind the coast and along tidal estuaries. Occurs inland on Sula-wesi to 1,350 m. Nests on Pulau Dua, Java. A flock numbering 5,000 has been reported from Lake Tempe, south Sulawesi. Usually moves in small flocks, fly-ing low with the flapping and gliding flight pattern typical of the family.

Tim Loseby

Distribution: Worldwide tropical and subtropical regions; nomadic. Confirmed breeding on Java; a locally fairly common resident, pre-sumed breeding on Sulawesi. A non-breeding visitor in other areas; vagrant on Sumatra and Kalimantan.

BLACK-HEADED IBIS

Threskiornis melanocephalus 80 cm F: Threskiornithidae

Description: Distinguished from the similar Australian White Ibis, *T. molucca,* resident on Seram and vagrant throughout eastern Indonesia, by its white (not black) tail.

Voice: Silent.

Habits: Found on tidal mudflats, along sheltered estuaries and in freshwater marshes and wet fields just behind the coast. Feeds on aquatic invertebrates by probing the mud with its specialised bill; also takes some fish. Always moves in flocks with other water birds and nests in colonies in trees near water. Today is much reduced on Java, but is still pre-sent on Pulau Dua and in other prime locations.

Morten Strange

Distribution: Oriental region; partly migratory. A local resident on Java; an uncommon non-breeding visitor on Sumatra.

OSPREY

Pandion haliaetus 55 cm F: Pandionidae

Morten Strange

Distribution: Worldwide; partly migratory. Widespread but scarce throughout Indonesia; mainly a non-breeding visitor, but also a resident on many islands in eastern parts.

Description: Note the characteristic long, narrow wings. Has a dark mask across its eyes. Underparts are pale.

Voice: Usually silent; a loud plaintive whistle when near nest.

Habits: The only member of its family. Found mainly in brackish lagoons and along sheltered coastal estuaries. Sometimes seen over the open sea and far inland along rivers and reservoirs. Lives entirely on fish, which it catches by diving spectacularly into the water from a great height. Usually builds its large nest in the top of a tall tree or on a cliff face near water.

JERDON'S BAZA

Aviceda jerdoni 45 cm F: Accipitridae

Morten Strange

Distribution: Oriental region. A presumed resident on Kalimantan, Sumatra and Sulawesi, but is generally scarce with few sightings.

Description: Note characteristic broad wing shape and barring in flight. At rest, its long wings and crest are diagnostic.

Voice: An airy, 2-note scream.

Habits: Frequents primary forest and forest edges in the lowlands. Observed particularly in the hills between 200 and 1,100 m. Unobtrusive habits. Perches in large trees, dropping to the ground for insects and small reptiles. Can sometimes be spotted soaring low over the forest.

PACIFIC BAZA (Crested Hawk)
Aviceda subcristata 40 cm F: Accipitridae

Description: Note distinctive barring on belly, and grey breast and head. Crest is visible when perched. The only *Aviceda* baza within its range.

Voice: A diagnostic disyllabic *whee-chu*.

Habits: Prefers forest, both primary forest and secondary growth. Often seen along forest edges and in disturbed areas near mature forest, mainly in the lowlands. In New Guinea, recorded to 1,200 m. Hunts for insects and small vertebrates in the trees. Sometimes soars conspicuously above the canopies or engages in an obvious display flight while calling repeatedly.

Morten Strange

Distribution: Australasia into northeast Australia. A widespread and fairly common resident in Nusa Tenggara, Maluku, West Papua and nearby islands.

BLACK BAZA
Aviceda leuphotes 33 cm F: Accipitridae

Description: Note black plumage with crest and diagnostic white spots. Also a distinct barring across underparts and wings rounded in flight.

Voice: A soft, airy scream of 1 to 3 notes.

Habits: Found along forest edges and open woodlands, often perching in large trees near clearings, riverbanks or villages. Gregarious during migration when they sometimes form small groups. Flies low with flapping wings when hunting insects and small vertebrate prey. Soars high when changing location.

Morten Strange

Distribution: Oriental region; migratory. An uncommon winter visitor on Sumatra and west Java.

LONG-TAILED BUZZARD (Long-tailed Honey-buzzard)

Heniocopernis longicauda 56cm   F: Accipitridae

Description: Similar in appearance and habits to the *Pernis* honey-buzzards of Eurasia and Oriental regions. Note its small head and fairly long tail that is fanned when soaring. Broadly streaked underparts are noticeable when perched.

Voice: Mainly silent; occasional screams during breeding displays.

Habits: Perhaps the most common raptor within its range, but numbers appear to have declined in recent years. Found in forest and along forest edges, from sea level to 3,000 m. Soars low over the forest and feeds on insects and some vertebrates in the canopies. Builds its nest high in a forest tree, after the rainy season, from April to May.

Distribution: New Guinea. A widespread and fairly common resident in West Papua and on most adjacent islands.

ORIENTAL HONEY-BUZZARD

Pernis ptilorhynchus 50 cm   F: Accipitridae

Description: Plumage varies from almost white (left photo), to a uniform dark brown colour (right photo). In flight, look for diagnostic long neck and tail, small head and fairly long wings.

Voice: Silent during migration; a high-pitched call while breeding.

Habits: Can turn up in a variety of forested habitats, from primary rainforest (residents) to open woodlands (migratory birds). Usually solitary, but sometimes forms flocks during peak migration, while moving across narrow straits between islands. Has a unique preference for raiding bee-hives and feeding on the larvae inside.

Distribution: Oriental region and northeast Asia; northern populations migrate. The Sunda resident race (with a crest) is uncommon; the migratory race is a winter visitor extending into parts of Nusa Tenggara.

BLACK-WINGED KITE (Black-shouldered Kite)

Elanus caeruleus 30 cm F: Accipitridae

Description: Unmistakable in this region (left photo). Note slender, falcon-like appearance in flight (right photo).

Voice: A short, soft whistle near nesting area.

Habits: Found in dry, savanna-like woodlands and open country with scattered trees and grassy fields. Easy to spot and observe. Usually solitary or in resident pairs. Perches on an open branch or a pole. Flies low with lifted wings; hovers over the ground before dropping into the grass to catch insects and small vertebrates.

Morten Strange

Distribution: Africa and Oriental region; sedentary. A widespread although scarce resident throughout most of Indonesia, including parts of Kalimantan.

BLACK KITE

Milvus migrans 65 cm F: Accipitridae

Description: Distinguished from the Brahminy Kite by its large size and overall dark plumage. Note the buff streaks and molting primaries on this immature bird. Its tail is slightly forked when closed.

Voice: A rather faint, prolonged scream.

Habits: This adaptable species is very successful and numerous in other regions, but is poorly established in Indonesia. It frequents open country with scattered trees, preferably near water, and is often seen in disturbed areas and on the outskirts of villages near the coast. This strong flier feeds on meat, mainly carrion, often scavenging at garbage dumps and fishing areas.

Morten Strange

Distribution: Africa, Eurasia, and Australasia; partly migratory. An uncommon resident and non-breeding visitor in parts of Wallacea and West Papua; vagrant in Sumatra and Kalimantan.

WHISTLING KITE

Haliastur sphenurus 56 cm F: Accipitridae

Description: Distinguished from the previous species and the immature Brahminy Kite by its slender body and long, narrow, rounded tail.

Voice: A distinctive shrill whistle.

Habits: This open country raptor is found in savanna woodlands in the lowlands and often in marshy areas near the coast. A good location to observe this bird is Wasur National Park near Merauke. This kite feeds on a variety of animals, fish and carrion, dropping down from a low flight to grab prey from the grass, water surface or roadside.

Jon Hornbuckle

Distribution: Australasia into Australia. A locally fairly common resident in parts of West Papua, especially the Trans-Fly region in the southeast.

BRAHMINY KITE

Haliastur indus 45 cm F: Accipitridae

Description: Note its diagnostic chestnut-brown upperparts and black wingtips. The immature bird is a mottled brown.

Voice: A nasal, mewing call.

Habits: Mainly a coastal bird, frequently seen in mangroves and over harbour areas. Also found along inland rivers and in wooded terrain far from water; occurs locally up into montane elevations. Flies low, dropping down to catch prey or pick up carrion. Although this kite is Jakarta's avian symbol and was previously present there in flocks of over 100 birds, it is now rare over the whole island of Java.

Morten Strange

Distribution: Oriental region and Australasia; sedentary. A widespread and locally common resident on all major Indonesian islands, except on Java where it is now vagrant.

WHITE-BELLIED SEA-EAGLE (White-bellied Fish-eagle)
Haliaeetus leucogaster 70 cm F: Accipitridae

Description: A massive bird. Note its white underparts and wings lifted to V-shape; upperparts are light grey. The immature bird is a brownish colour.

Voice: A loud, honking call used frequently around nesting site.

Habits: Mainly a coastal bird found on remote sea shores and offshore islands; also ventures up large rivers and visits reservoirs some distance inland. Seen singly or in resident pairs. Easily spotted soaring conspicuously over habitat, but not numerous anywhere. Catches live fish in spectacular swoops across the water's surface and takes a variety of other prey; also scavenges.

Distribution: Oriental region and Australasia; sedentary. Widespread throughout the Indonesian archipelago, but generally a low-density species.

CRESTED SERPENT-EAGLE
Spilornis cheela 58 cm F: Accipitridae

Description: Its rounded shape and somewhat spotted plumage, with an insignificant crest, are diagnostic (top photo). Note white wing band on flying bird (bottom photo). A similar species, *S. rufipectus,* is endemic to Sulawesi.

Voice: Often utters a loud and penetrating *wheew-wheew* when soaring.

Habits: Probably the most common forest raptor in its range. Occurs from lowland primary rainforest to mature secondary growth, in clearings and along forest edges, into submontane elevations. This rather conspicuous bird can be seen soaring high above the forest or sitting motionless on a midstorey branch looking for small prey.

Distribution: Oriental region; sedentary. A fairly common resident throughout Sumatra, Kalimantan, Java and Bali; recorded once on Lombok.

CRESTED GOSHAWK

Accipiter trivirgatus 40 cm F: Accipitridae

Description: Note its short, rounded wings and streaked underparts. Its crest is hardly noticeable.

Voice: A shrill, prolonged scream *he-he-he-he-he* near nest.

Habits: This low-density forest hawk is sometimes encountered in lowland and submontane rainforest and along forest edges, where it perches in the trees and flies into the canopy to hunt for small vertebrates and large insects. Occasionally soars over its territory, screaming loudly.

Distribution: Oriental region; sedentary. An uncommon resident in Sumatra and Kalimantan; rare on Java; vagrant on Bali.

GREY GOSHAWK (Variable Goshawk)

Accipiter novaehollandiae 45 cm F: Accipitridae

Description: Plumage highly variable with race and morph. Photo shows *A. n. griseogularis* of northern Maluku. Some West Papuan birds are all white.

Voice: A variable series of high-pitched notes.

Habits: An adaptable raptor found in primary forest, along forest edges and in nearby cultivation. Sometimes seen soaring low over the canopy. Hunts for birds, reptiles, small mammals and large insects among the trees.

Distribution: Australasia, south to Tasmania; sedentary. A locally fairly common resident in parts of Wallacea and throughout West Papua.

BLACK-MANTLED GOSHAWK

Accipiter melanochlamys 36 cm F: Accipitridae

Description: Distinguished from other *Accipiter* hawks within its range by its dark wings and back, and chestnut collar. Underparts are the same chestnut colour, without any streaks.

Voice: A high, rapid *wee-wee-wee*.

Habits: Found in primary rainforest and sometimes along forest edges. Usually occurs between 1,200–3,000 m and occasionally down to 300 m. This secretive bird lives in remote forested areas and is not often observed. Moves within the forest canopy or the upper storey and sometimes soars above the trees. Feeds mainly on birds, catching them in flight or on branches; also takes small mammals, frogs and insects.

Morten Strange

Distribution: New Guinea. A generally scarce resident in montane parts of West Papua.

GREY-HEADED GOSHAWK

Accipiter poliocephalus 35 cm F: Accipitridae

Description: Its pale grey head and whitish underparts are diagnostic; also note orange cere and legs.

Voice: A rapid series of high, thin notes.

Habits: Occurs in primary forest, along forest edges and in nearby cultivation. Prefers lowland elevations and foothills. Occasionally moves into lower montane forest to 1,500 m. Reported to feed mainly on lizards and snakes; also takes insects and birds. Its nest has been found 27 m high in a forest tree. Seldom observed and little studied.

Morten Strange

Distribution: New Guinea. A widespread, generally scarce resident in West Papua and on adjacent islands.

JAPANESE SPARROW-HAWK

Accipiter gularis 27 cm F: Accipitridae

Description: Photo shows immature bird. Female has barred, not streaked chest. Male underparts are more rufous, with thin barring.

Voice: Silent during migration.

Habits: Frequents forests and open woodlands and is often seen near the coast. Usually spotted singly, but loose congregations gather at crossing points between islands such as the strait between Java and Bali. Sometimes soars high late in the morning or during migration. Hunts by flying very low, grabbing small birds in flight.

Distribution: Breeds in northeast Asia; migratory. A widespread winter visitor in the Sunda and parts of the Wallacea subregions. Probably overlooked on many islands; generally fairly common and locally abundant during peak migration.

BESRA

Accipiter virgatus 33 cm F: Accipitridae

Description: Distinguished with difficulty from the previous migratory species, by its larger size and a streak on its throat that is sometimes visible. Rufous barring on underparts varies with age and subspecies, but is usually heavier than on this male.

Voice: Usually silent. A squealing *ki-weer* and a rapid *tchew-tchew* has been recorded.

Habits: This forest bird is usually found in denser cover than the previous species, often at montane elevations between 700 and 2,200 m. Has also been seen in the lowlands and reported at 3,000 m in Sumatra. Rarely observed during trips and surveys. Perches quietly in the forest, darting out to catch small birds on the wing.

Distribution: Oriental region; mainly sedentary. A generally rare resident on Sumatra, Java, Bali, Flores and montane parts of Kalimantan.

SMALL SPARROW-HAWK

Accipiter nanus 25 cm F: Accipitridae

Description: Best distinguished from the similar Vinous-breasted Sparrow-hawk, *A. rhodogaster* (also endemic to Sulawesi), by its orange-yellow (not greenish) feet and lack of barring on its thighs.

Voice: A thin, high-pitched *kiliu*; also a sharp rapid *ki-ki-ki*.

Habits: Occurs in montane forest between 900 and 2,000 m, possibly also lower. Mainly found in primary forest, but frequently emerges along forest edges and roadsides to hunt for large insects and snails; also takes small birds. Swoops out from a low perch to grab prey on the ground or in the air. Not often reported and little studied.

Filip Verbelen

Distribution: Indonesian endemic. An uncommon resident in montane parts of Sulawesi, except for southwestern parts. Near-threatened with global extinction due to forest clearance.

BLACK EAGLE

Ictinaetus malayensis 69 cm F: Accipitridae

Description: Plumage a uniform dark brown/blackish colour. A unique bird, the only member of its genus. Note its characteristic flight silhouette, with broad wings narrowing at the body.

Voice: Occasionally an airy *kleee-kee*.

Habits: This forest eagle is found mainly in primary rainforest at montane elevations, it has been recorded to 2,800 m on Sumatra. Also occurs at lower levels and sometimes moves into the lowlands. This low-density species requires a large wilderness territory and is sometimes seen soaring high over the forest. Flies low at canopy level when hunting, looking for birds, reptiles and mammals among the branches.

Samson So

Distribution: Oriental region into eastern Indonesia; mainly sedentary. A widespread but generally scarce resident in the Sunda subregion, on Sulawesi and in parts of Maluku.

GURNEY'S EAGLE

Aquila gurneyi 80 cm F: Accipitridae

Description: Distinguished with difficulty from other dark eagles by its long, straight wings and long, wedge-shaped tail; note greyish cere.

Voice: A high-pitched, piping call.

Habits: Found in lowland coastal forest and low hills, some distance inland; also strays into nearby cultivation. Usually seen soaring high on late morning thermals. Reportedly feeds on marsupial mammals, but only one confirmed observation. Little studied; its nest has never been described.

Morten Strange

Distribution: Indonesia and Papua New Guinea. Scarce resident on some islands in Maluku and on West Papua. Near-threatened with global extinction.

CHANGEABLE HAWK-EAGLE

Spizaetus cirrhatus 68 cm F: Accipitridae

Description: Photo shows dark morph. The pale morph is very different with whitish underparts, greyish-brown upperparts and dark moustache. Note short crest barely visible. Intermediate phases occur, hence the name.

Voice: A prolonged scream *hwee-hwee-hweee*.

Habits: Found in forest on Flores, from the lowlands to 1,700 m; occurs at over 1,800 m on Sumatra. A fairly adaptable species that sometimes turns up in cultivation and along disturbed forest edges; also reported in gardens on Sumatra. A low-density species that is not common anywhere within its range. Swoops onto prey such as birds, reptiles, frogs and small mammals, from a perch at the edge of the forest.

Ong Kiem Sian

Distribution: Oriental region; sedentary. A scarce resident on Sumatra, Kalimantan, Java, Bali, Sumbawa, Flores and a few smaller nearby islands.

JAVAN HAWK-EAGLE

Spizaetus bartelsi 60 cm F: Accipitridae

Description: Distinguished from the previous species by its slender body, chestnut-coloured face, black crown, and yellow-brown nape. Crest is seldom visible in flight.

Voice: During courtship a frequent disyllabic *ee-eeew.*

Habits: Occurs in forest and along forest edges from sea level to 3,000 m, but prefers the lower slopes from 200 to 1,200 m. Now rarely seen since its forest habitat has been much reduced. Recent surveys have estimated its world population to be about 600–1,000 individuals. BirdLife International Indonesia Programme has a recovery plan for this endangered species.

Vincent Nijman

Distribution: Indonesian endemic. A rare resident on Java only. Endangered with global extinction.

BLYTH'S HAWK-EAGLE

Spizaetus alboniger 52 cm F: Accipitridae

Description: Note slaty-black plumage with barred underparts and tail. Long crest is visible when perched.

Voice: Various shrill whistles and high-pitched notes.

Habits: A lower montane rainforest specialist typically found at altitudes between 500 and 1,000 m. Although scarce, it is sometimes observed circling low over the trees while hunting.

Morten Strange

Distribution: Sunda subregion; mainly sedentary. A widespread, low-density resident in Sumatra and Kalimantan.

BROWN FALCON

Falco berigora 47 cm F: Falconidae

Description: Plumage somewhat variable, sometimes paler underparts than the individual shown in photo. Its large size and hawk-like behaviour are always characteristic.

Voice: A rapid series of hoarse cackles and screeches.

Habits: Found in open forest and grasslands with scattered trees. Occurs from the lowlands into lower montane elevations, occasionally to 3,000 m. Perches in the open and can be quite approachable. Pounces from its perch onto small mammals, birds, reptiles, and other animal prey; also takes carrion. Patrols low across its territory, with uplifted wings like a hawk; also hovers clumsily.

Distribution: Australasia into Tasmania. A locally fairly common resident along northern and southern parts of West Papua.

SPOTTED KESTREL

Falco moluccensis 30 cm F: Falconidae

Description: Distinguished from kestrels in other regions by its darker brown background plumage and lack of grey in head.

Voice: A piercing *ke-ke-ke-ke* near its nest.

Habits: Mainly an open woodlands species found in coastal lowlands; also occurs locally into montane elevations. Frequents a variety of habitats, from dense forest edges into cultivation. Hunts in grassy areas, dropping down from an exposed perch or from a hovering position in the air, to catch small prey on the ground. Breeding behaviour has been little studied.

Distribution: Indonesian endemic. A rare resident on Java and Bali; fairly common locally throughout Wallacea.

Morten Strange

SPOTTED WHISTLING-DUCK

Dendrocygna guttata 46 cm F: Anatidae

Description: Distinguished from other whistling-ducks by its prominently spotted underparts and flanks. Captive photo.

Voice: A variety of piping and whistling notes.

Habits: Usually found in lowland freshwater swamps and marshes with plenty of vegetation cover and nearby trees; occasionally seen in tidal estuaries. Usually observed singly or in pairs; sometimes forms small flocks. Sometimes mingles with the following species. Feeds by dabbling for vegetable matter at the water's surface, habitually at night; can also dive.

Morten Strange

Distribution: Southeast Asia, from Mindanao in the Philippines to Papua New Guinea. A widespread but generally scarce resident in parts of Wallacea and West Papua.

WANDERING WHISTLING-DUCK

Dendrocygna arcuata 45 cm F: Anatidae

Description: Distinguished from the following species by its whitish flanks, black cap and scaly upperparts. In flight, its chestnut secondaries show clearly in wings. Captive photo.

Voice: A high-pitched whistle, especially when flying in flocks.

Habits: Under the right conditions this duck gathers in large numbers at freshwater swamps and reservoirs, and in tidal lagoons and brackish ponds just behind the coast. Feeds by dabbling for edible matter at the water's surface or by making quick dives; often feeds at night. Usually roosts in the grass near the water, seldom in trees.

Morten Strange

Distribution: Southeast Asia into northern Australia; roams widely outside breeding season. A generally scarce resident and non-breeding visitor on many islands; can be locally numerous.

LESSER WHISTLING-DUCK (Lesser Treeduck)

Dendrocygna javanica 41 cm F: Anatidae

Description: Distinguished from other treeducks by a lack of white streaks on flanks. Note light brown plumage with scaly wings. In flight, its wings are characteristically rounded.

Voice: Vocal; constantly utters a high-pitched, three-note whistle during flight.

Habits: Found in freshwater habitats such as marshes, reservoirs and flooded fields with plenty of vegetation. Hides during most of the day in lake-side grasses or roosts in low trees near water. Flies out slowly in dense flocks to feed on the water's surface at night, dabbling or diving for edible matter.

Distribution: Oriental region; nomadic outside breeding season. A generally scarce resident in parts of Sumatra, Kalimantan and Java, extending into Sumbawa and Flores; can be locally fairly common.

WHITE-WINGED DUCK

Cairina scutulata 75 cm F: Anatidae

Description: Unmistakable; white wing coverts show in flight; pale head is prominent. Captive photo shows female; male has all-white head and neck.

Voice: Short honks.

Habits: This specialist duck only occurs in lowland rainforest, along forested ponds and streams, feeding mainly by night. This shy and retiring bird is difficult to find in the wild. Way Kambas, Sumatra is a well-known location for observing this globally endangered species. Much reduced in numbers due to hunting and habitat conversion. Its total world population may number less than 1,000 birds.

Distribution: Oriental region; sedentary. A rare resident in parts of Sumatra, mainly in the southeast; locally extinct in Java.

GREY TEAL

Anas gibberifrons 42 cm F: Anatidae

Description: A uniformly dark face and small green speculum are diagnostic. Photo shows West Papuan/Australian subspecies. Considered by some to be a full species, the Grey Teal, *A. gracilis*—then *A. gibberifrons* is called the Sunda Teal. Treatment here follows del Hoyo (1992).

Voice: A loud series of quacks.

Habits: Usually found in freshwater lakes and marshes, and sometimes in brackish lagoons and ponds behind mangroves. Occurs from coastal areas to montane lakes at 2,000 m. Often seen in pairs or a small group, dabbling for vegetable matter and tiny invertebrates in the surface waters.

C. & D. Frith; Frithfoto

Distribution: Andaman Islands, through Indonesia to Australia and New Zealand. A locally numerous but generally uncommon resident on Java, Bali, parts of Wallacea and southern West Papua; a non-breeding visitor on Sumatra and Kalimantan.

PACIFIC BLACK DUCK

Anas superciliosa 53 cm F: Anatidae

Description: Unmistakable within its range; note characteristic head pattern. Male and female are similar.

Voice: Sometimes quacks.

Habits: Found in freshwater marshes, vegetated lakes and nearby wet fields. Usually seen in pairs or small groups, although flocks numbering 200 with other waterbirds have been reported. Mainly occurs in the lowlands, but observed locally at montane elevations in Wallacea to 2,000 m; in West Papua found at alpine lakes. Dabbles in the surface water for vegetable food or grazes on the banks. Changes location with a strong and direct flight.

Morten Strange

Distribution: Australasia into New Zealand and Pacific. A generally uncommon, locally numerous resident and non-breeding visitor in parts of eastern Indonesia; a rare visitor to Java and Bali; vagrant on Sumatra and Kalimantan.

GARGANEY

Anas querquedula 41 cm F: Anatidae

Morten Strange

Description: Note this female's pale brown plumage with diagnostic light-brown stripes across its head (right, with Lesser Whistling-Duck). Breeding male has prominent white eyebrows.

Voice: Usually silent during migration, sometimes a slight *kwak*.

Habits: Frequents swamps and wetlands, sometimes far inland, but is usually found on ponds and lagoons just behind the coast. Flies very fast in small dense flocks. Feeds on both vegetable and aquatic food at the surface of the water. Erratic occurrence and only during the northern winter from October to April.

Distribution: Breeds in temperate Eurasia; winters in Africa and Southeast Asia reaching Australia. A widespread but scarce winter visitor throughout much of Indonesia; vagrant on Sumatra, Java and Bali.

PHILIPPINE SCRUBFOWL (Tabon Scrubfowl)

Megapodius cumingii 35 cm F: Megapodiidae

Chua Ee Kiam

Description: Unmistakable within its range. This species and the allospecies, the Orange-footed Scrubfowl, *M. reinwardt*, of Nusa Tenggara, New Guinea and northern Australia is sometimes included under the following species.

Voice: A long, mournful whistle; often calls at night.

Habits: A forest bird that usually occurs in primary rainforest and mature secondary growth, mainly in the coastal lowlands. Found on Sulawesi to 2,000 m elevation. This family replaces pheasants in the Australasian region. Moves along the ground, feeding on insects, larvae, worms and snails. A shy and elusive bird that flies quickly to a low perch when disturbed.

Distribution: From Indonesia north into the islands off Sabah (Malaysia) and the Philippines. A locally fairly common but generally scarce resident on Sulawesi, Sangihe and Talaud Islands.

DUSKY SCRUBFOWL (Common Scrubfowl)

Megapodius freycinet 34 cm F: Megapodiidae

Description: Within its range can only be confused with Moluccan Scrubfowl, *Eulipoa wallacei,* which has pale brown plumage with a banded back.

Voice: Vocal; a series of chuckling notes.

Habits: A chicken-like bird that feeds on the ground in dense coastal or primary hill forest. Often seen in resident pairs. Walks long distances, picking up fruits and invertebrates from the leaf litter. Perches on low branches. Incubates its eggs using natural heat generated by a pile of rotting plant material, a habit unique to this family. The chick fends for itself immediately after hatching.

Morten Strange

Distribution: Indonesian endemic. A locally fairly common resident on Halmahera and adjacent islands in Wallacea and West Papua.

WATTLED BRUSH-TURKEY

Aepypodius arfakianus 42 cm F: Megapodiidae

Description: Note the diagnostic bare white skin on face and throat; its maroon-brown rump flashes on take-off. This species and the little known, endangered Waigeo Brush-turkey, *A. bruijnii,* of Waigeo Island, are the only members of this genus.

Voice: A harsh, explosive crowing near its mound.

Habits: Found in montane primary forest, from 750 to 2,800 m; occurs on islands to 300 m. At lower elevations it may overlap with 3 brush-turkeys of the *Talegalla* genus that occur exclusively in different parts of West Papua. A shy and inconspicuous bird, mainly terrestrial, that feeds on fallen fruits, seeds and probably insects. Flies up to a perch when disturbed.

Brian J. Coates

Distribution: New Guinea. A generally scarce resident in montane parts of West Papua, and in the hills of the nearby Misool and Yapen islands.

MALEO

Macrocephalon maleo 56 cm F: Megapodiidae

Description: Unmistakable; a monotypic genus.

Voice: A haunting *kee-ourrrrr*, a duck-like *kuk-kuk,* and a goose-like *gak-gak.*

Habits: Found along forest edges near open areas with loose soil. Often seen on coastal beaches as well as inland areas to 1,200 m. This shy bird is usually found at communal breeding grounds, but is difficult to approach. Some large sites support 150–200 pairs. Moves on the ground like a large chicken and flies up onto a branch in the forest when disturbed. Feeds on fallen fruits and invertebrates. Its large eggs, buried deep in sand, are kept warm by the sun at the beach or by geothermal heat in volcanic areas.

Distribution: Indonesian endemic. A widespread but uncommon resident on Sulawesi and the nearby smaller Bangka, Lembeh and Butung islands. Has disappeared from the south of Sulawesi due to habitat loss. Vulnerable to global extinction.

BLACK PARTRIDGE (Black Wood-partridge)

Melanoperdix nigra 24 cm F: Phasianidae

Description: Female (photo) is dark brown; note black bars on rufous wings. A monotypic genus. Male is all black.

Voice: A double whistle.

Habits: Found in primary forest. Reported from the lowlands on Sumatra, including peat swamp forest; in Kalimantan occurs at lower montane elevations. Moves along the forest floor, picking up insects, grubs and fallen seeds. There have been few observations from the field, so status is uncertain—has possibly declined in numbers. There are no nesting records from Sumatra, but this rare photograph is from a nesting site in Kalimantan.

Distribution: Sunda subregion, Malaysia and Indonesia only. A rare resident in Sumatra and Kalimantan. Near-threatened with global extinction.

FERRUGINOUS PARTRIDGE
Caloperdix oculea 26 cm F: Phasianidae

Description: The small white and black scales in an otherwise dark chestnut plumage are diagnostic. The genus is monotypic. Captive photo.

Voice: An ascending and accelerating trill, eventually ending in 2-4 harsher notes.

Habits: A forest bird reported to prefer lower montane hill forest in Borneo and secondary scrub in Sumatra. However, in Indonesia this species is only known from collected specimens and has never been spotted in the wild. It moves along the ground, picking up seeds, fallen fruits and insects.

Distribution: Sunda subregion. A rare resident in Sumatra and northern Kalimantan.

CRESTED PARTRIDGE (Crested Wood-partridge)
Rollulus rouloul 26 cm F: Phasianidae

Description: Unmistakable. The photo shows a captive male. The female is pale green with chestnut wings. A monotypic genus.

Voice: Utters a shrill, plaintive whistle *si-il* just at daybreak.

Habits: Found in primary rainforest and mature secondary forest, mainly in the lowlands. Occasionally moves into lower montane elevations. Shy and much reduced in numbers. Today it is rarely seen in the wild in Indonesia. Moves in small parties on the ground, feeding on fallen fruits and insects in the leaf litter.

Distribution: Sunda subregion. A widespread but uncommon resident in Sumatra and Kalimantan.

CRESTED FIREBACK

Lophura ignita ♂ 55 cm, ♀ 40 cm F: Phasianidae

Margaret Kinnaird

Morten Strange

Description: Captive male (top photo) has blue facial skin and diagnostic dark blue breast. Sumatran race has dark blue belly and white tail. Kalimantan race (bottom photo) has chestnut belly and yellow tail. The female (bottom photo) is brown with white scales on underparts.

Voice: Male has croaking call followed by a shrill chirp.

Habits: Restricted to lowland rainforest; occurs in both primary and mature secondary forest, often near rivers and streams. Formerly common in Indonesia, but now much reduced in numbers, although sightings are still reported. A shy bird; habits little known.

Distribution: Sunda subregion. An uncommon resident in Sumatra and Kalimantan. Vulnerable to global extinction.

RED JUNGLEFOWL

Gallus gallus ♂ 79 cm, ♀ 42 cm F: Phasianidae

Morten Strange

Description: Male (at left of photo, with a group of females) looks much like a purebred domestic chicken. Note its distinct ear patch (more reddish in south Sumatran and Javan birds).

Voice: Vocal during early morning. The call of the male is similar to the domestic chicken, but with a more abrupt ending.

Habits: The ancestor to the domestic chicken. An adaptable species found along primary forest edges and in nearby disturbed areas such as secondary growth, plantations and scrub. When disturbed, it runs or makes a short flight into cover. Omnivorous; often seen foraging in small parties, typically one male with a harem of females.

Distribution: Oriental region. Widespread and fairly common on Sumatra; rare on Java and Bali; introduced on Sulawesi and other islands in Wallacea.

GREEN JUNGLEFOWL

Gallus varius ♂ 70 cm, ♀ 40 cm F: Phasianidae

Description: Distinguished from the previous species by its dark greenish (not orange) neck, and purple rounded comb.

Voice: A brief, harsh version of the previous species' voice.

Habits: Found along forest edges, in drought deciduous woodlands and savanna. Often observed near the coast, as well as inland up to 2,000 m. Shy but sometimes seen near roads and rural villages. Still an easy bird to find in many places, but numbers are much reduced in recent years due to habitat loss and capture for the pet trade. Males make good fighting competitors when interbred with the domestic chicken.

Distribution: Indonesian endemic. A widespread and fairly common resident throughout Java, Bali, Lombok, Sumbawa, Flores, Alor, Sumba and some smaller adjacent islands.

BRONZE-TAILED PEACOCK-PHEASANT

Polyplectron chalcurum ♂ 50 cm, ♀ 35 cm F: Phasianidae

Description: Captive female in photo. Note diagnostic greyish head and brown plumage with scales, but no ocelli. Male has long tail, with blue-green sheen.

Voice: A loud *karau karau*.

Habits: Found in primary lower montane forest, between 800 and 1,700 m. Numbers have declined due to habitat loss, although it does show some tolerance to disturbance. Recent field sightings have been reported. Walks along the ground, feeding on small fruits and insects in the leaf litter. Otherwise little known; its movements and nesting habits in the wild have never been described.

Distribution: Indonesian endemic. A scarce resident in mountains of north and south Sumatra.

GREAT ARGUS

Argusianus argus ♂ 120 cm, ♀ 60 cm F: Phasianidae

Distribution: Sunda subregion. In Indonesia, a low density resident in Sumatra and Kalimantan.

Description: Unmistakable—a huge pheasant. Captive male in photo. Male has elongated tail feathers; female is a uniform chestnut brown. The genus is monotypic.

Voice: A powerful *kow-wow* that carries far in the forest.

Habits: Restricted to dense rain-forest, mainly primary lowland forest. Also occurs in mature disturbed areas and lower montane hills. Usually moves along the forest floor and sometimes flies up onto a low perch. This generally shy bird is rarely seen, but its explosive call is often heard in good forest and the male can sometimes be viewed at close range, at its display ground.

GREEN PEAFOWL

Pavo muticus ♂ 210, ♀ 120 cm F: Phasianidae

Distribution: Southeast Asia. In Indonesia, found only on Java. Regarded as vulnerable to global extinction.

Description: Unmistakable within its range. Distinguished from the better-known Indian Peafowl, *P. cristatus*, by its green (not blue) neck. Male (photo) has long tail.

Voice: Male calls with a loud *aow-aaw*.

Habits: Found on Java, mainly in the protected areas of Ujung Kulon (west Java) and Baluran National Parks (east Java). Here it can be found along forest edges and in dry savanna types of woodlands. Generally shy, but can be seen well in the evenings, when small groups roost low in trees. Much reduced throughout its fragmented range due to hunting and habitat loss.

BARRED BUTTON-QUAIL

Turnix suscitator 16 cm F: Turnicidae

Description: Distinguished from other button-quail and the female Blue-breasted Quail, *Coturnix chinensis*; F: Phasianidae, which is widespread in Indonesia, by its barred underparts (see Strange 2000).

Voice: A soft purring, a repeated *woot-woot* and a peculiar, accelerating, wooping call.

Habits: Within its range, this bird and the Blue-breasted Quail are the most likely small quail to be seen. Runs along the ground in open country with scrub. Often seen in heavily disturbed secondary forest with grassy patches and nearby cultivation. Usually stays under cover, but sometimes comes out early in the morning to feed on seeds along the roadside.

Martin Hale

Distribution: Oriental region. A locally fairly common resident in Sumatra, Java, Bali, Sulawesi, Lombok, Sumbawa, Flores, Alor and a few smaller islands nearby.

BROLGA

Grus rubicunda 140 cm F: Gruidae

Description: Similar to the Sarus Crane, *G. antigone,* of the Oriental region and northern Australia (see Strange 2000), but note small red dot on neck (not full red head) and dark grey (not reddish) feet.

Voice: A loud, trumpeting *ga rongg*.

Habits: The only member of the crane family in Indonesia. Freshwater marshes, coastal lagoons and grasslands are ideal habitats for this bird and are the best places to see it. The Brolgas congregate into large flocks here, sometimes in hundreds at prime locations. Feeds on small animal prey dug out of or picked up from the wet ground. Nests on the ground in the swamps during the wet season.

Jon Hornbuckle

Distribution: Australasia into southern Australia. A locally common resident in the Trans-Fly region of West Papua.

SLATY-BREASTED RAIL

Gallirallus striatus 24 cm F: Rallidae

Description: Distinguished from other rails by white barring on all upperparts; also note chestnut cap, contrasting with slate-coloured breast.

Voice: A harsh *gelek,* repeated 10–15 times.

Habits: Mainly found in freshwater marshes with plenty of vegetation; also extends into paddy fields and drier grasslands nearby. Shy and secretive, but may be quite numerous in the ideal habitat. Runs into cover at the slightest danger; rarely flies. Partly nocturnal; best viewed early in the morning when it sometimes emerges briefly from its cover onto the edge of a road, pond or field.

Distribution: Oriental region. A widespread and fairly common resident on Sumatra, Kalimantan and Java; rare on Bali; very rare and possibly resident on Sulawesi; vagrant on Lombok.

BUFF-BANDED RAIL

Gallirallus philippensis 28 cm F: Rallidae

Description: Note diagnostic head pattern. Its barred flanks and somewhat spotted wings are also distinctive.

Voice: A harsh alarm call *krek* and a variety of other squeaking and grunting notes.

Habits: Found in open country, mainly near swamps, but also seen in drier areas and around cultivation. Occurs in Wallacea to 1,000 m and in West Papua from sea level to 3,600 m. Often comes out into the open near a roadside or a wet patch, to feed on a variety of small animal prey, especially in the early morning and late afternoon (see photo). Never ventures far from cover and runs back to safety quickly, with head extended forward, when disturbed.

Distribution: Australasia, from the Philippines to New Zealand and Pacific islands. A widespread and scarce to locally common resident in large parts of eastern Indonesia; vagrant on Sumba.

BAILLON'S CRAKE

Porzana pusilla 18 cm F: Rallidae

Description: The white streaks on its back and wings together with its tiny size are diagnostic.

Voice: A short *krek-krek*.

Habits: Frequents freshwater marshes, small ponds and densely vegetated lakes and reservoirs. Walks restlessly at the edge of the water or on floating vegetation, feeding on aquatic insects and their larvae. Rarely emerges from cover and doesn't seem to fly by day.

Distribution: Africa, Eurasia and Australasia; partly migratory. A widespread but rare winter visitor in Indonesia; vagrant in West Papua and Bali. Possibly also a local resident, but only one confirmed breeding record (from Sumatra).

RUDDY-BREASTED CRAKE

Porzana fusca 21 cm F: Rallidae

Description: Note diagnostic lack of bars on breast and belly, and a faint barring under tail only.

Voice: Usually quiet; sometimes a long rattle.

Habits: Frequents a variety of freshwater wetland habitats, from marshes and wet paddy fields to grasslands and nearby drier scrub. Could be quite numerous, but is not easy to observe. Usually stays within cover; rarely flies and is usually crepuscular and secretive. This behaviour is typical of the family.

Distribution: East Asia and the Oriental region; partly migratory. A locally fairly common resident on Sumatra, Java and Bali; rare on Sulawesi and Flores; vagrant in Sumba and Kalimantan.

WHITE-BROWED CRAKE
Porzana cinerea 20 cm F: Rallidae

Description: Note black mask across eye, contrasting with white eyebrow.

Voice: Vocal during breeding season; a soft, high-pitched piping.

Habits: An attractive rail found in freshwater marshes, especially in the lowlands or near the coast. Observed less often in flooded fields. Often seen walking on floating vegetation, across the surface of the water. A resident pair usually travels together, feeding mainly on aquatic invertebrates. This usually crepuscular bird is alert and wary, and walks quietly into cover when disturbed.

Distribution: Southeast Asia into Australasia; sedentary. A widespread and locally fairly common resident on all the major islands.

WHITE-BREASTED WATERHEN
Amaurornis phoenicurus 33 cm F: Rallidae

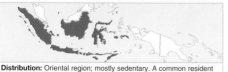

Description: Unmistakable; the only rail with a white breast.

Voice: Vocal, especially during the semi-darkness at dawn and dusk. Makes a series of peculiar croaking and grunting chuckles that last several minutes; also a high-pitched, single-note alarm call.

Habits: The most numerous member of its family in Indonesia. A tolerant and omnivorous species occurring mainly in freshwater wetlands; also found in coastal mangroves. Has adapted well to living in drainage canals and flooded fields near villages and gardens. Comes out into open areas, running around like a chicken, often in pairs. Also perches low on branches and makes short flights into cover when disturbed.

Distribution: Oriental region; mostly sedentary. A common resident throughout Sunda and parts of Wallacea; has recently expanded to the east, reaching Seram.

WATERCOCK
Gallicrex cinerea 40 cm F: Rallidae

Description: Its brown plumage together with its large size are always diagnostic. In spring the males show breeding plumage (see photo; shown with Redshanks and Common Sandpiper). Non-breeding male and female are light brown with dark, scaly-black upperparts.

Voice: Silent during migration.

Habits: During migration frequents freshwater marshes and rivers with dense vegetation cover, usually not too far from the coast. Also comes out into nearby small ponds and flooded fields to feed, especially at night. This shy bird can be seen well as it flies across the reeds when flushed.

Distribution: East Asia and Oriental region; partly migratory. Breeding recorded in Sumatra; otherwise a generally uncommon winter visitor to Kalimantan, Java, Bali, Sulawesi, Sumbarwa and Flores.

DUSKY MOORHEN
Gallinula tenebrosa 31 cm F: Rallidae

Description: Distinguished from the following species by the lack of white on its flanks.

Voice: A variety of loud shrieks and yelps.

Habits: Frequents freshwater lakes and vegetated swamps and ponds, mainly in the lowlands. Occurs to 1,000 m on Sulawesi. Often observed in resident pairs (see photo) and at prime locations many will congregate together. This quite conspicuous bird stays out in the open and is often active all through the day, but is wary and difficult to approach. Feeding habits are much like the following species.

Distribution: Australasia, south to Tasmania; mainly sedentary. A locally fairly common resident and non-breeding visitor in parts of Wallacea and West Papua; vagrant on Flores, Sumba and south Kalimantan.

COMMON MOORHEN

Gallinula chloropus 33 cm F: Rallidae

Description: Note the conspicuous white line on its flanks.

Voice: An abrupt, metallic *pruuk*.

Habits: Only found around freshwater wetlands, large marshes and small ponds. At home on the surface of the water, where it swims like a duck, feeding on all kinds of organic matter such as plants, seeds and tiny invertebrates. Equally at home on land, where it can find food and run fast when required. A resident pair often feeds together.

Distribution: Worldwide except Australasia; partly migratory. A locally fairly common resident in Sumatra, south Kalimantan, Java, Bali, Sulawesi, Lombok, Sumbawa, Flores and Sumba.

PURPLE SWAMPHEN

Porphyrio porphyrio 43 cm F: Rallidae

Description: Unmistakable; note its purple and blue plumage, red bill and massive legs. Captive photo.

Voice: An explosive *wak* and a variety of grunts and hoots.

Habits: Requires extensive freshwater marshes, but sometimes moves into nearby fields to forage, especially at dusk. Usually occurs in small flocks. Not migratory, however populations will change location readily, depending on conditions and water levels. Clambers about wetland vegetation looking mainly for plant food. Also makes short flights, dropping quickly back into cover.

Distribution: Africa, Eurasia and Australasia; somewhat nomadic. In Indonesia, a widespread but generally scarce resident on most major islands.

COMMON COOT

Fulica atra 40 cm F: Rallidae

Description: Unmistakable within its range; note its prominent white bill and facial shield.

Voice: Quite vocal; a variety of harsh, metallic notes.

Habits: Found on open water in the montane lakes of West Papua. In other areas, frequents freshwater marshes and tidal, coastal lagoons. Remarkably duck-like, for a member of this family. Spends most of its time swimming on the water surface and frequently dives under water, mainly in search of plant food. A strong flier that accelerates by pattering across the surface before lifting off.

Morten Strange

Distribution: Africa, Eurasia and Australasia; partly migratory. A local and scarce resident in the interior mountains of West Papua; breeds on east Java; a rare visitor on Bali and Flores; vagrant on Sulawesi and Buru.

AUSTRALIAN BUSTARD

Ardeotis australis 105 cm F: Otididae

Description: Unmistakable; the only member of this family in Indonesia.

Voice: Silent except for a booming call during display.

Habits: Found in open grasslands and savanna with scattered tree cover. Prefers the transitional zone between grasslands and dry woodlands. Often observed near marshes, but not in the wet areas. This photo from Wasur illustrates its habit of moving into burnt areas. Walks along the ground and makes a short, heavy flight when disturbed. Feeds on large insects and small reptiles, as well as seeds, shoots and other plant matter. The male performs a spectacular mating display puffing out neck feathers and wings, and strutting about.

Jon Hornbuckle

Distribution: Australasia into southern Australia; mainly sedentary. In Indonesia, a locally fairly common resident in the Trans-Fly region of West Papua.

BRONZE-WINGED JACANA

Metopidius indicus 29 cm F: Jacanidae

Description: Unmistakable; note dark plumage and prominent white eye-brow. This genus is monotypic. Replaced in Eastern Indonesia by the Comb-crested Jacana, *Irediparra gallinacea*.

Voice: Piping and low guttural notes.

Habits: Found in freshwater swamps and overgrown lakes and ponds, where it runs across the surface on floating vegetation. Typical of this small family. Probably the most important location in Indonesia is around the Tulang Bawang river in south Sumatra, where extensive but usually inaccessible breeding colonies of waterbirds can be found. During the drier season, thirty or more can sometimes gather at a single pond.

Distribution: Oriental region. A generally scarce but very locally numerous resident on Sumatra; rare on Java.

Tim Loseby

GREATER PAINTED SNIPE

Rostratula benghalensis 25 cm F: Rostratulidae

Description: Photo shows female together with Wood Sandpiper. Male has rufous-tinged parts replaced with dull brown. Genus is monotypic.

Voice: Usually silent; during breeding the female utters a penetrating *kook-kook-kook* at dawn and dusk.

Habits: This peculiar bird and a South American species are the only members of its family. Secretive and largely nocturnal, this snipe is best viewed as it slowly emerges from cover near a vegetated marsh, usually at dusk or dawn. Sometimes makes a heavy flight out of the reeds, dropping quickly and silently back in.

Morten Strange

Distribution: Africa, Oriental region, East Asia and Australia; sedentary. A generally scarce resident in Sumatra, Java, Lombok, Sumbawa and Flores; few records from Kalimantan.

MASKED LAPWING
Vanellus miles 34 cm F: Charadriidae

Description: Unmistakable within its range; note its prominent yellow wattles. Black wingtips show in flight.

Voice: Typical of the genus; a loud, staccato alarm call *ke-ke-ke-kek*.

Habits: Frequents open country with fairly short grass near lakes and marshes. Usually found at freshwater wetlands, sometimes also in tidal areas. Resident pairs can be seen at breeding sites, faithfully defending their territory. Disperses somewhat outside of breeding season and forms small flocks. Runs forward in a plover-like manner and stops abruptly to peck for insects and worms.

Margaret Kinnaird

Distribution: Australasia. A locally fairly common resident in the southeastern part of West Papua; a non-breeding visitor on the islands offshore.

GREY PLOVER
Pluvialis squatarola 28 cm F: Charadriidae

Description: Distinguished from the following species by its grey (not golden) upperparts; in summer plumage the underparts are black.

Voice: A slurred whistle *kwee-u-ee;* often calls in flight.

Habits: Seems to be everywhere on exposed seashores during peak migration, from September to October and March to April, but can be seen at any month of the year. Prefers remote sandy beaches and coral reefs; settles less often on mudflats and is never found around fresh water. Doesn't usually bunch up in dense flocks like some shorebirds. Often just a few birds are spread out over the beach.

Morten Strange

Distribution: Worldwide; breeds in the high Arctic, winters in the tropics, reaching Australia. A common passage migrant and winter visitor throughout coastal Indonesia.

PACIFIC GOLDEN PLOVER (Lesser Golden Plover)
Pluvialis fulva 25 cm F: Charadriidae

Description: Note golden-brown upperparts with orange dots.

Voice: A clear and penetrating whistle *tu-ee*

Habits: During migration, this plover frequents estuaries, mangroves and tidal mudflats, as well as grasslands and fields behind the shoreline. Often seen at airfields and golf courses near the sea. Unlike the previous species, this bird is very sociable and congregates in dense flocks at prime locations during peak migration. Spreads out when feeding and forms groups when flying.

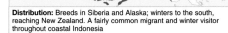

Distribution: Breeds in Siberia and Alaska; winters to the south, reaching New Zealand. A fairly common migrant and winter visitor throughout coastal Indonesia

LITTLE RINGED PLOVER
Charadrius dubius 18 cm F: Charadriidae

Description: A yellow orbital ring is diagnostic in all plumages. Photo shows breeding plumage, with distinct black collar and mask. A Redshank is on the right.

Voice: Resident race emits a harsh *chit-chit*; migrants, a soft *pee-u*.

Habits: Breeds along riverbanks, from the coast up to 1,500 m. During migration, it can turn up at coastal wetlands, along tidal estuaries and in drier fields far inland. This active feeder runs forward quickly, then stops briefly to peck in the mud or sand.

Distribution: Breeds in temperate and subtropical Eurasia and New Guinea; winters in Africa and tropical Asia. An uncommon resident in West Papua; a scarce winter visitor throughout Indonesia.

KENTISH PLOVER

Charadrius alexandrinus 15 cm F: Charadriidae

Description: Photo shows migratory race in non-breeding plumage. The resident race is treated by Andrew (1992) as an endemic species, the Javan Plover, *C. javanicus.*

Voice: A soft *twit*

Habits: Mainly found along the coast, especially on tidal estuaries and mudflats and at adjacent sandy points. It can sometimes be found some distance inland, along rivers and in wet fields. Is often solitary, but will mix with other shorebirds, gathering in small flocks at prime locations.

Morten Strange

Distribution: Worldwide except Australasia; northern populations migrate. The resident race breeds in Java and Sumbawa, and possibly Bali. An uncommon winter visitor there and on Sumatra; vagrant in Kalimantan, Sulawesi and Halmahera.

MALAYSIAN PLOVER

Charadrius peronii 15 cm F: Charadriidae

Description: The male (back) has a diagnostic thin, black band across its neck; the female's band (front) is rufous brown. Note its pale legs.

Voice: Similar to that of the previous species.

Habits: A specialised bird found only on exposed tropical beaches composed of sand, crushed coral debris and shells. Usually observed in remote and desolate coves. This habitat is not favoured by many shorebirds, but vacationing humans have displaced this tiny and confiding bird from many previously known locations. Today it is considered near-threatened with global extinction.

Morten Strange

Distribution: Southeast Asia; sedentary. A widespread but scarce resident on Sumatra, Kalimantan, Sulawesi, Bali, Lombok, Sumbawa, Flores, Sumba, Timor and some smaller adjacent islands.

LESSER SAND-PLOVER (Mongolian Plover)

Charadrius mongolus 20 cm F: Charadriidae

Morten Strange

Description: Photo shows non-breeding plumage. In breeding plumage this plover has a rufous breast band and a black facial mask.

Voice: A short, trilling *dri-it*.

Habits: Likely to be found on all Indonesian islands, usually between August and June, but has been recorded during all months of the year. Found in all types of coastal habitat, often on mudflats near mangroves and around commercial prawn pond areas, but also on exposed sandy beaches and in saline marshes behind the beach.

Distribution: Breeds in the high Arctic and temperate northeast and central Asia; migrates south reaching Australia. A fairly common passage migrant and winter visitor throughout Indonesia.

GREATER SAND-PLOVER (Large Sand-plover)

Charadrius leschenaultii 23 cm F: Charadriidae

Morten Strange

Description: Similar to the previous species, but note the diagnostic stronger bill, longer legs and greyish upperparts.

Voice: Sometimes a soft *trrrt*.

Habits: Much like the previous species, in fact the two often mix. In Indonesia this bird is generally more numerous, especially on exposed sandy coastlines. Flocks spread out when feeding, but form flocks when flying to high tide roosting sites.

Distribution: Breeds in central Asia; migrates to tropics and south to Australia. A common passage migrant and winter visitor in Indonesia.

LITTLE CURLEW

Numenius minutus 30 cm F: Scolopacidae

Description: Distinguished from the following species by its size and much shorter bill, which are diagnostic.

Voice: A fluty *di-di-di* in flight.

Habits: Settles near the coast during migration, in dry, open country with short grass. Often seen in airport areas and sometimes far inland. More rarely sighted at tidal mudflats. Unlike some shorebirds that migrate in short hauls with frequent stops, this species is believed to fly nonstop from China to southern New Guinea, and is therefore rare in Southeast Asia.

Distribution: Breeds in eastern Siberia; winters in New Guinea and northern Australia. An uncommon passage migrant in West Papua; rare in Wallacea; vagrant on Java and Bali.

WHIMBREL

Numenius phaeopus 43 cm F: Scolopacidae

Description: Distinguished from the Curlew by its shorter bill and black crown-stripe.

Voice: A fluty and penetrating *tu-tu-tu-tu* when taking off.

Habits: One of the most widespread and numerous shorebirds visiting Indonesia, especially during the northern winter from September to April. Some birds can be found throughout the year. Frequents mudflats, mangroves and estuaries, as well as sandy shores and coral reefs. Also seen occasionally in freshwater marshes and fields behind the coast. Quite shy; takes off with a whistling call when approached.

Distribution: Worldwide; breeds in temperate northern hemisphere; winters in the south. A common passage migrant and winter visitor throughout coastal Indonesia.

EURASIAN CURLEW

Numenius arquata 55 cm F: Scolopacidae

Description: Distinguished from the Whimbrel (foreground) by its much longer bill and lack of black crown-stripe.

Voice: A fluty and plaintive *cour-li* in flight.

Habits: Found on mudflats, exposed beaches and offshore islets during migration, usually mixing with other shorebirds. Probes deep into the mud for worms and crustaceans with its specialised bill. Congregates at high tide roosting sites (see photo).

Allen Jeyarajasingam

Distribution: Breeds in temperate Eurasia; winters south. A widespread but generally uncommon winter visitor on Sumatra, Java and Bali; rare in Nusa Tenggara; vagrant in Kalimantan and Halmahera.

FAR EASTERN CURLEW

Numenius madagascariensis 57 cm F: Scolopacidae

Description: Distinguished with difficulty from the previous species by its longer bill and diagnostic dark (not pale) rump, which is visible on take-off.

Voice: Similar to previous species.

Habits: Breeds in subarctic freshwater marshes. Moves to the coast during migration, often mixing in small flocks with other shorebirds on tidal mudflats and along estuaries or around saline lagoons behind the coast. Follows a more easterly migration route than many other north Asian waterbirds. The main wintering ground is in Australia, where the previous species does not occur.

Peter Basterfield/Windrush Photos

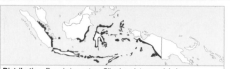

Distribution: Breeds in eastern Siberia; winters mainly in Australasian region reaching New Zealand. A widespread but generally uncommon winter visitor throughout Indonesia, mainly in eastern regions; locally common on Sumatra; rare in rest of Sunda.

BLACK-TAILED GODWIT

Limosa limosa 40 cm F: Scolopacidae

Description: A large bird distinguished from the following species by its prominent black-and-white tail and a white wing band that shows in flight.

Voice: Usually quiet; occasionally a loud *kell-kell-kell* when taking off.

Habits: Gathers at coastal mudflats during migration, usually in small flocks. Seems to be mainly a passage migrant, passing through from September to November and March to April. Spreads out and feeds with the other shorebirds at low tide, but congregates into dense groups at high-tide roosting sites.

Distribution: Breeds in temperate and subarctic Eurasia; winters south reaching Australia. A widespread passage migrant and winter visitor throughout Indonesia; locally abundant off south Sumatra, Sulawesi and Timor; occurs on other islands in small numbers.

BAR-TAILED GODWIT

Limosa lapponica 37 cm F: Scolopacidae

Description: Best distinguished from the Black-tailed Godwit by its barred tail, visible in flight, and lack of wingbar. Look for slightly upturned bill and more scaly upperparts, visible at rest. The third bird in the background is a Common Redshank.

Voice: Usually quiet; in flight a soft *kit-kit-kit.*

Habits: Found with other shorebirds at extensive mudflats on remote shorelines. At prime locations will congregate in dense flocks numbering hundreds of individuals, but usually just a few are seen together.

Distribution: Breeds in arctic Eurasia and Alaska, wintering south reaching New Zealand. In Indonesia, a widespread, mainly passage migrant; locally abundant on Sumatra, Kalimantan and Sulawesi; less common on other islands.

COMMON REDSHANK
Tringa totanus 28 cm F: Scolopacidae

Description: Note red legs, brownish upperparts and spotted breast.

Voice: Vocal; a loud, ringing *teu-hoo* when taking off.

Habits: Indonesia is an important wintering ground for this species. In the mangroves of eastern Sumatra, flocks of 10,000 individuals have been reported. During migration, frequents ponds just behind the tidal area and mud-flats along sheltered beaches. Birds spread out during low tide and probe the mud for minute invertebrates.

Distribution: Breeds in temperate Eurasia; winters south reaching Indonesia. In Indonesia, a common winter visitor and locally abundant in the Sunda subregion and on Sulawesi and Flores; less common further east.

MARSH SANDPIPER
Tringa stagnatilis 23 cm F: Scolopacidae

Description: Best distinguished from the following species by its thinner bill and paler grey upperparts. Generally has a more slender build and quicker movements.

Voice: A high-pitched *tyeuk,* thinner and higher than the Common Greenshank's voice.

Habits: During migration, mixes with other shorebirds on tidal mudflats, around prawn ponds and sometimes on freshwater wetlands. Usually forms smaller flocks than other shorebirds; often just a few are seen together. Frantically probes the surface of the mud at low tide.

Distribution: Breeds in central and northern Asia; migrates south reaching Australia. A locally common passage migrant and winter visitor in Sumatra and Kalimantan; less numerous in the east.

COMMON GREENSHANK

Tringa nebularia 32 cm F: Scolopacidae

Description: Much like the Marsh Sandpiper, but has somewhat darker upperparts. Its larger size and stronger bill are diagnostic. Shown here with a Redshank.

Voice: A penetrating *teu-teu* when taking off.

Habits: Found on all wetlands, mainly on tidal mudflats, along mangrove edges and in fish cultivation areas; also seen on exposed sandy beaches. Sometimes observed far inland around rivers and lakes, unlike most other shorebirds. Usually solitary; sometimes gathers in small groups, but never in dense flocks. Walks slowly when feeding and rushes forward to stir up small fish, much like an egret.

Distribution: Breeds in subarctic Eurasia; migrates south to Australia. A widespread and fairly common passage migrant and winter visitor throughout Indonesia, although not abundant.

WOOD SANDPIPER

Tringa glareola 20 cm F: Scolopacidae

Description: Note its diagnostic golden scaly upperparts and white supercilium.

Voice: A high-pitched, shrill *wee-wee-wee*.

Habits: Probably the most widespread and numerous shorebird in Indonesia. Can be found with other species on tidal mudflats and around freshwater marshes far inland. Often seen singly or in small flocks. During peak migration, hundreds can be seen in loose gatherings on wet paddy fields.

Distribution: Breeds in northern Eurasia; migrates south, reaching Australia. A common passage migrant and winter visitor throughout Indonesia; abundant in the west; less numerous in West Papua.

TEREK SANDPIPER

Xenus cinereus 23 cm F: Scolopacidae

Distribution: Breeds in northern Eurasia; migrates south reaching Australia. A widespread and fairly common passage migrant and winter visitor throughout Indonesia.

Description: Distinguished from the Redshank by its smaller size, orange legs, smooth grey upperparts, slightly upturned bill and frantic movements. Shown here with a Common Greenshank (right) for comparison. Often placed in its own genus.

Voice: A loud, trilled *twee-hwee-hwee*.

Habits: Generally less numerous than many other shorebirds, although flocks of thousands have been reported at prime locations in eastern Sumatra. This species is strictly coastal and is often found on exposed points of estuaries where sandy beaches begin. Runs about frantically, picking minute prey out of the surface of the mud.

COMMON SANDPIPER

Actitis hypoleucos 20 cm F: Scolopacidae

Distribution: Breeds all across northern and central Eurasia; winters south to Australia. A common, widespread migrant and winter visitor throughout Indonesia.

Description: Distinguished from other sandpipers by its small size and smooth chocolate-brown upperparts. Shown here with prey, a small crab.

Voice: A penetrating *twee-wee-wee* when taking off.

Habits: The most widespread and adaptable of all shorebirds that visit Indonesia, mainly from August to April. Found wherever water is nearby, from tidal mudflats and sandy shores, to inland reservoirs and even montane rivers. Occurs in West Papua to 3,300 m. Often solitary, but found in loose flocks during peak migration. This restless feeder runs constantly along the water's edge, bobbing its tail and pecking in the sand.

GREY-TAILED TATTLER

Heteroscelus brevipes 25 cm F: Scolopacidae

Description: Distinguished from the Common Redshank by its smooth grey upperparts and greenish legs (bottom photo). Note complete lack of white in wing when flying (top photo).

Voice: Sharp whistle *too-weet*.

Habits: Strictly coastal during migration. Often seen on mudflats and exposed sandy beaches with washed-up coral debris. Found in small flocks only, near, but not among, other shorebirds. During high tide, perches low in mangrove trees.

Distribution: Breeds in northeastern Siberia; winters south reaching New Zealand. A fairly common passage migrant and winter visitor throughout Indonesia, mainly in the east; uncommon on Sumatra.

Morten Strange

RUDDY TURNSTONE

Arenaria interpres 23 cm F: Scolopacidae

Description: Unmistakable; note black breast band and white spots in upperparts. White pattern in wings, tail and back flash prominently in flight.

Voice: A metallic *ti-ti-ti-ti-ti* when taking off.

Habits: This shorebird usually passes through Indonesia during the northern spring and fall, but can turn up at any month of the year. Sometimes appears in unlikely places such as rocky coastlines or harbour areas. Also feeds near other sandpipers and plovers on mudflats. Usually runs quickly in small groups, sometimes turning over small stones to flush out prey.

Morten Strange

Distribution: Worldwide; breeds high in the Arctic and winters in the south. A widespread and fairly common passage migrant throughout Indonesia.

ASIAN DOWITCHER

Limnodromus semipalmatus 35 cm F: Scolopacidae

Description: Its powerful, all-black bill and black (not pale) legs best distinguish it from the rare Long-billed Dowitcher, *L. scolopaceus*, recorded on Bali.

Voice: Usually silent; sometimes a quiet *miau*.

Habits: Indonesia is the main wintering ground for this near-threatened species, with 13,000 individuals counted in Sumatra and 1,000 in Java (out of an estimated total world population of 20,000). Mixes with godwits on wintering grounds. Although similar to godwits, look for its up-right stance, with lowered bill at rest, and its peculiarly mechanical movements when feeding.

Distribution: Breeds in subarctic Siberia; winters in Southeast Asia into northern Australia. A generally scarce but locally numerous winter visitor in east Sumatra and north-east Java; vagrant in Kalimantan, Sulawesi and Timor.

SWINHOE'S SNIPE

Gallinago megala 28 cm F: Scolopacidae

Description: In the field cannot be conclusively distinguished from the Pintail Snipe, *G. stenura*, the common snipe in Sumatra and western Indonesia.

Voice: A short, rasping cry when taking off.

Habits: Both species frequent wetlands, mainly vegetated swamps and wet fields inland, and brackish marshes near the coast; rarely seen on tidal mud-flats. In West Papua also inhabits dry grasslands in the interior. Snipes are secretive birds that usually stay under cover, but will come out to feed in the open when undisturbed. When flushed they take off in a sudden and rapid flight.

Distribution: Breeds in Mongolia and Siberia; winters south reaching northern Australia. A widespread and fairly common winter visitor, especially in eastern Indonesia.

RED KNOT

Calidris canutus 24 cm F: Scolopacidae

Description: Note its stocky build, pale non-breeding plumage and strong, fairly short bill. Legs appear short when walking.

Voice: A muted *chut-chut* and a whistling *twit-wit* when taking off.

Habits: Occurs on mudflats and along estuaries with other shore-birds, often with the Great Knot, *C. tenuirostris*; see Strange (2000). Flies and feeds close together in small flocks.

Distribution: Worldwide; breeds in the high Arctic; migrates to the extreme south of southern continents. In Indonesia, a widespread but rare passage migrant in most subregions; vagrant in Kalimantan.

SANDERLING

Calidris alba 20 cm F: Scolopacidae

Description: Unmistakable; note very pale appearance in non-breeding plumage and distinct black shoulder patch.

Voice: A distinctive *cheep cheep* when taking off.

Habits: Not recorded very often in Indonesia, but is quite likely numerous during peak migration at remote sandy beaches. Also seen at somewhat sheltered coves and coral reefs, but never near mangroves or brackish water. These birds are sometimes seen in small groups, running along in the surf so quickly they look like white balls rolling erratically around.

Distribution: Worldwide; breeds high in the Arctic; winters in the south, reaching New Zealand. A widespread and possibly fairly common passage migrant throughout Indonesia; one recorded from Kalimantan.

RUFOUS-NECKED STINT

Calidris ruficollis 15 cm F: Scolopacidae

Description: Note its greyish upperparts and diagnostic short black legs. Head and breast are a rufous colour in breeding plumage.

Voice: A soft *chit-chit-chit*.

Habits: The most numerous of the small sandpipers in Indonesia. Strictly coastal during migration when it is found on mudflats near mangroves and sand flats at the mouths of estuaries. Feeds in large flocks. Runs continuously across the mud, pecking frantically from side to side. The birds at the rear fly to the front in a continuous motion. When disturbed, the birds take off and manoeuvre rapidly across the coastline in a packed flock.

Morten Strange

Distribution: Breeds in northeast Siberia; migrates south reaching New Zealand. A widespread, common passage migrant and winter visitor throughout Indonesia.

LONG-TOED STINT

Calidris subminuta 16 cm F: Scolopacidae

Description: Distinguished from the previous species by its brownish, rather scaly upperparts and fairly long, greenish legs.

Voice: A soft *chi-rup* on take-off.

Habits: During migration usually found in coastal regions, behind the beach in saline marshes and at freshwater ponds. Seen less often on tidal mudflats and in dry, vegetated areas. Also recorded near water at lower montane terrain far inland. Does not form dense flocks; usually a few move together in a loose group.

Morten Strange

Distribution: Breeds in Siberia; winters mainly in Southeast Asia; a few reach Australia. A widespread but generally scarce winter visitor throughout Indonesia.

CURLEW SANDPIPER
Calidris ferruginea 21 cm F: Scolopacidae

Description: Note its silver-grey uparts and decurved bill. Shown here with a Marsh Sandpiper (left) for comparison.

Voice: A liquid *chirrip*.

Habits: During migration, congregates along the coastline, feeding mainly on tidal mudflats, along estuaries, and around brackish ponds and flooded fields near the sea. Usually forms small groups with other shorebirds and is found in dense flocks at prime locations. Feeds by walking forward at a brisk pace, pecking rapidly in the mud from side to side, in a typical *Calidris* style.

Distribution: Breeds high in arctic Siberia; migrates south reaching New Zealand. A widespread and fairly common passage migrant in west Indonesia; probably overflies most of the east.

WHITE-HEADED STILT
Himantopus leucocephalus 37 cm F: Recurvirostridae

Description: Long red legs and needle-thin bill are diagnostic. Included as a subspecies under the following species by Andrew (1992) and C&B (1997); here follows M&P (1993). Distinguished from the following species by its black hindneck stripe.

Voice: A penetrating *kik-kik-kik* in flight.

Habits: Found on coastal wetlands, especially around flat brackish lakes and saline marshes just behind tidal estuaries. Also seen in wet paddy fields nearby. This noisy and conspicuous bird flies across its habitat, calling loudly, its long legs trailing behind its tail. The nest is built on the ground, usually on a small patch of dry land, out in a shallow lagoon.

Distribution: Australasia and Sunda subregion; somewhat nomadic. An uncommon resident on Java, Sumatra, probably Sulawesi and possibly elsewhere in the east; a rare visitor to other islands, including Kalimantan.

BLACK-WINGED STILT

Himantopus himantopus 37 cm F: Recurvirostridae

Description: Distinguished from the previous species by its all-white head (in spite of names). The photo shows an immature bird, which has more grey on its head and neck than a White-headed immature.

Voice: Similar to that of the White-headed Stilt.

Habits: Much like the previous species. Note its unusually long legs that look like stilts as it walks and runs about in shallow water, feeding on small aquatic prey.

Distribution: Worldwide tropics and subtropics except Australasia; northern populations migrate south. In Indonesia its status is uncertain. May be a rare non-breeding visitor to northern Kalimantan.

RED-NECKED PHALAROPE

Phalaropus lobatus 18 cm F: Phalaropidae

Description: A small bird that swims high in water. Look for its needle-thin bill. Non-breeding plumage (photo) is white with black mask and upperparts.

Voice: A short *chek*.

Habits: This peculiar shorebird breeds in tundra marshes, where it feeds by swimming quickly around in small ponds. Turns pelagic during winter and spends the non-breeding season at sea, feeding on plankton, often in loose flocks far from the shore. Indonesia is a major wintering area, where it is often observed. Loose flocks numbering thousands have been reported from Wallacea. Can also be seen resting on coastal mudflats and coral reefs.

Distribution: Breeds worldwide, high in the north; winters to the south, reaching southern Australia. In Indonesia, a widespread and fairly common winter visitor in most inland seas; not recorded in Sumatra.

BEACH THICK-KNEE

Esacus magnirostris 51 cm F: Burhinidae

Description: Unmistakable within its range; the only thick-knee in Indonesia, except for the Bush Thick-knee, *Burhinus magnirostris* (listed in J&O 1997, but not Andrew 1992. *B. grallarius* by Beehler 1986) found in Trans-Fly, West Papua.

Voice: A loud, high-pitched *pee-pee-pee*.

Habits: A coastal specialist that is found mainly on small offshore islands and reefs, and on remote parts of the main islands of Indonesia. This low-density species is not numerous anywhere within its range. Frequents mudflats near estuaries, barren rocky shores and coral reefs, where it feeds almost exclusively on crabs. When disturbed, this shy, quiet bird flies quickly away, low across the water.

David Tipling/Windrush Photos

Distribution: Oriental region and Australasia; sedentary. In Indonesia a widespread but scarce resident, especially on the small offshore islands throughout the archipelago.

AUSTRALIAN PRATINCOLE

Stiltia isabella 24 cm F: Glareolidae

Description: Distinguished from the following species by the lack of a black border around its throat and a smooth sandy-rufous plumage. Immature bird (photo) has some streaks on breast. Appears tern-like in flight.

Voice: A clear whistle: *kiree-pett*.

Habits: Observed during the southern winter, from May into early December, when a fair number settle in the Trans-Fly region of West Papua. Here flocks can occur, but further west it becomes gradually rarer. Like the following species, it can turn up in open country. Having slightly longer legs, it tolerates longer grass and spends more time on the ground walking around to feed, although it also hawks for insects in the air.

Jon Hornbuckle

Distribution: Australasia; breeds in Australia; migrates north. A widespread but generally scarce southern-winter visitor in parts of eastern Indonesia; rare in the Sunda subregion.

ORIENTAL PRATINCOLE

Glareola maldivarum 25 cm F: Glareolidae

Description: Distinguished from the previous species by a black border around its throat and forked tail in flight.

Voice: A sharp *chek-chek*.

Habits: During migration frequents open country with short or no vegetation. Also found around coastal marshes and on dry fields inland. Often seen around airfields. They usually gather in small groups, although flocks of over 80 individuals have been reported from Sumatra, Bali and Flores. Catches insects in the air and on the ground.

Distribution: Breeds in northern parts of the Oriental region and East Asia; migrates south reaching northern Australia. A widespread but generally scarce passage migrant and winter visitor throughout Indonesia.

POMARINE JAEGER (Pomarine Skua)

Stercorarius pomarinus 55 cm F: Stercorariidae

Description: Distinguished with some difficulty from the following species by its larger size, slower flight, and rounded (not pointed) tip of tail. Photo shows immature bird.

Voice: Silent during migration.

Habits: Four species of this small family (there are seven members worldwide) have been recorded in Indonesia, but this species and the next are the only two that occur here with any regularity. The family is probably much overlooked. This species turns up during the northern winter, from September to May. It is strictly a pelagic bird; although sometimes seen near the beach, it never ventures onto land.

Distribution: Breeds worldwide in high Arctic regions; winters to the south reaching New Zealand. A widespread but generally scarce winter visitor throughout Indonesian seas.

ARCTIC JAEGER (Arctic Skua)

Stercorarius parasiticus 45 cm F: Stercorariidae

Description: Distinguished with some difficulty from the previous species by pointed (not rounded) tip of tail and smaller size. Photo shows dark morph; light morph has pale neck and underparts.

Voice: Silent during migration.

Habits: During migration is mainly pelagic, but sometimes flies briefly across the beach. This strong flier, more quick and slender than the previous species, has the appearance of a falcon-like gull. During the winter both jaegers feed almost exclusively by chasing terns and shearwaters until they drop their catch.

Morten Strange

Distribution: Breeds worldwide in Arctic and subarctic regions; winters south reaching New Zealand. A rare passage migrant seen near Java, Bali, Sulawesi, Sula, Flores and some smaller islands.

WHISKERED TERN

Chlidonias hybridus 26 cm F: Laridae

Description: Note short bill, pale wings with black spots under wing coverts, and a slightly forked tail.

Voice: A short, harsh *chek*.

Habits: Most terns in Indonesia seem to come from Australia during the southern winter, but some are present all year. During migration this tern is found around lakes, rivers and ponds near the coast, and around tidal estuaries and shallow coastal waters. Flies with elaborate wingbeats, low over the water, picking up small prey. Also catches insects in the air.

Morten Strange

Distribution: Breeds in Africa, Eurasia and Australia; migrates to the south (Australian birds migrate north). Widespread in Indonesia; a common visitor in West Papua, Wallacea and Bali; status uncertain on Sumatra; vagrant in Kalimantan.

WHITE-WINGED TERN

Chlidonias leucopterus 23 cm F: Laridae

Description: Note the distinct black dot behind ear, a white rump and low flight.

Voice: A sharp *kwek-kwek*.

Habits: In Indonesia, this tern is mainly a passage migrant seen during northern fall and spring. During peak migration it is locally abundant; moves in flocks of hundreds of birds. Can turn up during all months of the year, in sheltered coastal areas and far inland around rivers and lakes. Picks prey out of the water without plunging in. Insects, water spiders and tiny fish also reported taken.

Distribution: Breeds in temperate Eurasia; migrates south, reaching New Zealand. A widespread and locally common passage migrant and winter visitor throughout Indonesia.

GULL-BILLED TERN

Gelochelidon nilotica 38 cm F: Laridae

Description: Photo shows breeding plumage. Note heavy black bill that is diagnostic in all plumages. During the non-breeding season the forecrown is white. A monotypic genus.

Voice: Usually silent during migration.

Habits: Found on Sumatra during the northern winter, from October to July. In West Papua occurs mainly during the southern winter, from February to September. During migration, it settles primarily on coastal mudflats and along mangrove edges. Usually seen spread out in small groups, although loose flocks of up to 200 have been reported. Flies slowly over the mud, swooping down for small prey. Often rests on the ground between sallies.

Distribution: Worldwide tropics and subtropics; northern populations migrate south (Australian residents move north reaching eastern Indonesia). A widespread and fairly common migrant throughout Indonesia.

BRIDLED TERN

Sterna anaethetus 37 cm F: Laridae

Description: Distinguished from the rarer, non-breeding Sooty Tern, *S. fuscata*, by its slaty-grey (not black) upperparts and white supercilium that extends back on head behind eye.

Voice: Usually quiet; sometimes a short *wep-wep*.

Habits: This tern can turn up almost anywhere, but its major breeding colonies are located mainly in the Malacca Straits off Sumatra and the Banda Sea within Wallacea. Breeds with other sea birds on remote islets, often mixing with the previous species. Roams widely during the non-breeding season, usually far from the coast, where it feeds by dipping into the surface water for small fish, squid and plankton.

Howard Nicholls/Windrush Photos

Distribution: Worldwide tropical seas; nomadic outside breeding season. A widespread but uncommon resident throughout Indonesia; patchy in distribution; very numerous locally.

LITTLE TERN

Sterna albifrons 23 cm F: Laridae

Description: Its very small size and rapid wing-beats are diagnostic. In breeding plumage the bill is yellow with a black tip. In non-breeding plumage (photo) the bill is black.

Voice: A high-pitched *kik-kik*.

Habits: Usually seen in coastal regions and sometimes around freshwater lakes and rivers as much as 100 km inland. Breeds from May to September in small colonies on open sandy patches near the coast. Outside its breeding season, migrants often flock with other terns, resting on the beach or feeding in shallow water, hovering and plunging in energetically for small fish.

Morten Strange

Distribution: Breeds in Africa, Eurasia and Australasia; partly migratory. A widespread and fairly common winter visitor throughout Indonesia; also resident on Java, Bali and Wallacea.

GREAT CRESTED TERN (Crested Tern)

Sterna bergii 45 cm F: Laridae

Description: Its large size and slow flight are characteristic. Note yellowish bill and dark grey upperparts.

Voice: A sharp *kirrik*.

Habits: One of the most numerous marine terns in Indonesia. Can be seen around virtually all inland waters, often close to the beach. Found on land only during the breeding season, when it settles in colonies on remote offshore islets, and nests on the ground. Although nesting has only been confirmed off Java and in Wallacea, this tern probably breeds near Sumatra and West Papua as well. Dives for fish from a great height, deep into the sea.

Distribution: Tropical and subtropical seas around Africa, Eurasia, Australasia and the Pacific; nomadic. A widespread resident and non-breeding visitor throughout coastal Indonesia.

LESSER CRESTED TERN

Sterna bengalensis 40 cm F: Laridae

Description: Shown here with *S. bergii*. The individuals on the right with orange bill are the Lesser Crested Terns. Note its smaller size; paler upperparts are also sometimes characteristic.

Voice: Similar to that of the previous species.

Habits: Much like the previous species; the two often mix as shown in the photo. Lesser Crested terns are generally less numerous. Nesting has been recorded off Sulawesi and possibly occurs in other places as well. Roosts between fishing stints on offshore fishing equipment or on tidal sand banks.

Distribution: Tropical seas from Africa to Australia; nomadic outside breeding season. A widespread, non-breeding visitor throughout coastal Indonesia, also resident.

BROWN NODDY
Anous stolidus 42 cm F: Laridae

Description: Distinguished with some difficulty from the following species by its larger size and smaller pale cap that contrasts less sharply with its blackish back.

Voice: Usually quiet; harsh croaks near nest.

Habits: This pelagic tern breeds in large numbers on Gunungapi and other remote islets in the Bandar Sea, Wallacea. Breeding has been reported off Sumatra and West Papua as well. Never seen on the beaches of major islands. On the open ocean it moves singly or in small groups, swooping down to the surface to pick up small fish. At the breeding ground, birds greet each other by nodding their heads, as shown in this photograph.

Colin Poole

Distribution: Worldwide tropical seas; somewhat nomadic. Resident and locally common in the Wallacea; otherwise rarely encountered in offshore Indonesian waters.

BLACK NODDY
Anous minutus 32 cm F: Laridae

Description: When comparing with the previous species, note its longer, thinner bill and its pale cap that extends down the neck, contrasting sharply with blackish back.

Voice: Usually quiet; a harsh rattling near nest.

Habits: Indonesia is the western limit of this sea bird's range. Appears to be rare, although may be confused with previous species, as the two readily mix. Nests on the ground or in low trees and bushes on remote islets. Usually feeds far offshore, almost exclusively on small fish. This elegant flier sometimes rests on floating debris.

Martin Hale

Distribution: Tropical Atlantic and Pacific Oceans, into Southeast Asia; mainly sedentary. Generally scarce offshore West Papua, Java and Sumatra, where breeding has been recorded; vagrant offshore Kalimantan and Wallacea.

THICK-BILLED GREEN PIGEON (Thick-billed Pigeon)

Treron curvirostra 27 cm F: Columbidae

Description: Note the diagnostic red cere in both male (top) and female (bottom). May be conspecific with the Grey-cheeked Green Pigeon, *T. griseicauda*, of Sulawesi, Java and Bali, which is very similar.

Voice: A soft, throaty *cloo-cloo*.

Habits: An adaptable arboreal bird found in a variety of wooded habitats, both in primary rainforest and disturbed secondary growth. Occurs mainly in the lowlands on Sumatra, but is also found in Kalimantan, at lower montane elevations. Often seen in pairs or small groups, thrashing around in fruiting fig trees. Flies in a fast and direct manner between canopies.

Distribution: Southeast Asia. A widespread and fairly common resident in Sumatra and Kalimantan, and most nearby islands.

Morten Strange

LITTLE GREEN PIGEON

Treron olax 22 cm F: Columbidae

Ong Kiem Sian

Description: The male's grey head together with its orange breast are diagnostic (see photo). The female is distinguished with difficulty from other female *Treron* pigeons by its small size, grey cap and white chin.

Voice: A quiet, high-pitched cooing.

Habits: A forest bird found in primary rainforest and along disturbed forest edges, mainly in the lowlands. On Sumatra recorded to 1,400 m. Perches high in large trees, so good views are rare, but sometimes comes down low to feed on figs. Also seen in small groups flying rapidly above the canopies in the early morning and late afternoon.

Distribution: Sunda subregion. A locally fairly common resident on Sumatra and Kalimantan, including some nearby islands; rare on west Java.

PINK-NECKED GREEN PIGEON (Pink-necked Pigeon)

Treron vernans 25 cm F: Columbidae

Description: Male (top photo, foreground) has diagnostic purple neck and pink breast. Note the black primaries and yellow band of the female, visible in flight (bottom photo).

Voice: Some chuckling and gurgling notes.

Habits: This coastal bird, found mainly in mangroves and coastal woodlands, has expanded successfully into disturbed forest, plantations, parks and gardens. Occurs from sea level up to 1,200 m locally. Seen in pairs or loose groups, feeding on small fruits high in the trees. This strong flier changes location quickly.

Distribution: Southeast Asia. A common resident of the Sunda subregion; extends into Sulawesi, Lombok, Sumbawa and some adjacent islands; two recent sightings from Halmahera suggest expansion of range.

Morten Strange

BLACK-BACKED FRUIT-DOVE

Ptilinopus cintus 34 cm F: Columbidae

Guy Dutson

Description: Note characteristic black band separating pale greyish breast from dark yellow below. The sexes are similar.

Voice: A muted *whoo-oo*.

Habits: Occurs in forest, from primary forest to mature secondary growth with tall trees. Found at sea level and often at higher elevation elevations to 1,800 m. Not easy to observe, in spite of its conspicuous plumage. Moves high within the canopies of large fruiting trees, often in pairs or small groups. Flies rapidly to another concealed perch. Otherwise little studied.

Distribution: Indonesian endemic. A locally fairly common resident on Lombok, Sumbawa, Flores, Timor and some smaller nearby islands; rare on Bali.

PINK-HEADED FRUIT-DOVE

Ptilinopus porphyreus 29 cm F: Columbidae

Description: Note diagnostic pink head contrasting with white breast band. Photo shows male; female is a duller colour.

Voice: A soft *hoo*.

Habits: A forest bird restricted to montane elevations between 1,400 and 2,200 m. Often found in oaks and heath forest. This shy bird is sometimes seen perched quietly in the middle storey (see photo) but has been little studied. Feeding habits and movements are unknown. The nest has been described on Java as an untidy structure of twigs, 5–6 m above the ground.

Distribution: Indonesian endemic. An uncommon resident in montane parts of Sumatra and Java; rare on Bali.

Edward Vercruysse

RED-EARED FRUIT-DOVE

Ptilinopus fischeri 34 cm F: Columbidae

Description: The prominent red mask is diagnostic. North and central Sulawesi birds have greenish upperparts; birds in the south are greyish-black.

Voice: A soft *oowup* and a deep *oooo*.

Habits: This forest bird is usually found from 1,800 to 3,000 m. It is rarer in lower hills down to 600 m. Occurs in both primary and recently logged forest and is somewhat tolerant to disturbance. Moves inconspicuously and quietly in the middle storey below the canopy, feeding on small fruits. Moves slowly or not at all and is easy to overlook. Flies off between the trees when disturbed.

Distribution: Indonesian endemic. A widespread but generally uncommon resident in montane parts of Sulawesi.

B. Van Elegem

JAMBU FRUIT-DOVE

Ptilinopus jambu 28 cm F: Columbidae

Description: Male (top) is distinguished from other fruit-doves by its red face and breast patch; female (bottom) is duller.

Voice: A quiet *hoo*.

Habits: Found in coastal mangroves and lowland secondary rainforest, also in nearby plantations. Usually observed singly or in pairs, never in flocks like many other pigeons. Feeds quietly on fruits within the canopies of large trees. Quite mobile; changes location in the forest and visits offshore islands. A low-density and inconspicuous species often missed during surveys.

Distribution: Sunda subregion. A widespread but uncommon resident in Sumatra, Kalimantan and west Java.

PINK-SPOTTED FRUIT-DOVE

Ptilinopus perlatus 26 cm F: Columbidae

Description: Distinguished from the sympatric and somewhat similar Ornate Fruit-dove, *P. ornatus*, by the delicate pink spots on its wings, barely visible here.

Voice: A low-pitched *hoo*.

Habits: A forest bird found mainly at lowland elevations, from the coast to 1,200 m. Usually occurs in primary forest, but is also often seen along forest edges and in disturbed secondary growth. Here flocks feed in fig trees, sometimes in large groups, mixing with other pigeons. Somewhat nomadic during the dry season, from June to August. Travels long distances to find fruiting trees.

Distribution: New Guinea. A widespread and fairly common resident in West Papua and on the nearby Waigeo, Yapen and Aru islands.

BLUE-CAPPED FRUIT-DOVE

Ptilinopus monacha 17 cm F: Columbidae

Description: A small bird. Note diagnostic blue crown. The male (photo) has a small blue spot on its lower belly and a yellow line behind the eye.

Voice: A slow *who-oo*.

Habits: Found in forest edges, secondary growth, mangroves and coastal cultivation. Could be more numerous locally than the few field observations indicate. Perches in the middle storey of large trees. Little is known about this bird; its movements and its feeding and nesting habits have never been studied.

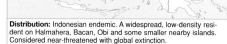

Distribution: Indonesian endemic. A widespread, low-density resident on Halmahera, Bacan, Obi and some smaller nearby islands. Considered near-threatened with global extinction.

CLARET-BREASTED FRUIT-DOVE

Ptilinopus viridis 23 cm F: Columbidae

Description: A fairly small pigeon. Note the diagnostic red spot on its upper breast.

Voice: A distinctive series of hooting notes.

Habits: Found in tall forest and along forest edges; also seen occasionally in nearby cultivation. This lowland species thrives in coastal forest on islands, but in West Papua occurs mainly between 300 and 1,000 m. Usually seen in fruiting trees, mixing with starlings, cuckoo-shrikes and other pigeons. Never found in large flocks; appears to be a low-density species. Quite a conspicuous bird—frequently perches in the open as shown in the photo.

Distribution: Eastern Indonesia, east to the Solomon Islands in the Pacific. Locally fairly common, but a generally scarce resident on Buru, Seram, some smaller nearby islands and northern West Papua.

ORANGE-BELLIED FRUIT-DOVE

Ptilinopus iozonus 21 cm F: Columbidae

Description: An orange belly and plain green breast together are diagnostic. Also note purple shoulder patch. Captive photo.

Voice: High-pitched *hoo* calls.

Habits: An arboreal bird usually found in the lowlands, mainly in forest edges and secondary growth. Also visits mangroves and is often observed around cultivated areas and roadsides. Locally the most numerous fruit-dove. Feeds on a variety of fruits, mainly figs. Flocks in fruiting trees, often with other pigeons. The nest is a flimsy platform of twigs built high in a forest tree.

Distribution: New Guinea. A widespread and fairly common resident in West Papua, Waigeo, Yapen and the Aru islands.

GREY-HEADED FRUIT-DOVE

Ptilinopus hyogaster 24 cm F: Columbidae

Description: Distinguished by its grey face and wing pattern from the sympatric, but rarer, Scarlet-breasted Fruit-dove, *P. bernsteinii*.

Voice: A soft *who-huu*.

Habits: Found at forest edges and in secondary growth; also ventures into nearby plantations. Occurs mainly in the lowlands, extending to foothills at 450 m (Halmahera) and 1,000 m (Bacan). Often resident pairs perch out in the open together, especially in the late afternoon. Flocks of 20 have been reported. Otherwise no information available on movements or feeding and nesting habits.

Distribution: Indonesian endemic. A common resident on Halmahera, Bacan and smaller nearby islands.

BLACK-NAPED FRUIT-DOVE

Ptilinopus melanospila 27 cm F: Columbidae

Distribution: Indonesia, north into parts of the Philippines. A locally fairly common resident on Java, Bali and parts of Wallacea; vagrant on Sumatra.

Description: Note the characteristic white head and yellow chin of this male (photo). The black spot on back of head not visible from this angle. Female is a uniform dark green colour.

Voice: A frequent *wu-woo.*

Habits: An arboreal pigeon that frequents primary forest and forest edges, mainly in the coastal lowlands. On Sulawesi recorded to 1,600 m. This adaptable bird has also been observed in cultivated areas near forest. Appears to be fairly numerous. Is often seen with other fruit-doves and imperial pigeons in fruiting trees, sometimes in flocks, but more often in resident pairs. Good views are not easy, however, as it usually moves about slowly under cover, as shown in the photo.

WHITE-BELLIED IMPERIAL PIGEON

Ducula forsteni 48 cm F: Columbidae

Distribution: Indonesian endemic. A locally fairly common resident on Sulawesi; also recently discovered on the Sula Islands where it is uncommon.

Description: Distinguished by a broad green breast band that separates the white head and belly, from the similar sympatric, but rarer, Grey-headed Imperial Pigeon, *D. radiata*. Captive photo.

Voice: A slow, deep *uu-uum.*

Habits: Found in primary rainforest and mature secondary forest, from 150 to 2,200 m; occurs mainly from 800 to 1,600 m. Perches in the middle storey or at canopy level. A flock of 30 has been reported in fruiting trees. Otherwise nothing is known about its feeding habits and movements; the nest has never been described.

GREEN IMPERIAL PIGEON

Ducula aenea 45 cm F: Columbidae

Description: Note pale grey body and green wings. The Sulawesi subspecies has a rufous head.

Voice: A deep cooing that varies with the subspecies.

Habits: A forest bird found in lowland and lower montane rainforest and along forest edges. Also occurs locally in mangroves and savanna woodlands. Quite numerous, but perches high in large trees and is not easy to approach. Best observed flying between fruiting trees and roosting sites, especially in the early morning and late afternoon.

Distribution: Oriental region. A widespread and fairly common resident in the Sunda subregion, including the larger islands; extends to Sulawesi, Lombok, Sumbawa, Flores and Sumba.

SPECTACLED IMPERIAL PIGEON (White-eyed Imp'l Pigeon)

Ducula perspicillata 45 cm F: Columbidae

Description: Note the diagnostic eye-ring that contrasts with its dark grey head.

Voice: A series of 6–8 low, hooting notes.

Habits: A forest bird found in primary rainforest and along forest edges with large trees. Also seen occasionally in nearby wooded cultivation. Occurs from sea level into lower montane elevations. Quite conspicuous, especially in early morning and late afternoon, when it flies about and perches in the open, often in resident pairs, although a flock of 14 has been reported. Feeds in fruiting trees; otherwise little studied.

Distribution: Indonesian endemic. A fairly common resident throughout the Maluku Islands.

YELLOW-EYED IMPERIAL PIGEON

Ducula concinna 43 cm F: Columbidae

Description: A pale grey body with black bill and orange eye are diagnostic.

Voice: A series of deep growls, sometimes in duet.

Habits: Confined to small islands, where it is found in primary and secondary coastal forest and along forest edges; also extends into nearby wooded cultivation. Gregarious; flocks of up to 40 have been reported foraging high in the trees. Feeds on fruits such as figs and young coconuts. Its movements within and between islands are poorly understood and its nest has not been described.

Distribution: Indonesian endemic. One vagrant record from northern Australia; possibly nomadic. Widespread and locally common on small islands in eastern Indonesia.

Margaret Kinnaird

PINON'S IMPERIAL PIGEON

Ducula pinon 46 cm F: Columbidae

Description: A grey head, maroon belly and red eye patch are diagnostic.

Voice: A low-pitched, resonant, hooting call.

Habits: Found in rainforest and along forest edges, mainly in the lowlands. Moves around the forest in search of fruiting trees and is quite often encountered along forest trails. Usually seen in small groups of 3–6 birds, although a flock of more than 10 has been reported. The nest is a scanty platform of twigs located 11–18 m up in a forest tree, usually holding one egg.

Distribution: New Guinea. A fairly common resident in West Papua and on the larger nearby islands.

Morten Strange

MOUNTAIN IMPERIAL PIGEON

Ducula badia 45 cm F: Columbidae

Description: Note the distinctive brown wings and pale head. These characteristics set it apart from the similar Dark-backed Imperial Pigeon, *D. lacernulata*, which takes over this niche on Java, Bali, Lombok and Sumbawa.

Voice: A deep, booming *oomp-oomp*.

Habits: Mainly a montane bird found at altitudes between 400 and 2,200 m. It is resident in the mountains, but will travel a considerable distance to feed. Often spends the day in the lowlands and retreats to the hills in the late afternoon, flying conspicuously over the forest.

Distribution: Oriental region. Widespread and previously fairly common; now apparently a generally scarce resident on Sumatra and Kalimantan; rare in west and central Java.

PIED IMPERIAL PIGEON

Ducula bicolor 40 cm F: Columbidae

Description: Unmistakable throughout most of its range; the only black and white pigeon.

Voice: A variety of deep hooting and cooing calls.

Habits: An island specialist sometimes seen flying along the coast. Appears to roost and breed on small offshore islands, flying great distances to larger islands to feed in fruiting trees. Usually seen in pairs or small groups, although flocks of up to 150 have been reported. Conspicuous and easy to observe where present, but this species is rare now on Java and Bali, and in other densely populated areas due to excessive hunting pressure. Numbers are much reduced, but it is still locally common.

Distribution: Southeast Asia, east to New Guinea; disperses widely within its range. A widespread resident throughout coastal Indonesia except Nusa Tenggara; vagrant on Flores.

SILVER-TIPPED IMPERIAL PIGEON

Ducula luctuosa 43 cm F: Columbidae

Description: Distinguished from the previous species by silver grey (not black) feathers in wing.

Voice: Subdued and muted cooing calls.

Habits: Found in forest edges, open woodlands and nearby cultivated areas. Often occurs near the coast and inland up to 800 m. Usually seen in small flocks of 5–20 individuals, although a flock of 250 has been reported from an evening roost in Sula Islands. Otherwise, not much is known about this bird.

Distribution: Indonesian endemic. A resident on Sulawesi and smaller adjacent islands. Locally numerous but generally uncommon.

BARRED CUCKOO-DOVE

Macropygia unchall 38 cm F: Columbidae

Description: Distinguished by its greyish (not rufous) underparts and head, from the similar Ruddy Cuckoo-dove, *M. emiliana*, which overlaps on Java. The female shown in the photo is heavily barred. The male lacks barring on head and belly. Captive photo.

Voice: A loud, resonant *croo-uum*.

Habits: Found in primary forest, secondary growth and along forest edges; occasionally seen in nearby cultivation. Usually occurs in montane rainforest, from 800 to 3,000 m. Often spotted flying quickly through the trees, often in resident pairs. Feeds on small berries and shoots in the middle storey; also flies down to the ground to pick up seeds.

Distribution: Oriental region. Locally fairly common in elevated parts of Sumatra, Java, Bali, Lombok and Flores.

BROWN CUCKOO-DOVE (Slender-billed Cuckoo-dove)

Macropygia amboinensis 36 cm F: Columbidae

Description: Photo shows a male; the female has some barring on its neck. Slight variations occur among the island subspecies within its range.

Voice: A repertoire of soft coos and hoots that vary with subspecies.

Habits: An adaptable bird doing well in many wooded habitats, from primary forest to secondary growth and nearby cultivation. Occurs in coastal lowlands and hills, locally up to 2,000 m. Feeds on a selection of small fruits and seeds, usually low in the trees; also feeds on the ground and in dense forest at canopy level.

Distribution: Australasia, from Sulawesi to eastern Australia. A widespread and locally common resident in Sulawesi, Maluku and West Papua.

Morten Strange

BARRED-NECKED CUCKOO-DOVE (Dusky Cuckoo-dove)

Macropygia magna 40 cm F: Columbidae

Description: The only *Macropygia* cuckoo-dove within its range and elevation. Note heavy barring on neck of male (photo). The female is a duller colour.

Voice: A hooting 3-note call.

Habits: Found in primary forest and along forest edges; restricted to the lowland areas below 160 m. Little of this habitat remains within its range. Appears to be a low-density species, sometimes seen in resident pairs. Flies between the canopies of tall trees on flapping wings, alighting in the middle storey. Shy and inconspicuous. Feeding and breeding habits have not been studied.

Filip Verbelen

Distribution: Indonesian endemic. A generally scarce resident on Alor, Timor, Wetar, Leti, Moa, Tanimbar and some smaller nearby islands; possibly also on south Sulawesi.

LITTLE CUCKOO-DOVE

Macropygia ruficeps 30 cm F: Columbidae

Description: Distinguished with some difficulty from the Ruddy Cuckoo-dove by its small size and paler underparts. The Borneo race (male in photo) has dark-brown spots on breast.

Voice: A rapidly repeated *kroo-wuk*.

Habits: Restricted to lower montane forest, from 300 to 2,000 m. Breeds above 900 m, but often ventures lower to feed. Found in primary forest, along forest edges and in nearby cultivated areas; reported feeding in rice fields. Usually seen flying rapidly into the forest or foraging on fruits and berries low in trees. The nest is a flimsy structure built 1–7 m up in a small tree.

Distribution: Southeast Asia. A fairly common montane resident of Sumatra and Kalimantan; uncommon on Java, Bali, Lombok, Sumbawa, Flores, Sumba and Timor.

SPOTTED DOVE

Streptopelia chinensis 30 cm F: Columbidae

Description: Distinguished by its scaly wings and the white dots in its broad neck collar, from the similar, but rarer, Island Collared-dove, *S. bitorquata*, of Java, Bali and Nusa Tenggara.

Voice: A soft *te-croo-crooo*.

Habits: A successful species inhabiting all types of cleared areas, dry woodlands and cultivation; also found in villages. Numerous where allowed to proliferate, but many are hunted for the captive trade. Often seen near rural roadsides, where they walk on the ground, picking up seeds. Flies off low to perch in the open when disturbed.

Distribution: Oriental region; introduced to Hawaii, Australia, Fiji and other states. Widespread and common throughout the Sunda subregion; introduced or has expanded into many islands in eastern Indonesia.

ZEBRA DOVE (Peaceful Dove)

Geopelia striata 21 cm F: Columbidae

Description: Unmistakable; can only be confused with the following allospecies.

Voice: A soft, rolling *croo-croo-croo*.

Habits: Found in rural lowland areas near fields, roadsides and along the edges of villages. Spends much time walking on the ground, picking up seeds. Flies up and perches in a tree when disturbed. Although an adaptable species, it is much reduced in numbers, as many are trapped for the bird trade.

Morten Strange

Distribution: Sunda subregion; introduced in other regions. A locally common resident in eastern Sumatra; scarce elsewhere including Java, Bali and Lombok; introduced to Kalimantan and Sulawesi.

BARRED DOVE

Geopelia maugei 22 cm F: Columbidae

Description: An allospecies of the previous species. Note diagnostic barring extending down centre of belly.

Voice: A disyllabic *ooo-loo*.

Habits: Similar to the previous species, which it replaces geographically. Observed along dry deciduous forest edges, in scrub and in somewhat wooded cultivation near rural villages, often in small flocks. Usually occurs in the coastal lowlands, often in areas adjacent to mangroves. Recorded on Flores to 1,400 m. Feeds on the ground, but flies quickly into low trees to perch when disturbed. Feeding and breeding habits have been little studied.

Morten Strange

Distribution: Indonesian endemic. A widespread and generally common resident throughout Nusa Tenggara, from Sumbawa east to the Kai Islands.

EMERALD DOVE (Emerald Ground-dove)

Chalcophaps indica 25 cm F: Columbidae

Morten Strange

Description: Note bright-green wings and warm vinous underparts. Photo shows captive male; female lacks grey cap.

Voice: A soft, deep *tu-hoop.*

Habits: An arboreal bird found in rainforest, secondary growth and along forest edges. Occurs mainly in the lowlands and locally to 1,500 m. Lives alone or in resident pairs. Feeds on the ground under fruiting trees. Flies to a distant low branch when disturbed. This wary bird is usually encountered accidentally when it suddenly flies past, low among the trees.

Distribution: Oriental region and east into northern Australia. A widespread and locally fairly common resident throughout Indonesia, except mainland West Papua.

NEW GUINEA BRONZEWING

Henicophaps albifrons 38 cm F: Columbidae

Morten Strange

Description: Distinguished from the following species by its white forehead and a greenish iridescence in wing. Captive photo.

Voice: A rapid series of *whoops,* also a throaty *krrrr.*

Habits: This forest bird is usually seen walking on the ground in wet primary rainforest. Is also found in drier forest edges. Occurs mainly in the lowlands, inland to 1,200 m. Moves alone or in pairs. Not often seen and appears to be a low-density species. Feeds on fallen fruits and invertebrates and flies to a low branch when disturbed. Nesting behaviour has never been described.

Distribution: New Guinea. A scarce resident in West Papua and nearby islands. Near-threatened with global extinction.

THICK-BILLED GROUND-PIGEON
Trugon terrestris 33 cm F: Columbidae

Description: Unmistakable; the only member of its genus. Captive photo.

Voice: A loud *hiin*.

Habits: This terrestrial pigeon walks on the floor of primary rainforest, usually alone or in resident pairs. Occurs inland to 600 m. Feeds on seeds that it pries from fallen fruits. When disturbed, makes a brief flight further into the forest, but rarely perches on branches. Rarely observed. One white egg is laid in a nest of sticks and mosses, built on the ground, up against a tree trunk or a fallen log.

Distribution: New Guinea. A generally scarce resident in West Papua.

NICOBAR PIGEON
Caloenas nicobarica 40 cm F: Columbidae

Description: Unmistakable. Photo shows a captive male. The female's hackles are shorter. Quite unique; the only member of its genus.

Voice: Usually quiet.

Habits: This specialist usually breeds on small, forested islands free of predators, although it occasionally wanders onto larger islands. Feeds on the ground within dense vegetation, mainly at dusk. Formerly numerous, but now rarely seen during field surveys in many places.

Distribution: Southeast Asia east to New Guinea; makes nomadic movements between islands. Resident on small islands; also recorded from a few larger ones, including once on Sulawesi.

WESTERN CROWNED PIGEON
Goura cristata 70 cm F: Columbidae

Description: Distinguished by its grey-blue (not dark maroon) underparts, from the allospecies, the Southern Crowned Pigeon, *G. scheepmakeri*, of southern New Guinea. Captive photo.

Voice: A deep *hooom*, audible only when near.

Habits: A forest bird found mainly in lowland rainforest. Often seen near flooded areas, in mangroves and along rivers. Walks on the ground, feeding on fallen fruits and insects. Flies up to a high perch with noisy wing-beats when disturbed. Also roosts in trees. Much reduced in numbers due to capture for the bird trade.

Distribution: Indonesian endemic. An uncommon resident in West Papua, including the islands of Misool and Waigeo. Vulnerable to global extinction.

VICTORIA CROWNED PIGEON
Goura victoria 70 cm F: Columbidae

Description: One of three members of this peculiar genus. Recognised by the white tips of its crown feathers, its pale maroon breast patch and its range. Captive photo.

Voice: Similar to previous species.

Habits: Much like those of the previous species. Mainly occurs in lowland and swamp forest, but occasionally found in drier areas and up to 600 m. Previously numerous, but now much reduced due to habitat clearance and capture for the bird trade, since this species is popular in zoos and safari parks. Today it is difficult to find even in remote areas.

Distribution: New Guinea. An uncommon resident in northern West Papua, including the islands of Biak and Yapen. Vulnerable to global extinction.

BROWN LORY

Chalcopsitta duivenbodei 32 cm   F: Psittacidae

Description: Note the diagnostic yellow shoulder and moustache seen well from this angle. Appears dull brown when perched.

Voice: A harsh, penetrating screech during flight.

Habits: Found in lowland forest, often at sea level in tall primary rainforest, at forest edges and in open habitats nearby. Has been recorded to 200 m. Sometimes seen with other honeyeaters and parrots in large flowering trees. Flies morning and evening, to and from communal roosts. Otherwise a little studied and poorly understood species.

Distribution: North coast of New Guinea only. A locally fairly common but generally scarce resident in northeastern parts of West Papua.

VIOLET-NECKED LORY

Eos squamata 25 cm   F: Psittacidae

Description: A violet collar and red back together are diagnostic.

Voice: A penetrating screech during flight; chattering squeals while feeding in a flock.

Habits: A forest bird found in primary as well as mature secondary forest and along forest edges, but flies long distances to feed in coconut plantations and other wooded cultivated areas. Usually occurs near the coast, but also found inland to 1,200 m. Usually a resident pair travels together, however, flocks will gather in large flowering forest trees. Congregations of 50 have been reported. Otherwise little studied; its nest has never been described from the wild.

Distribution: Indonesian endemic. A fairly common resident on Halmahera, Bacan, Obi, Misool, Waigeo and some smaller adjacent islands.

MOLUCCAN RED LORY
Eos bornea 30 cm F: Psittacidae

Distribution: Indonesian endemic. A fairly common resident on Buru, Seram, the Kai Islands and the smaller nearby islands within south Maluku.

Description: Note the diagnostic all-red head and neck with no blue markings. Captive photo.

Voice: Short screeches in flight.

Habits: An arboreal bird found in primary and mature secondary rainforest. Often flies into nearby cultivated areas near villages. Occurs mainly in the lowlands, but is also observed locally in lower montane hills to 1,800 m. This social and conspicuous bird can be seen feeding in fruiting and flowering trees. Although still numerous in remoter areas, it is now reduced in numbers near towns due to capture for the domestic and international bird trade.

RAINBOW LORIKEET
Trichoglossus haematodus 24 cm F: Psittacidae

Distribution: Bali and Australasia into south Australia. A rare resident on Bali; locally fairly common around Nusa Tenggara, and east to Maluku and West Papua.

Description: Differs from the Sulawesi allospecies, the Ornate Lorikeet, *T. ornatus*, which has a red throat. Many subspecies variations within its range. Captive photo (left) shows *T. h. haematodus* of south Maluku and West Papua. Note differences in *T. h. weberi* (right) from Flores.

Voice: Harsh screeches during flight; chattering squeaks while feeding.

Habits: Frequents forest edges, dry woodlands and plantations. Flies low in a fast, conspicuous and noisy fashion. Settles in flowering and fruiting trees to feed in small groups, although flocks of 150 have been reported. Populations are much reduced due to capture for the pet trade.

IRIS LORIKEET
Psitteuteles iris 20 cm F: Psittacidae

Description: Note small size and diagnostic red forehead. Captive photo.

Voice: Shrill screeches and whistles.

Habits: A forest bird found in primary forest and along forest edges, from the lowlands to lower montane elevations. On Timor occurs mainly between 600 and 1,500 m. Flies about quickly, landing in flowering trees. Previously flocks of 50 were reported, but numbers seem to have declined in recent years and it is rarely seen today. Feeding and nesting habits have never been studied in the wild.

Morten Strange

Distribution: Indonesian endemic. A scarce resident on Timor and the Wetar islands only. Vulnerable to global extinction.

DUSKY LORY
Pseudeos fuscata 25 cm F: Psittacidae

Description: Note the orange bill and distinctive pattern of red and brown in plumage. A unique parrot; the only member of its genus. Captive photo.

Voice: A powerful and noisy screech.

Habits: Lives in noisy, mobile flocks that move frequently between flowering trees and roosting sites, screeching loudly in the process. Occurs in a variety of wooded habitats, from primary rainforest to forest edges and nearby cultivation. Feeds on nectar, pollen and occasionally fruits in large trees. Not often reported from Indonesian New Guinea, but can be locally abundant in Papua New Guinea, in the southeastern part of the island

Distribution: New Guinea. A generally scarce resident in West Papua and on Yapen Island.

Morten Strange

BLACK-CAPPED LORY (Western Black-capped Lory)

Lorius lory 28 cm F: Psittacidae

Description: Unmistakable within its range. The extent of purple on neck and belly varies somewhat with subspecies. Captive photo.

Voice: A variety of melodious, clear whistles and squeals.

Habits: Inhabits primary rainforest, forest edges, swampy forest and drier woodlands. Often seen in coastal lowlands. Occurs inland to 1,000 m; recorded rarely to 1,600 m. Feeds on nectar and pollen; also takes some fruits and insects. This sedentary bird is usually seen in resident pairs, flying below the canopy, to and from its roosting site. A popular cage bird in eastern Indonesia.

Distribution: New Guinea. A locally fairly common resident in West Papua and on most nearby islands.

CHATTERING LORY

Lorius garrulus 30 cm F: Psittacidae

Description: Unmistakable within its range—the only *Lorius* parrot with all-red head.

Voice: A loud bray during flight.

Habits: Inhabits primary and secondary rainforest, but also visits coconut groves and other plantations near the forest. Occurs from the lowlands into the hills; found on Bacan to 1,300 m. Flies rapidly among the tree tops and lands in a canopy to clamber about, sometimes upside down, chewing on flowers. Usually found in pairs, although flocks of 10 have been reported. Still numerous in remote regions, but much reduced in other areas due to trapping for the bird trade.

Distribution: Indonesian endemic. A locally fairly common resident on Halmahera, Bacan, Obi and some smaller nearby islands within north Maluku.

RED-FLANKED LORIKEET

Charmosyna placentis 17 cm F: Psittacidae

Description: The male of this species (photo) is distinguished from the Red-fronted Lorikeet, *C. rubronotata*, of northern New Guinea, by its red facial patch. Female lacks the red and blue colours in its streaked ear coverts. An allospecies, the Blue-fronted Lorikeet, *C. toxopei* (endemic to Buru), has a blue crown.

Voice: A sharp *tst* in flight.

Habits: Found in primary and mature secondary forest and along forest edges in the lowlands; also in nearby cultivated areas. Less conspicuous than other species; flies quietly in small groups, perching high inside the canopies of flowering trees. Raises two chicks, often in a cavity in a tree fern.

Distribution: Indonesia and Papua New Guinea. A generally scarce resident in Maluku and West Papua.

Morten Strange

LITTLE RED LORIKEET (Fairy Lorikeet)

Charmosyna pulchella 18 cm F: Psittacidae

Description: Distinguished with difficulty from the sympatric but larger (24 cm) Josephine's Lorikeet, *C. josefinae*, by its red forehead and faint streaks on breast.

Voice: A weak and high-pitched *ksss*.

Habits: A forest bird that specialises in the lower montane habitat, from 500 to 1,800 m. Occasionally seen below and above this preferred range. Abundant in some areas, rare in others. Roams widely in search of flowering trees. Flies quickly into flowering trees and clambers about in the canopies, feeding on nectar and pollen. Often seen with Josephine's Lorikeet, which frequents the same range, habitat and elevation.

Morten Strange

Distribution: New Guinea. A locally fairly common resident in lower montane parts of West Papua.

PAPUAN LORIKEET

Charmosyna papou 38 cm (with streamers) F: Psittacidae

Description: Some plumage variations with sex and subspecies. Note distinct red (left) and black (right) morphs. The very long central streamers in tail are always diagnostic. Captive photos.

Voice: A loud *queea* in flight.

Habits: Strictly montane. Found in forest and along forest edges, from 1,750 m to the tree limit at 3,500 m. Regularly seen during treks in the mountains, when it flies overhead, usually in pairs. Feeds on buds and nectar in flowering trees or on small fruits and seeds.

Distribution: New Guinea. A fairly common resident in montane parts of West Papua.

PLUM-FACED LORIKEET

Oreopsittacus arfaki 17 cm F: Psittacidae

Description: Note diagnostic white streaks across purple cheeks. The only member of this genus. Photo shows male; female has green crown.

Voice: A soft, high-pitched chattering.

Habits: This adaptable, upper montane specialist usually occurs from 1,800 to 3,400 m. It is found mostly in primary rainforest, but also ventures into forest edges near trails and villages. Seems fairly numerous and is regularly spotted feeding on flowers in its preferred habitat, in the canopies of low trees covered in mosses and epiphytes. Flies off into the forest canopy when disturbed. Otherwise little studied; its nesting behaviour has not been reported.

Distribution: New Guinea. A locally fairly common resident in montane parts of West Papua.

ORANGE-BILLED LORIKEET

Neopsittacus pullicauda 18 cm F: Psittacidae

Description: Distinguished with great difficulty from the sympatric Yellow-billed Lorikeet, *N. musschenbroekii* (21 cm), by its smaller size and light orange (not bright yellow) bill. These lorikeets are the only members of this genus.

Voice: A frequent, high-pitched shriek when flying and perched.

Habits: Found in the upper montane zone, from 2,100 m to the tree-line at 3,800 m. The most numerous parrot in the Snow Mountains of West Papua. Occurs in the alpine meadows and the cloud forest just below. The similar Yellow-billed Lorikeet is usually seen from 1,400 to 2,300 m, often near cultivation. Conspicuous and tame, it flies restlessly about in small flocks.

Morten Strange

Distribution: New Guinea. A locally common resident in upper montane parts of West Papua.

RED-BREASTED PYGMY PARROT

Micropsitta bruijnii 9 cm F: Psittacidae

Description: Note its tiny size, blue nape, and the yellow forehead and cheeks of this male; its underparts are red. The female is a duller colour and has a green belly.

Voice: A thin *tsee-tsee*.

Habits: The only montane member of this peculiar genus of parrots. Three other species occur in lowland parts of West Papua. Prefers the montane range of forest between 500 and 2,300 m; on Buru also reported from lowlands. Frequents tall primary forest and occasionally moves into nearby cultivation. Looks more like a nuthatch (Sittidae) than a parrot as it crawls along branches and tree trunks cleaning fungus and lichen from the bark (see photo).

Morten Strange

Distribution: Indonesia and Papua New Guinea, east to the Solomon Islands. A generally scarce resident in montane parts of West Papua; rare on Buru and Seram Islands in the Maluku Province.

PALM COCKATOO

Prosciger aterrimus 58 cm F: Psittacidae

Description: Unmistakable; commonly seen in bird parks and aviaries around the world. Note its diagnostic red face and erect crest. A unique, monotypic genus. This species and other cockatoos have been placed in a separate family (Cacatuidae) by some authors.

Voice: A loud and screaming *keeyaank* and softer whistles.

Habits: Found in tall primary rainforest and along forest edges. Also seen in drier coastal woodlands, mainly in the lowlands to 750 m. Flies into nearby open areas to feed. Best seen in early morning and evening, when it flies about, calling and perching high in the open. Feeds on seeds and nuts, sometimes dropping down on the ground for fruits.

Distribution: New Guinea and the Cape York Peninsula, Australia. A scarce resident in West Papua and nearby islands. Near-threatened with global extinction.

YELLOW-CRESTED COCKATOO

Cacatua sulphurea 34 cm F: Psittacidae

Description: Smaller than the following species; its crest is usually yellow. Subspecies *C. s. citrinocristata* of Sumba (photo) has an orangey crest.

Voice: Variety of loud screeches.

Habits: Found in primary rainforest, monsoon forest and along forest edges. Sometimes feeds in nearby cultivation. Occurs from the lowlands to lower montane hills at 1,000 m. Usually seen flying in pairs, low across the forest. Perches in the canopy, except for late in the day when it sits in the open. Much reduced in numbers due to trapping and habitat destruction.

Distribution: Indonesian endemic. A locally fairly common resident on Komodo Island; uncommon on Sulawesi, Sumbar and Timor; rare on Sumbawa, Flores and Alor; possibly extinct on Lombok. Globally endangered with extinction.

SULPHUR-CRESTED COCKATOO

Cacatua galerita 50 cm F: Psittacidae

Description: Unmistakable within its range. The only other white parrot on New Guinea is the much smaller Little Corella, *C. pastinator* (38 cm), which occurs in the Trans-Fly region only.

Voice: A variety of powerful screams. The alarm call *raaa* is often heard.

Habits: Found in forest habitats, mainly in tall primary lowland rainforest, inland to 1,000 m. Seen rarely at 1,400 m. Best observed in early morning and late afternoon, when it perches in the open in the tops of huge trees, feeding on seeds. In Australia this species readily enters cultivated areas, but in Indonesia it is shot on sight, so does not occur near villages.

Morten Strange

Distribution: New Guinea to Australia, reaching Tasmania. A widespread but generally scarce resident in West Papua.

WHITE COCKATOO

Cacatua alba 46 cm F: Psittacidae

Description: Distinguished from other cockatoos by its large size and complete lack of colour. Its shaggy crest makes its head appear large.

Voice: A short, raucous screech.

Habits: Found in primary and mature secondary forest, mainly in the lowlands and foothills, occasionally to 900 m. Also inhabits forest remnants in disturbed areas. Generally declining in numbers. Flies strongly between the trees or perches in the middle storey, often in pairs. These cockatoos gather in small flocks, mainly in the evening, when they fly, call and interact in the open before roosting.

Morten Strange

Distribution: Indonesian endemic. A locally fairly common resident on Halmahera, Bacan and a few smaller islands nearby; observations from Obi believed to be escapees.

TANIMBAR CORELLA (Tanimbar Cockatoo)
Cacatua goffini 32 cm F: Psittacidae

Description: Unmistakable; the only white parrot within its range. Note pinkish lores and pale bill showing well in this rare habitat shot from Yamdena.

Voice: Variety of harsh screeches.

Habits: Found in all wooded habitats, from closed forest to open woodlands. Feeds on flowers and fruits high in the trees and regularly raids nearby maize crops. Often flies just above the canopy calling loudly. Still numerous; flocks of up to 200 have been reported. A survey in 1992 estimated the total population to be 300,000–400,000 individuals. However, thousands are captured each year for a possibly unsustainable trade.

Filip Verbelen

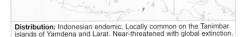

Distribution: Indonesian endemic. Locally common on the Tanimbar islands of Yamdena and Larat. Near-threatened with global extinction.

PESQUET'S PARROT (Vulturine Parrot)
Psittrichas fulgidus 46 cm F: Psittacidae

Description: Unmistakable and unique. Note its prominent red belly and the secondary wing feathers that flash in flight. A monotypic genus. Captive photo.

Voice: A penetrating, harsh scream that has been compared to tearing cloth.

Habits: Patchy occurrence in rainforested foothills and at lower montane elevations, usually from 600 to 1,000 m. Also reported close to sea level and inland to 2,000 m. Previously observed in the Lake Sentani area near Jayapura, but numbers are much reduced and it is now rarely seen. Hunted for skins, feathers, food and for the captive trade. Forages widely, feeding on fruits and flowers.

Alain Compost

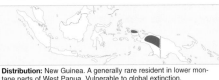

Distribution: New Guinea. A generally rare resident in lower montane parts of West Papua. Vulnerable to global extinction.

ECLECTUS PARROT

Eclectus roratus 39 cm F: Psittacidae

Description: Quite unique; the only member of its genus, but there are several subspecies. Photo shows male; female is mainly red, with purple bands across back and belly.

Voice: A loud penetrating squawk *graaah*.

Habits: An adaptable parrot found from primary rainforest to disturbed areas near villages. Occasionally seen in coastal scrub. A conspicuous and noisy bird, often observed flying low over the forest on broad wings, in pairs or small parties. Perches in the open, in the morning and evening; otherwise found chewing on vegetable food in the forest canopy. The nest is built in a cavity high in a large tree.

Distribution: Australasia, from Indonesia into northern Australia. A common resident on Halmahera and parts of West Papua. Widespread but less numerous on Sumba, Tanimbar and the Kai islands, and the remainder of Maluku.

RED-CHEEKED PARROT

Geoffroyus geoffroyi 25 cm F: Psittacidae

Description: Many subspecies occur on different islands, but the red head of the male (right) and the brown of the female are always conspicuous.

Voice: A characteristic, metallic *kee-kee-kee* in flight.

Habits: Found in all wooded areas, from primary forest to coastal mangroves and plantations. Has a rapid and swerving flight and often calls as it flies about. Perches in the open and feeds on vegetable matter. Nests high within a cavity in a dead branch. This behaviour is typical of its family.

Distribution: Australasia, from Indonesia into northern Australia. Widespread throughout Maluku, Nusa Tenggara and West Papua and generally common.

GREAT-BILLED PARROT

Tanygnathus megalorynchos 38 cm F: Psittacidae

Morten Strange

Description: Note the diagnostic yellow streaks in its wings and the huge red bill.

Voice: A repeated, harsh *ke-rarr* in flight and right after landing.

Habits: Found in forest, along forest edges, in mangroves and cultivation near the beach, and in low hills inland. Quite a common sight, mainly in coastal areas on smaller islands. Never found in large numbers. Often conspicuous late in the day, when birds fly about, calling and landing on exposed branches in the tops of the trees. The nest is built in a cavity high in a forest tree.

Distribution: Indonesia and Balut Island, the Philippines. A widespread and locally fairly common resident on the smaller islands of eastern Indonesia.

RED-BREASTED PARAKEET

Psittacula alexandri 34 cm F: Psittacidae

Description: Distinguished from the following species by its red breast and greyish head.

Voice: A harsh disyllabic scream.

Habits: Avoids the dense tropical rainforest around the Equator. Absent from the Malay Peninsula, Sumatra and most of Borneo, instead prefers the drought deciduous and open woodlands of subtropical and coastal regions. Also reported from swamps in south Sumatra and parts of Kalimantan. Formerly numerous in Indonesia, but its numbers are now much reduced around settlements due to trapping for the pet trade. Can still be seen in flocks visiting flowering and fruiting trees in remote rural and protected areas.

Ong Kiem Sian

Distribution: Oriental region. A locally fairly numerous but generally scarce resident on Java, Bali, Kangean as well as Simeulue, Banyak and the Nias islands off Sumatra.

LONG-TAILED PARAKEET
Psittacula longicauda 40 cm F: Psittacidae

Description: Note the extremely long tail and red face of the male (left). The female (right) has a shorter tail and duller facial patterns.

Voice: A penetrating screech during flight.

Habits: Much reduced in numbers due to habitat clearance and hunting. Does not do well in captivity. Can still be found locally along lowland forest edges, mangroves and nearby cultivated areas below 300 m. Always congregates in noisy flocks at communal roosts, especially in the evening.

Distribution: Southeast Asia. A widespread but generally scarce resident on Sumatra, Kalimantan and some nearby islands.

RED-WINGED PARROT
Aprosmictus erythropterus 31 cm F: Psittacidae

Description: Unmistakable; the two similar king-parrots that occur in Indonesia (genus: *Alisterus*) both have red heads and red underparts. Photo shows captive male; female has green back and shoulders. Forms a separate genus along with the Olive-shouldered Parrot, *A. jonquillaceus*, a Timor endemic and allospecies.

Voice: A metallic, staccato *ching* or *crilling*.

Habits: Frequents open savanna woodland; never strays far from water. Flies at canopy level with a characteristic elastic and buoyant flight, different from that of other parrots. Lands high in large trees to feed on flowers, seeds and fruits.

Distribution: New Guinea and northern Australia. A locally fairly common resident in the Trans-Fly region of West Papua only.

BREHM'S TIGER-PARROT

Psittacella brehmii 24 cm F: Psittacidae

Description: Distinguished with difficulty from the following species by its size and entirely brown head, including face. Photo shows female; male has yellow neck stripe and lacks barring on breast.

Voice: A distinctive *ee-yurr.*

Habits: Frequents montane forest between 1,500 and 2,600 m. Found mainly in tall primary forest, but also along forest edges and in nearby scrub. A quiet and inconspicuous bird, unlike other members of its family. Feeds on buds, seeds and fruits in the middle storey. Flies off stealthily, moving quickly within the forest canopy.

Distribution: New Guinea. A fairly common resident in montane parts of West Papua.

PAINTED TIGER-PARROT

Psittacella picta 19 cm F: Psittacidae

Description: Male (left) is distinguished from the previous species by its green (not brown) face. The female (right) lacks yellow neck stripe, but has barring across its breast. The sympatric Modest Tiger-parrot, *P. modesta* (14 cm), found from 1,700 to 2,800 m, is much smaller and has a brown breast.

Voice: A musical *err-eee.*

Habits: An upper montane specialist that occurs in forest from 2,500 m to the treeline at 3,800 m. Frequently moves into low alpine scrub and the stunted moss forest just below. Quite tame, like many upper montane birds; allows a close approach as it feeds at eye level on seeds, small fruits and berries. Little studied otherwise.

Distribution: New Guinea. A locally common resident in the central Snow Mountain area of West Papua.

BLUE-RUMPED PARROT

Psittinus cyanurus 18 cm F: Psittacidae

Description: A small, compact parrot. The genus is monotypic. The male (photo) has a blue rump, bluish head and red bill. The female has a brown head and bill.

Voice: A loud, metallic *chi-chi-chi.*

Habits: Found in rainforest, mainly in the lowlands; often seen in mangroves and on nearby plantations. On Sumatra occurs to 700 m. This species roams widely between locations and most sightings are of birds flying rapidly past, directly above the trees. Little is known about its feeding and nesting habits.

Morten Strange

Distribution: Sunda subregion. A widespread but generally scarce resident on Sumatra and Kalimantan.

BLUE-CROWNED HANGING-PARROT

Loriculus galgulus 12 cm F: Psittacidae

Description: The small *Loriculus* parrots are quite similar, but this is the only one within its range. Note the blue crown and red patch on the chest of this male (photo), missing on the female.

Voice: A high-pitched *dzi* in flight.

Habits: Seen mostly in small groups, flying quickly on rapidly moving wings, calling frequently. Lands in the tops of tall forest trees to feed on figs, small fruits, berries and nectar. This bird is difficult to observe among the foliage, because of its very small size and cryptic plumage. Also visits cultivated areas and villages to feed. Breeds in primary and mature secondary rainforest, from the lowlands to low hills.

Morten Strange

Distribution: Sunda subregion. A locally fairly common resident in Sumatra and Kalimantan; introduced in west Java.

MOLUCCAN HANGING-PARROT
Loriculus amabilis 13 cm F: Psittacidae

Description: Unmistakable; the only *Loriculus* parrot in its range. Female shown in photo; male has red forehead and throat patch. The larger subspecies on Sula is treated by del Hoyo (1997) as a separate species, the Sula Hanging-parrot, *L. sclateri*.

Voice: Similar to previous species.

Habits: Moves widely in all kinds of wooded habitat, from primary forest to mangroves and cultivated areas. Found mainly in the lowlands, and locally to 450 m. Feeds high in fruiting or flowering trees. Little information is available on feeding and nesting habits.

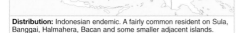

Distribution: Indonesian endemic. A fairly common resident on Sula, Banggai, Halmahera, Bacan and some smaller adjacent islands.

WALLACE'S HANGING-PARROT
Loriculus flosculus 12 cm F: Psittacidae

Description: Unmistakable; the only *Loriculus* parrot in its range. The female is a uniform green, except for its red rump; the male has a small red throat patch.

Voice: A screeching *strrt*.

Habits: Found in closed forest, especially in lower montane regions from 400 to 1,000 m. Good locations for viewing are near Labuhanbajo and Pota Wangka in western Flores. In the east of the island it has been found at Gunung Egon-Ilimudu. In general, however, this species is not numerous and is difficult to find. Small flocks land in large, fruiting fig trees, calling softly and continuously as they clamber along the branches like tree-rats (see photo).

Distribution: Indonesian endemic. A rare resident on the island of Flores only. Vulnerable to global extinction.

YELLOW-THROATED HANGING-PARROT

Loriculus pusillus 12 cm F: Psittacidae

Description: Unmistakable; the only *Loriculus* parrot in its range. Captive photo shows female; male has larger yellow breast patch.

Voice: A ringing *sree-ee* in flight.

Habits: Inhabits lowland rainforest, open casuarina woodlands and montane forest to 1,800 m. Feeds high in large fruiting figs and flowering trees, often flying in a swirling fashion above the canopy before settling in. Two eggs are laid in a cavity high in a tree, often in an old barbet hole.

Distribution: Indonesian endemic. A generally uncommon resident on Java and Bali.

INDIAN CUCKOO

Cuculus micropterus 33 cm F: Cuculidae

Description: In the field, best distinguished from the Eurasian Cuckoo, *C. canorus* (a vagrant to Java) and the following species by its call.

Voice: The penetrating 4-note whistle, with 4th lower note, is diagnostic.

Habits: Found in forested areas, from the lowlands to 1,000 m. More often heard than seen. Usually perches high and flies like a small hawk within the forest canopy, looking for small invertebrate food. This cuckoo is known to be nest-parasitic, but there are no confirmed breeding records from Indonesia.

Distribution: Oriental region and East Asia; northern populations migrate south. A winter visitor and presumed resident in the Sunda subregion; uncommon in Kalimantan; rare on Sumatra and Java.

ORIENTAL CUCKOO

Cuculus saturatus 30 cm F: Cuculidae

Morten Strange

Description: Upperparts may be more greyish than those of the previous species. Best identified by in-hand measurements or call.

Voice: A three-note *cuk, coo-coo.*

Habits: The resident population breeds in closed forest, especially in the hills and montane areas to 1,900 m. Brood-parasitic on flycatchers and warblers. Migrant individuals can turn up in any wooded area, during the northern winter from September to June. Feeds on caterpillars and insects. When disturbed, it flies off quickly into the canopy like a small raptor.

Distribution: Breeds in East Asia; migrates south reaching northern Australia. One subspecies resident in the Sunda subregion and Nusa Tenggara; the northern subspecies is a widespread winter visitor throughout.

PLAINTIVE CUCKOO

Cacomantis merulinus 21 cm F: Cuculidae

Morten Strange

Description: Best distinguished from the following species by lack of eye-ring. The subspecies found on Java and Sulawesi has a grey breast.

Voice: A mournful series of whistling notes, rising in pitch.

Habits: This very adaptable cuckoo is often found in open woodlands, as well as cultivated areas and villages. Can be quite numerous. Flies quickly from one tree to the next, preferring to stay within low canopies feeding on invertebrates. Rarely seen clearly. Nest-parasitic on prinias and tailorbirds.

Distribution: Oriental region. A widespread and fairly common resident on Sumatra, Kalimantan, Java, Bali and Sulawesi.

BRUSH CUCKOO

Cacomantis variolosus 24 cm F: Cuculidae

Description: Where it overlaps with the previous species, look for its larger size and distinct eye-ring. The western subspecies is treated by Andrew (1992) as a separate species, the Rusty-breasted Cuckoo, *C. sepulcralis*.

Voice: A series of 10–15 rising, whistling notes.

Habits: Found mainly in closed forest, but also seen in cultivated areas and scrub, although less often than the previous species. Occurs in coastal woodland and mangroves, and up to 2,500 m inland on Sulawesi. Solitary, secretive and more often heard than seen. Confirmed brood-parasitic on sunbirds, the Pied Bushchat, white-eyes and probably flycatchers, fantails and the Long-tailed Shrike.

Distribution: Southeast Asia east into Australia; Australian populations migrate north into eastern Indonesia. Resident throughout on all major islands, but generally uncommon.

Morten Strange

CHESTNUT-BREASTED CUCKOO

Cacomantis castaneiventris 24 cm F: Cuculidae

Description: Distinguished from the previous species by deep chestnut underparts extending up to throat.

Voice: A descending, whistled trill.

Habits: Occurs inside closed primary forest; sometimes seen along forest edges near clearings and rivers, but never in cultivated areas. Prefers the lower montane zone from 1,200 to 2,100 m. Also found locally at sea level and as high as 2,500 m. Flutters about below the canopy, catching insects and caterpillars, sometimes landing on the ground. Confirmed nest-parasitic on scrub-wrens.

Distribution: New Guinea into the Cape York Peninsula, Australia. A generally fairly common resident throughout West Papua and most adjacent islands.

Morten Strange

FAN-TAILED CUCKOO

Cacomantis flabelliformis 27 cm F: Cuculidae

Description: Distinguished with difficulty from the previous species by its longer and broader tail.

Voice: Similar to and possibly indistinguishable from the previous species.

Habits: In Indonesia, a strictly montane forest bird found mainly from 1,500 to 3,500 m; occasionally seen down to 1,200 m. Seems to replace the previous species at higher elevations. In Australia it also occurs in the lowlands and in open country. Confirmed nest parasite on scrub-wrens, fairy-wrens and robins.

Distribution: New Guinea, southeast into southern Australia and Pacific islands. An uncommon resident in upper montane parts of West Papua.

LITTLE BRONZE CUCKOO (Malayan Bronze Cuckoo)

Chrysococcyx minutillus 15 cm F: Cuculidae

Description: Distinguished with difficulty from other small cuckoos by the combination of darker, dull wings and heavy barring.

Voice: A slow, descending whistle of 3–5 notes.

Habits: Found in coastal forest and mangroves; sometimes seen in nearby scrub and cultivated areas. Very inconspicuous, so possibly overlooked during surveys. Hops about in trees, flying swiftly to the next one. Nest-parasitic on the *Gerygone* warblers and *Nectarinia* sunbirds.

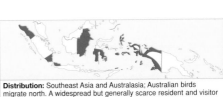

Distribution: Southeast Asia and Australasia; Australian birds migrate north. A widespread but generally scarce resident and visitor on many islands; possibly fairly common in West Papua and Sulawesi.

GOULD'S BRONZE CUCKOO

Chrysococcyx russatus 15 cm F: Cuculidae

Description: Distinguished with difficulty from the previous species by an increased greenish iridescence on upperparts and sparsely barred underparts. Should possibly be included as a subspecies under the previous species, but here follows Andrew (1992), M&P (1993) and C&B (1997).

Voice: An accelerating, descending *see-see-see*.

Habits: Occurs in a variety of wooded habitats, from closed primary forest to open woodlands and nearby cultivated areas. Usually lays its eggs in the nests of *Gerygone* warblers. Feeds on insects and larvae found in trees.

Distribution: Southeast Asia, east into northern Australia. A locally fairly common resident on Sulawesi, Flores and Timor, and parts of Kalimantan and West Papua.

DRONGO CUCKOO

Surniculus lugubris 25 cm F: Cuculidae

Description: Similar to the sympatric Bronzed Drongo (F: Dicruridae), but note its thin bill and white barring under tail. A monotypic genus.

Voice: An ascending, whistling call of 4–8 notes.

Habits: Found in lowland rainforest and along forest edges; occasionally disperses into scrub. On Sulawesi occurs to 1,200 m. Perches high in trees and flies quickly into the next when disturbed, so good views are difficult. Can usually be located by its call during the breeding season. Its nest-parasitic habits have not been studied in Indonesia.

Distribution: Oriental region; partly migratory. An uncommon resident and winter visitor throughout the Sunda subregion; can be locally common on Sulawesi; rare on Halmahera.

COMMON KOEL (Asian Koel)

Eudynamys scolopacea 42 cm F: Cuculidae

Distribution: Oriental region, into parts of eastern Indonesia; partly migratory. Widespread but generally scarce throughout the Sunda subregion and parts of Wallacea.

Description: A large cuckoo. Photo shows female (left) and displaying male. The Sulawesi population has a black bill and is treated by Andrew (1992) as a separate species, the Black-billed Koel, *E. melanorhyncha*.

Voice: A far-reaching *ko-wel* that varies somewhat with subspecies; also a bubbling series of notes.

Habits: Found in forest edges and coastal woodlands, as well as plantations and near villages. This shy and secretive bird stays within the canopy, feeding on small fruits. Only its loud call gives it away. Nest-parasitic, mainly on crows.

AUSTRALIAN KOEL

Eudynamys cyanocephala 42 cm F: Cuculidae

Distribution: Indonesia into northern Australia; partly migratory. A widespread but generally scarce resident and possible migrant from Australia in parts of Wallacea and West Papua.

Description: Possibly conspecific with the previous species. Distinguishing between the males is probably not possible in the field. Photo shows a male; the female is much paler below and lacks barring. Treated as separate species here, following Andrew (1992) and C&B (1997).

Voice: Like previous species.

Habits: Similar to those of the previous species. Turns up in a variety of wooded habitats, from closed forest to open woodlands. Occurs mainly in coastal lowlands; in Wallacea to 500 m; in West Papua to 1,500 m. Sometimes spotted in the can-opies of fruiting trees. Breeding has not been studied in Wallacea. Is nest-parasitic on orioles and friarbirds in New Guinea.

CHESTNUT-BELLIED MALKOHA

Phaenicophaeus sumatranus 40 cm F: Cuculidae

Description: Note the chestnut colour under the tail coverts that distinguishes this species from the Black-bellied Malkoha, *P. diardi*, which has a similar appearance and distribution.

Voice: A low *kok;* usually quiet.

Habits: This lowland rainforest specialist occurs in primary and secondary forest and mangroves, from the coast to 500 m. It hops about in the forest canopy, somewhat like a squirrel, making short flights into a neighbouring tree. Non-parasitic, but breeding has been little studied. This individual is collecting small sticks for a nest high in a tree.

Morten Strange

Distribution: Sunda subregion. A local and generally scarce resident in Sumatra and Borneo.

GREEN-BILLED MALKOHA

Phaenicophaeus tristis 55 cm F: Cuculidae

Description: Its green bill is not diagnostic; look instead for an extremely long tail and plain grey underparts.

Voice: Grunting or croaking notes.

Habits: In Indonesia, mainly a submontane forest bird occurring from 700 to 1,500 m; found locally to 200 m. Inhabits the lowlands on Kangean. This adaptable bird ventures into disturbed forest edges and plantations, feeding on insects and small vertebrates found in the vegetation. A resident pair is often seen together, hopping about in the middle storey, and frequently flying through openings to another tree.

Morten Strange

Distribution: Oriental region. A widespread and locally fairly common resident on Sumatra and Kangean Island north of Bali

RAFFLES'S MALKOHA

Phaenicophaeus chlorophaeus 33 cm F: Cuculidae

Description: Unmistakable; a small malkoha. The male (photo) is a chestnut colour; the female has a grey head and breast.

Voice: Quite vocal, with a soft, cat-like *kiaow-kiaow-kiaow.*

Habits: Found in primary lowland rainforest, but is fairly adaptable and often seen in disturbed areas and along forest edges. Occurs locally to 700 m. Usually seen in resident pairs, clambering about the foliage in the forest canopy searching for invertebrates. Does not fly far. To date, nest has never been described.

Distribution: Sunda subregion. A locally fairly common resident in Sumatra, Batu, Bangka and Kalimantan.

RED-BILLED MALKOHA

Phaenicophaeus javanicus 45 cm F: Cuculidae

Description: The only malkoha in Indonesia with a red bill.

Voice: A quiet *kuk.*

Habits: Less adaptable than other malkohas. Found mainly in primary rainforest, from lowlands to 1,000 m. Seen less often in mature secondary forest and occasionally in nearby scrub. Moves from the middle and upper storeys to just below the canopy, often in resident pairs. Hops and flies briefly from branch to branch, searching for large insects.

Distribution: Sunda subregion. A generally scarce resident in Sumatra, Kalimantan and Java.

YELLOW-BILLED MALKOHA
Phaenicophaeus calyorhynchus 53 cm F: Cuculidae

Description: The only malkoha within its range. Distinguished from the following allospecies by its size, bill and grey belly.

Voice: A short, nasal chatter.

Habits: Occurs in primary and mature secondary rainforest, from the lowlands to 1,300 m. Also ventures into nearby scrub and is regularly reported in surveys. Clambers about the vegetation, searching for large insects; sometimes seen feeding near troops of Sulawesi Macaque monkeys. Breeding habits have been little studied and its nest has never been described.

Margaret Kinnaird

Distribution: Indonesian endemic. A fairly common resident on Sulawesi.

CHESTNUT-BREASTED MALKOHA
Phaenicophaeus curvirostris 49 cm F: Cuculidae

Description: Distinguished from other malkohas within its range by its chestnut breast and yellow bill. Borneo race also has a chestnut belly.

Voice: A deep *tok-tok-tok*.

Habits: Found in primary rainforest, secondary growth, nearby scrub and along forest edges. Occurs from the lowlands to 1,000 m, and is occasionally seen to 1,500 m. Moves around the middle storey like a small mammal, usually in pairs, looking for large insects and small vertebrate prey. Quite approachable, unlike most forest birds, although it rarely perches in the open. The pair builds a nest of twigs.

Morten Strange

Distribution: Sunda subregion. A widespread and fairly common resident in Sumatra, Kalimantan, Java and Bali.

GOLIATH COUCAL

Centropus goliath 66 cm F: Cuculidae

Description: Unmistakable; the largest cuckoo in the world. Note its huge size and white wing coverts.

Voice: A series of very deep notes *ooom-ooom.*

Habits: Occurs in primary rainforest and along forest edges. Sometimes seen near rivers and clearings. Climbs about in the vegetation with some awkwardness. Often this massive bird is spotted flying weakly across the trail or when it calls as it sits passively within a large canopy. Feeds on large insects. Otherwise little studied and its nest has never been described.

Distribution: Indonesian endemic. A locally fairly common resident on Halmahera; uncommon on Bacan, Obi and other smaller nearby islands.

GREATER COUCAL

Centropus sinensis 52 cm F: Cuculidae

Description: Its large size and smooth plumage without spots are diagnostic. Shown holding lizard prey. The rare Short-toed Coucal, *C. rectunguis,* has the same plumage but is only 30 cm long and is found in closed forest.

Voice: A repeated, deep, booming *poop-poop-poop.*

Habits: Occurs in forest edges and secondary growth, often near riverbanks and in mangroves; also ventures into nearby plantations. Creeps around thickets, searching for vertebrate and invertebrate prey. Sometimes seen clearly, flying to and from the ground, near rural roadsides. The nest is a large ball of twigs and leaves built low in a bush.

Distribution: Oriental region. A widespread and fairly common resident in Sumatra, Kalimantan, Java and Bali.

LESSER COUCAL

Centropus bengalensis 42 cm F: Cuculidae

Description: Distinguished from the previous species by its size and white streaks in plumage. The rare, endemic Javan Coucal, *C. nigrorufus,* (Sunda Coucal; M&P 1993) has black on its back and in wings.

Voice: Hoots like the Greater Coucal, but more rapidly and with a higher pitch.

Habits: Mainly an open country species that has benefited from forest clearance. Quickly invades new grassland areas, marshes and cultivation. Makes short flights across the vegetation, but feeds on the ground in tall grass and scrub, searching for insects, frogs and lizards. Perches in the open in the early morning and late afternoon.

Morten Strange

Distribution: Oriental region. A widespread and common resident in the Sunda and Wallacea subregions.

BARN OWL

Tyto alba 34 cm F: Tytonidae

Description: Unmistakable; note its characteristic heart-shaped face; appears very white as it flies at night, like a ghost.

Voice: A screeching *wheech* and a penetrating *ke-ke-ke.*

Habits: Occurs in open woodlands and often in built-up areas. Spends the day roosting in a dark place such as a dense tree, a cliff ledge or under a building. At night it flies out on silent wings to hunt for rats and other small prey in open country. The nest is constructed in a cavity in a tree or building. Not often seen in Indonesia, but possibly overlooked.

Morten Strange

Distribution: Worldwide. A generally scarce resident in Sumatra, Java, Bali and parts of Nusa Tenggara.

SULAWESI SCOPS-OWL

Otus manadensis 21 cm F: Strigidae

B. Van Elegem

Description: The only scops-owl within its range. These owls are mainly identified by voice and in-hand examination. Three species are illustrated here. The Sangihe population was recently described as a new species, *O. collari*.

Voice: A single, clear, rising whistle.

Habits: Occurs in wooded areas, from closed rainforest to disturbed forest patches and nearby cultivation. Found mainly in the lowlands; sometimes inland to 2,000 m, and occasionally to 2,500 m. Usually calls for a few hours after dusk and again in the early morning before dawn. Perches low inside canopies; hawks from there for flying insects. Will respond to imitation of call.

Distribution: Indonesian endemic. A widespread and common resident on Sulawesi, and the smaller islands of Siau and Sangihe just to the north.

JAVAN SCOPS-OWL

Otus angelinae 20 cm F: Strigidae

Filip Verbelen

Description: Note small size and pale underparts with black streaks.

Voice: Not described, possibly silent.

Habits: Found in montane forest from 1,400 to 2,000 m. Known only at a few locations, mainly at Gunung Tangkubanprahu and Gunung Gede-Pangrango National Park, where this rare photograph was taken. Habits and status are poorly known. BirdLife International regards this species as vulnerable to global extinction.

Distribution: Indonesian endemic. A rare resident in montane areas of west Java only.

COLLARED SCOPS-OWL

Otus lempij 23 cm F: Strigidae

Description: A small brownish owl; ear tufts are sometimes visible; note pale collar around neck, hence the name.

Voice: A soft *hoo-o*, repeated at regular intervals.

Habits: The most numerous owl within its range and the one most likely to be encountered near villages and rural roads. Found in forest edges and cultivation, from the lowlands to 1,000 m. Most active early in the night; very vocal right after dusk during the breeding season. Drops from a low perch to the ground, where it feeds on crickets, cockroaches, larvae and small reptiles. Nests in cavities in trees and sometimes old buildings.

Morten Strange

Distribution: Africa, Eurasia and the Oriental region. A widespread and fairly common resident in Sumatra, Kalimantan, Java and Bali.

BARRED EAGLE-OWL

Bubo sumatranus 45 cm F: Strigidae

Description: Note prominent ear tufts. Distinguished from following species by cross-barring (not vertical streaks) on underparts.

Voice: A deep *whoo* and a variety of grunting calls.

Habits: This fairly adaptable species occurs in primary forest and dense secondary forest. Also found along forest edges and in nearby disturbed areas. Although rarely reported, could be quite common in the lowlands to 1,000 m. On Sumatra recorded to 1,600 m. A nest has also been found here, at the base of an epiphytic fern. Sometimes seen roosting during the day. Flies out at dusk to hunt from a low perch.

Frank Lambert

Distribution: Sunda subregion. A generally uncommon resident in Sumatra, Bangka, Kalimantan, Java and Bali.

BUFFY FISH-OWL

Ketupa ketupu 45 cm F: Strigidae

Description: Distinguished from the Spotted Wood-owl, *Strix seloputo*, and the Brown Wood-owl, *S. leptogrammica*, both uncommon in western parts of Indonesia, by black streaks in dark brown plumage, and ear tufts.

Voice: A soft *to-wee*.

Habits: Found in closed forest and wooded areas, mainly in the lowlands. Occurs on Sumatra to 1,100 m. This adaptable species seems to prefer forest edges. At dusk it comes out into open country and hunts near a stream, rice field or fish pond. Lands near the water to catch fish, frogs and crustaceans, but also takes small terrestrial prey and birds. Roosts in a tree during the day, often in resident pairs.

Distribution: Southeast Asia. A generally scarce resident on Sumatra and some adjacent islands, Kalimantan and Java; rare on Bali.

BROWN HAWK-OWL

Ninox scutulata 30 cm F: Strigidae

Description: Unmistakable; the only hawk-owl within its breeding range. An additional eight *Ninox* owls are listed by Andrew (1992) for Wallacea and West Papua, where they are called boobooks. This species is also known as the Brown Boobook.

Voice: A double hoot *hu-oop* repeated just after dusk and before dawn.

Habits: Resident in closed forest and along forest edges. Winter visitors also turn up in mangroves, wooded cultivated areas and gardens. Found mainly in the coastal lowlands; on Sumatra recorded to 1,500 m. Emerges after dusk to hunt for large insects near clearings. Builds its nest in a cavity in a large tree.

Distribution: East Asia and Oriental region; northern populations migrate south. A generally uncommon resident in Sumatra and Kalimantan, rare on Java and Bali; winter visitor only in parts of Wallacea; breeding on Sulawesi suspected.

PAPUAN FROGMOUTH

Podargus papuensis 50 cm F: Podargidae

Description: Note large size. Distinguished from the sympatric Marbled Frogmouth, *P. ocellatus,* by its size and by greyish plumage, richly mottled with black.

Voice: A resonant *ooom* and a laughing hoot in early evening and before dawn.

Habits: This huge frogmouth is regularly heard in lowland rainforest and disturbed areas, including nearby gardens. Often found around sea-level terrain near swampy areas; rarely to 2,100 m. Strictly noctural. Sometimes can be seen during the day, roosting near trails in the open coastal woodlands of Wasur National Park. Flies out at dusk to hunt for small invertebrates on the ground.

Jon Hornbuckle

Distribution: New Guinea, east into the Solomon Islands and south to Cape York Peninsula, Australia. A widespread and locally fairly common resident in West Papua and on adjacent islands.

GOULD'S FROGMOUTH

Batrachostomus stellatus 25 cm F: Podargidae

Description: Note the pale, scaly underparts that set it apart from the next species. Also look for the characteristic long, barred tail.

Voice: A distinctive, rising *oooh-wheeow,* repeated at seven-second intervals.

Habits: A forest bird found in rainforest in the extreme lowlands. Occurs on Sumatra to 500 m elevation. This photograph was taken in Way Kambas National Park in Sumatra, a regular site for this cryptic species, but it is usually difficult to find. Roosts on a branch during the day and emerges in early evening to glean insects from the foliage inside the canopies.

Bill Simpson

Distribution: Sunda subregion. A scarce resident in Kalimantan and Sumatra, including the nearby islands of Riau, Lingga and Bangka.

JAVAN FROGMOUTH

Batrachostomus javensis 24 cm F: Podargidae

Description: Note the characteristic small bill and wide mouth. Female (photo) has somewhat browner plumage than male. An additional four rare members of this family occur in western Indonesia, but the family is curiously absent from Bali and Wallacea.

Voice: A croaking series of 4–5 notes, rising and trailing off.

Habits: Found in lowland rainforest; also inhabits low hills on Java. This peculiar night bird is difficult to find in Indonesia. However it is quite vocal at the beginning of the year, during the breeding season, and then its call gives it away. Sometimes it is sighted during the day, roosting in a low tree.

Distribution: Southeast Asia. An uncommon resident on Java; rare in Kalimantan and Sumatra.

Uthai Treesucon

MOLUCCAN OWLET-NIGHTJAR

Aegotheles crinifrons 30 cm F: Aegothelidae

Description: Unmistakable within its range. Looks like a cross between an owl and a nightjar. This unique family has only eight members worldwide. This species, from Maluku, is also called the Long-whiskered Owlet-nightjar.

Voice: A variety of squeals and cackles.

Habits: Occurs in closed forest, mainly in primary and mature secondary growth. Extends from the lowland into hills and lower montane elevations, where its weird call is heard regularly. Will respond somewhat to a call imitation or tape playback, but this little known species is shy and good views are difficult. Sits on an open perch in the forest, sallying out for insects, as shown in this rare photo.

Distribution: Indonesian endemic. A generally scarce resident on the islands of Halmahera, Kasiruta and Bacan only.

B. Van Elegem

LARGE-TAILED NIGHTJAR

Caprimulgus macrurus 30 cm F: Caprimulgidae

Description: Distinguished with difficulty from other nightjars by its bright white throat. Best identified by call. Photo shows a nesting bird. Indistinguishable in the field from the allospecies Philippine Nightjar, *C. manillensis* (Sulawesi Nightjar, *C. celebensis;* C&B (1997)).

Voice: A hollow, penetrating *chonk,* repeated through the evening.

Habits: Its call is heard every evening in many parts of Indonesia, but this bird does not seem to be numerous anywhere and is possibly in decline. Calls from a low perch and is often seen on the ground. Found in forest edges and nearby cultivated areas and villages. Flies out at dusk to hawk for insects in the air.

Morten Strange

Distribution: Oriental region and Australasia. Widespread throughout most of Indonesia; status uncertain; appears to be uncommon in the Sunda subregion, Wallacea and West Papua.

SAVANNA NIGHTJAR

Caprimulgus affinis 22 cm F: Caprimulgidae

Description: Small bird with grey-brown plumage. Distinguished from the previous species by lack of a white throat patch. Individual in photo has straw stuck to foot, trailing behind tail.

Voice: Vocal. A soft, penetrating *chew-eep* repeated during early evening.

Habits: An open country bird that has benefited from coastal forest clearance and developments. Found in savanna woodlands, grasslands and dry fields, especially near the coast, and inland along riverbeds. Often seen near human habitation. Loose colonies form at prime locations, with several pairs breeding in the vicinity. Calls from a perch or while flying back and forth, hawking for insects.

Morten Strange

Distribution: Oriental region, southeast into Indonesia. A widespread and locally fairly common resident in the Sunda subregion and parts of Wallacea.

EDIBLE-NEST SWIFTLET

Aerodramus fuciphagus 13 cm F: Apodidae

Distribution: Southeast Asia. A locally common resident throughout the Sunda subregion and parts of Nusa Tenggara.

Description: In the field regarded as indistinguishable from other *Aerodramus* swiftlets. (genus *Aerodramus* included under *Collicalia* by Beehler (1986), M&P (1993) and C&B (1997)).

Voice: A high-pitched *tscheerr.*

Habits: Found in all types of open country, especially near the coast and on offshore islands. Occurs locally to 2,800 m. Feeds on the wing. Perches at nest inside deep limestone caves and navigates in total darkness by an audible echolocation rattle. When nest-building (see photo), it constructs a unique translucent cup made up of hardened saliva. Nests are collected by local people and traded commercially for consumption.

Margaret Kinnaird

UNIFORM SWIFTLET

Aerodramus vanikorensis 13 cm F: Apodidae

Distribution: Philippines and Indonesia, east into the Pacific islands. A locally common resident throughout West Papua and parts of Wallacea.

Description: Distinguished from the previous species by its nest, which has moss added to the saliva.

Voice: Shrill calls in flight.

Habits: Much like the Edible-nest Swiftlet; also echolocates. Flies over all kinds of habitat, from open country to closed lowland forest, catching tiny insects in the air. The members of this genus have a swerving flight pattern, fluttering and gliding intermittently. Always seen in small flocks. Nests communally in caves.

Morten Strange

MOSSY-NEST SWIFTLET

Aerodramus salangana 12 cm F: Apodidae

Description: Distinguished from the Edible-nest Swiftlet by its nest, which is made largely from moss (see photo). May be conspecific with the previous species.

Voice: Shrill calls in flight.

Habits: The exact range and status of this species is somewhat uncertain, as it cannot be distinguished from the Edible-nest Swiftlet in the field. Echolocates to find its nest in the dark caves where it breeds. Flies and feeds much like the two previous species.

Morten Strange

Distribution: Sunda subregion. Appears to be an uncommon resident in west Sumatra, Kalimantan, Java; a common resident on Bali.

BLACK-NEST SWIFTLET

Aerodramus maximus 13 cm F: Apodidae

Description: Note square tail in flight. Distinguished from the Edible-nest Swiftlet by its nest, which is made of black feathers held together by saliva.

Voice: Shrill calls in flight.

Habits: Much like the Edible-nest Swiftlet. Also echolocates. Swerves high over coastal areas, lower late in the day. Occurs in large flocks locally. Never perches in trees or lands on the ground. Is attracted to limestone areas, where it nests deep inside caves. Its nests are collected for consumption, although less valuable than the clean nests of the Edible-nest Swiftlet.

Morten Strange

Distribution: Sunda subregion. A locally common resident in coastal Sumatra and Kalimantan; uncommon on Java.

GLOSSY SWIFTLET (White-bellied Swiftlet)

Collocalia esculenta 9 cm F: Apodidae

Description: A very small swiftlet with fast wing beats, shown here at its nest. Note very long wings.

Voice: High-pitched, twitting sounds.

Habits: Seen feeding over all terrain, from lowland open country to forests and montane areas above the tree line. Varies in abundance, but occurs in many places in small groups; rarely seen in larger flocks. Unlike *Aerodramus* swiftlets, this swift cannot echolocate, so it builds its nest near cave entrances, under cliff overhangs or in abandoned houses.

Morten Strange

Distribution: Oriental region and Australasia. A generally common resident throughout Indonesia, except where replaced by the following species.

LINCHI SWIFTLET (Cave Swiftlet)

Collocalia linchi 10 cm F: Apodidae

Description: Similar to the previous species; note pale belly, visible in flight. Possibly conspecific with the previous species.

Voice: High-pitched, twitting sounds.

Habits: Seen over forest and open country, as well as wetlands and cultivation. The most numerous swiftlet on Java and Bali. Flight is slow and erratic, and much lower than *Aerodramus* swiftlets. It sometimes flies at eye-level, like a swallow. Breeding is similar to the previous species.

Morten Strange

Distribution: Sunda subregion. A common resident on Java, Bali and Lombok; a local resident in montane Sumatra.

BROWN-BACKED NEEDLETAIL (Brown Needletail)

Hirundapus giganteus 25 cm F: Apodidae

Description: Note its characteristic 'cigar' body shape. Distinguished from other *Hirundapus* swifts by its large size and uniformly dark brown plumage, except for a small white patch under tail. White lores are sometimes visible.

Voice: A squeaky *cheek*.

Habits: One of four needletail swifts occurring in Indonesia. The largest and the most common in its range, although never numerous. Flies high over forest and sometimes open woodlands, catching insects in the air. Moves very fast and quickly covers great distances. Rarely seen perched. Reported to nest in tree-holes, but few nesting records exist.

Morten Strange

Distribution: Oriental region; partly migratory. A presumed resident and a widespread but generally scarce winter visitor in Sumatra, Kalimantan, Java and Bali.

SILVER-RUMPED SWIFT

Rhaphidura leucopygialis 11 cm F: Apodidae

Description: Distinguished from similar swiftlets by diagnostic broad wings and flapping flight. All-black except for a white rump that flashes brightly when turning and flying away. This species and the very similar West African species are the only members of this genus.

Voice: A high-pitched *tirr-tirr*.

Habits: Occurs in primary rainforest and forest edges, mainly in the lowlands. Recorded to 1,500 m in Java. Flies low over the forest canopies; in the evenings flies near the ground over cleared areas. Often seen near streams and wet areas, but never around settlements. Flight is fast and fluttering. Little studied; believed to nest in tree cavities.

Morten Strange

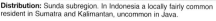

Distribution: Sunda subregion. In Indonesia a locally fairly common resident in Sumatra and Kalimantan, uncommon in Java.

PAPUAN NEEDLETAIL (Papuan Spine-tailed Swift)

Mearnsia novaeguineae 12 cm F: Apodidae

Morten Strange

Description: Note unmistakable shape, with broad wings and body. A uniformly dark colour.

Voice: Thin but penetrating squeaks.

Habits: Flies above open country near forest. Often seen over coastal areas and swampy patches. In the afternoon or during cloudy weather, it swoops in, fast and low to the ground, hunting for flying insects. Feeds in small flocks, often mixing with *Collocalia* swiftlets, but is always easy to recognise by its direct flight pattern. Roosts in a hollow tree in nearby forest.

Distribution: New Guinea. A locally fairly common resident in lowland parts of West Papua, but absent from the Vogelkop Peninsula and nearby islands.

FORK-TAILED SWIFT

Apus pacificus 18 cm F: Apodidae

C. & D. Frith: Frithfoto

Description: A fairly large swift. In flight the very long, narrow wings and long, deeply forked tail are characteristic.

Voice: Sometimes a high-pitched *dzee-dzee;* mainly quiet during migration.

Habits: Hunts for flying insects over open country, usually in coastal lowland regions, but has been recorded inland to 1,000 m. Observed during the northern winter (August to April). Locally abundant during peak migration to the south (September to November), sometimes mixing with other swifts. This species tends to fly very high and is possibly overlooked. Can turn up anywhere within the archipelago.

Distribution: Breeds in East Asia; migrates south into the Oriental and Australasian regions, reaching southern Australia. A widespread, common migrant and winter visitor throughout most of Indonesia.

LITTLE SWIFT

Apus affinis 15 cm (House Swift) F: Apodidae

Description: Shown perched at its nesting site. White rump shows clearly in flight. Look for square (not forked) tail.

Voice: Penetrating screams. Very vocal at roosting sites in the evening.

Habits: Hunts for insects on the wing over open country and marshy areas, rarely near forest. Flight pattern is steadier than swiftlets. Nests under cliff overhangs and often under man-made structures such as bridges, dams and houses.

Distribution: Africa, tropical and subtropical Eurasia. A widespread and locally common resident in Sumatra, Kalimantan, Java and Bali; has recently expanded into parts of Wallacea.

Morten Strange

ASIAN PALM-SWIFT

Cypsiurus balasiensis 11 cm F: Apodidae

Description: Note its characteristic narrow, forked tail. Also distinguished from swiftlets by its more direct flight pattern. A unique species that is the only member of its genus in Asia.

Voice: High-pitched screams.

Habits: Exclusively associated with tall, broad-leafed palm trees, often planted near villages or scattered around open grasslands. Flies quickly about near the palm trees, hawking insects at canopy level. Roosts under cover of the leaves and its tiny nest is fixed to the underside of a leaf.

Distribution: Oriental region. A widespread and fairly common resident in Sumatra, Kalimantan, Java, Bali and southern Sulawesi.

Morten Strange

GREY-RUMPED TREESWIFT

Hemiprocne longipennis 20 cm F: Hemiprocnidae

Morten Strange

Description: Note long, narrow wings and long tail. The deep fork in tail shows while turning. Male has chestnut ear coverts.

Voice: A high-pitched *fee-fee-few* when flying.

Habits: Occurs in disturbed forest with large free-standing trees and along edges of primary forest Sometimes found in mangroves and parks. Perches frequently on high branches, unlike true swifts. From there it performs long raids for flying insects with a characteristic flapping and gliding flight pattern. Most active during the early morning and late afternoon. Usually seen in resident pairs and sometimes in small flocks.

Distribution: Sunda subregion into parts of Wallacea. A widespread and locally fairly common resident in the Sunda subregion, extending into Sulawesi and Lombok.

MOUSTACHED TREESWIFT

Hemiprocne mystacea 31 cm F: Hemiprocnidae

Morten Strange

Description: Unmistakable within its range; much larger than previous species. Note its very long tail. The white eyebrow and moustachial streak are prominent when perched.

Voice: A loud, high-pitched, squeaky call when flying.

Habits: Much like the previous species. Hawks for insects high in the air, from an open perch near forest. Mainly found in the lowlands, but also occurs in the mountains on New Guinea. A single egg is placed in a tiny cup nest that is fixed with saliva to a branch high in a large tree.

Distribution: Indonesia and Papua New Guinea. Widespread and locally fairly common in Maluku and West Papua.

WHISKERED TREESWIFT
Hemiprocne comata 15 cm F: Hemiprocnidae

Description: A small treeswift; note upright posture and long, narrow wings reaching beyond tail.

Voice: A high-pitched *squeawk* in flight.

Habits: Restricted to lowland rainforest. In Sumatra extends to 1,000 m. Often seen in resident pairs along forest edges, logging tracks and nearby clearings and rivers. Predictable and conspicuous, but nowhere numerous. Perches high on open branches and flies out to grab small insects in the air nearby.

Distribution: Southeast Asia. A local and generally scarce resident in Sumatra and Kalimantan.

Morten Strange

RED-NAPED TROGON
Harpactes kasumba 33 cm F: Trogonidae

Description: Photo shows a male. The diagnostic red nape that contrasts with its black head is barely visible. Female has a brown head with orange, not red underparts.

Voice: Diagnostic call of 6 melancholy notes *kaup, kaup, kaup, . . .* trailing off.

Habits: Restricted to primary and mature secondary rainforest in the lowlands below 400 m. A low-density species that apparently adapts poorly to disturbance. Usually located by call. Sometimes spotted perched at middle storey level within the forest. Otherwise, little is known about this enigmatic bird.

Distribution: Sunda subregion. A local, scarce resident in Sumatra and Kalimantan.

Alan OwYong

DIARD'S TROGON

Harpactes diardii 30 cm F: Trogonidae

Description: Note violet eye-ring of both male (left) and female (right). Female has brown (not black) throat.

Voice: Ten–twelve *kaup* notes, quicker and higher pitched than the Red-naped Trogon.

Habits: Similar to the previous species. This low-density rainforest specialist is found in closed forest, from the lowlands to 850 m. Sits motionless below the canopy and is easy to miss in spite of its bright colours. Flies off abruptly and disappears from sight. The trogon family has been little studied. These birds do poorly in captivity.

Distribution: Sunda subregion. An uncommon resident in Sumatra and Kalimantan.

SCARLET-RUMPED TROGON

Harpactes duvaucelii 25 cm F: Trogonidae

Description: Small size; male (left) and female (right) are distinguished from the similar and sympatric (but rarer) Cinnamon-rumped Trogon, *H. orrhophaeus*, by the blue eye-brow, and scarlet rump of the male and the brown head of the female.

Voice: An accelerating, 12-note *yau, yau*.

Habits: Restricted to lowland rainforest below 600 m. Found in both primary and closed secondary forest. Appears to be the most numerous trogon within its range, although it is not really common anywhere. Perches in the lower and middle storey. Otherwise little studied. Feeding and nesting behavior rarely observed.

Distribution: Sunda subregion. A locally fairly common resident in Sumatra and Kalimantan.

RED-HEADED TROGON

Harpactes erythrocephalus 34 cm F: Trogonidae

Description: Note the diagnostic red head of the male in photo; female has brown head.

Voice: Five or more mellow notes *tiaup, tiaup.*

Habits: This trogon is restricted to montane rainforest. Occurs from 400 to 1,900 m. Like other members of this family, it sits quietly at middle storey level or slightly lower in primary rainforest, and shifts quickly to another perch when disturbed. Hawks for insects among the trees, but this is rarely observed.

Distribution: Oriental region. In Indonesia, a rarely recorded resident in montane parts of Sumatra.

COMMON KINGFISHER

Alcedo atthis 17 cm F: Alcedinidae

Description: Note small size and diagnostic rufous ear coverts. A Maluku subspecies has blue ear coverts and is very similar to following species, which does not occur in Maluku.

Voice: A very high-pitched *zeep* when taking off.

Habits: Turns up during migration in all kinds of open country wetlands. Is often seen around tidal estuaries, mangroves, fish ponds, coastal villages as well as rivers and lakes far inland. Occurs locally to 1,500 m. Drops into the water from a low perch to grab small fish. Flies off quickly, low across the surface of the water, when disturbed.

Distribution: Across Eurasia into Australasia; northern populations migrate south. A widespread winter visitor in the Sunda subregion and northern Wallacea; resident on Sulawesi and possibly the rest of Wallacea.

BLUE-EARED KINGFISHER

Alcedo meninting 16 cm F: Alcedinidae

Distribution: Oriental region; sedentary. A locally fairly common resident on Sumatra and most nearby islands, Kalimantan, Sulawesi, Java and Lombok; rare on Bali.

Description: Best distinguished from the previous species by its blue (not rufous) ear coverts; its plumage appears a darker blue.

Voice: Similar to the previous species, although thinner and pitched higher.

Habits: Prefers forested streams, large rivers and ponds in wooded areas. Also found in coastal mangroves, but never in open country. Occurs near the coast on Sulawesi, but is also found along inland rivers in the Sunda subregion. Occurs on Sumatra to 1,000 m. Sits on a low perch near water and plunges in to grab tiny fish. Shy and inconspicuous—often not seen until it takes off abruptly, flying out of sight, low across the water.

AZURE KINGFISHER

Alcedo azurea 17 cm F: Alcedinidae

Distribution: Australasia; extends from Indonesia into Australia, reaching Tasmania. An uncommon resident on Bacan, Halmahera, Tanimbar, and West Papua and adjacent islands.

Description: Distinguished from the Common Kingfisher by its lack of rufous ear coverts and smooth (not spotted), dark blue upperparts. The similar and sympatric Variable Dwarf Kingfisher, *Ceyx lepidus*, is only 12 cm long.

Voice: A high-pitched *tseet,* mostly in flight.

Habits: Much like the previous species. Found near forested streams along the coast or in mangroves. Occurs inland to the foothills and rarely to 1,500 m in West Papua. Sits on an exposed perch near water and dives for small fish, sometimes hovering before plunging in.

SMALL BLUE KINGFISHER

Alcedo coerulescens 13 cm F: Alcedinidae

Description: Tiny size, blue breast band and white belly together are diagnostic.

Voice: A short, high-pitched *ti-ti-ti.*

Habits: Occurs near mangroves, tidal mudflats, fish ponds and brackish estuaries. Found less often behind the coast along freshwater streams and in wet paddy fields. Sits low on an open perch, dropping down to grab small fish and other aquatic prey in shallow water or on the mud.

Distribution: Indonesian endemic; sedentary. A locally fairly common resident on south Sumatra, Java, Kangean, Bali, Lombok and Sumbawa; a single record from Flores.

ORIENTAL DWARF KINGFISHER (Black-backed Kingfisher)

Ceyx erithacus 14 cm F: Alcedinidae

Description: Photo shows the sedentary Sunda subregion resident race, treated by M&P (1993) and Strange (2000) as the Rufous-backed Kingfisher, *C. rufidorsus.* Northern migratory birds have almost black wings and a black ear patch.

Voice: A soft but penetrating whistle *tsie-tsie.*

Habits: This lowland rainforest specialist resident inhabits primary and mature secondary rainforest. Occasionally found to 700 m. The Black-backed race also turns up in disturbed habitats on north Sumatra and in Kalimantan during migration, and interbreeding has occurred. Often seen near small forest streams. The nest is built in a hole in an embankment.

Distribution: Oriental region. An uncommon resident and possible winter visitor in the Sunda subregion and parts of Nusa Tenggara.

STORK-BILLED KINGFISHER

Pelargopsis capensis 37 cm F: Alcedinidae

Description: Unmistakable in Indonesia; note its huge size and massive red bill. Wings and back are blue; pale blue rump flashes in flight.

Voice: A vocal bird with a variety of harsh calls, including a loud *kak-kak-kak*.

Habits: Found in both tidal mangroves and along wooded rivers and marshes far inland. Occurs mainly in the lowlands and locally to 1,200 m. Perches in trees and bushes near water and pounces onto the surface catching aquatic prey. Flies off low when disturbed, calling loudly.

Distribution: Oriental region; sedentary. A widespread resident and locally fairly common in Kalimantan and Sumbawa, although generally scarce; uncommon on Sumatra; rare on Java; also occurs on Bali, Lombok and Flores.

BANDED KINGFISHER

Lacedo pulchella 23 cm F: Alcedinidae

Description: Unmistakable; photo shows male. Female has black bars on chest and brown upperparts. A unique bird; the only member of its genus.

Voice: A long series of whistled *chi-wiu*.

Habits: A peculiar kingfisher that is restricted to closed forest. Inhabits primary forest and mature secondary rainforest, from the lowlands to lower montane elevations. Not associated with water. Usually located by call and is often seen sitting lethargically in the middle storey below the canopy for long periods. Hunts for insects in the forest.

Distribution: Southeast Asia. A generally scarce resident in Sumatra, Kalimantan and Java.

BLUE-WINGED KOOKABURRA

Dacelo leachii 40 cm F: Alcedinidae

Description: The largest kingfisher in Indonesia. Distinguished from following species by its larger size and pale neck. Its wings flash blue in flight.

Voice: A noisy variety of harsh cackles and screeches.

Habits: Found in the open savanna forest in the Trans-Fly region, west to the Mimika River. Occurs from sea level to 400 m. Sits motionless on a perch in the open woodland, flying down to grab small prey in the grass below. Often seen in resident pairs. The nest is built in a hollow in a tree or termite mound.

Charles Tyler/Windrush Photos

Distribution: New Guinea into northern Australia. A generally scarce resident in southern and southwestern West Papua.

SPANGLED KOOKABURRA

Dacelo tyro 33 cm F: Alcedinidae

Description: Distinguished from the previous species by its characteristic spangled head, neck and mantle.

Voice: A rattling gurgle; also a loud *kurk*.

Habits: Occurs in the open drought deciduous forests of the Trans-Fly lowlands. The Wasur National Park, where this photo was taken, is a good place to find this species. Sits at a low level in the forest, preferring slightly denser growth than the previous species. Since it does not perch in the open, it is best located by its loud call.

Jon Hornbuckle

Distribution: New Guinea. A locally fairly common resident in the Trans-Fly region of West Papua and nearby Aru Islands.

RUFOUS-BELLIED KOOKABURRA

Dacelo gaudichaud 28 cm F: Alcedinidae

Morten Strange

Description: Can be confused with the much rarer Shovel-billed Kingfisher, *Clytoceyx rex*, which has a short, dark bill and lacks blue in its wing coverts.

Voice: A loud, barking call and a descending chuckle.

Habits: A forest bird found in tall primary rainforest. Occurs mainly in the lowlands and inland to 750 m. Rarely seen to 1,300 m. Sits motionless in the middle storey below the canopy (see photo), often in resident pairs. Inconspicuous. Usually located by its call. Flies out from its perch to glean large insects from the trees. The nesting site is dug into a termite mound.

Distribution: New Guinea. A locally fairly common resident in West Papua and on most nearby islands.

LILAC-CHEEKED KINGFISHER

Cittura cyanotis 28 cm F: Alcedinidae

B. Van Elegem

Description: Note its characteristic red bill and pinkish cheeks. Photo shows female; male has dark blue (not black) eye-stripe and wing coverts. A unique, monotypic genus.

Voice: A fairly quiet bird with a call of 3–4 muted, descending notes.

Habits: Found in primary forest and mature secondary growth, from the lowlands to 1,000 m. On Sangihe also recorded in nearby wooded cultivation. An inconspicuous bird usually seen perched alone on a horizontal branch, low in the middle storey (see photo). Drops from there onto the ground to catch invertebrates and small reptiles.

Distribution: Indonesian endemic. A generally scarce resident on Sulawesi (except in the south) and on the nearby smaller islands of Sangihe, Siau and Lembeh.

WHITE-THROATED KINGFISHER

Halcyon smyrnensis 27 cm F: Alcedinidae

Description: Distinguished from other *Halcyon* kingfishers by its white breast in combination with a brown head and neck.

Voice: A piercing, staccato laugh, often on take-off, but also when perched.

Habits: A successful bird that has adapted well to disturbed habitats and seems to be expanding on Sumatra, where it was recently reported to 1,500 m. This noisy and conspicuous open woodland species is often seen in plantations and perched on wires along rural roads. It prefers marshes and wet areas, but is often seen away from water. Drops from its perch to grab prey on the ground.

Distribution: Subtropical and tropical Eurasia, and the Oriental region. A fairly common resident in Sumatra, vagrant west Java.

BLACK-CAPPED KINGFISHER

Halcyon pileata 30 cm F: Alcedinidae

Description: Look for diagnostic black head.

Voice: A piercing alarm call on take-off, similar to that of the White-throated Kingfisher.

Habits: Occurs during the northern winter in September to March. Can be locally numerous in prime habitat, which is rural open country. Often seen on coastal wetlands and around up-country rivers and swamps. Also sometimes found in dry fields and wooded cultivated areas. Sits on a low perch and flies down to grab insects and small vertebrate prey in the grass. Quite shy; flies off with a penetrating call if approached.

Distribution: East Asia and Oriental region; migratory. A locally fairly common winter visitor in Sumatra, Kalimantan and adjacent islands; vagrant on Java and Sulawesi.

JAVAN KINGFISHER

Halcyon cyanoventris 25 cm F: Alcedinidae

Margaret Kinnaird

Description: Unmistakable; note violet back and belly, and lack of white in plumage; white spot in wing is visible in flight.

Voice: A loud *tjie-tjie-tjie*.

Habits: An open country kingfisher often seen in rural areas. Seems to have declined on Java, but is still numerous in the Bali countryside. Associated with wet areas like river banks and flooded paddy fields, but does not fish. Sits low on an open perch, such as a pole or a rock, and flies out to catch insects in the grass. Conspicuous, but shy, and takes off when approached, flying low and fast, directly to the next perch.

Distribution: Indonesian endemic. A fairly common resident on Java and Bali only.

BLUE-AND-WHITE KINGFISHER

Halcyon diops 20 cm F: Alcedinidae

Morten Strange

Description: Distinguished from the Collared Kingfisher by its size and marine blue (not turquoise) head and wings. Photo shows female; male has white collar and breast.

Voice: A warbling *tu-tu-tuk*; less vocal than most other kingfishers.

Habits: Found in forest edges, along edges of mangroves and in nearby cultivated areas. Recorded from sea level to 700 m. Often a resident pair is seen perching and displaying on an open dead branch. At other times, it sits low near vegetation and is quite confiding. Otherwise, little has been reported on its feeding and breeding habits.

Distribution: Indonesian endemic. A fairly common resident on Halmahera, Bacan, Obi and some smaller nearby islands.

LAZULI KINGFISHER

Halcyon lazuli 20 cm F: Alcedinidae

Description: Note blue-black head and lack of white collar. Photo shows the male; female has a white throat and upper breast (not lower breast).

Voice: Like other *Halcyon* kingfishers, a shrill *kee-kee-kee;* an almost trilling series of notes.

Habits: Found in forest edges, secondary growth and nearby cultivation, often near wet areas. Occurs in the coastal lowlands to 600 m. Sits in the lower middle storey, often in resident pairs. Occasionally seen on roadside cables. Although tolerant to some habitat disturbance, it seems to have declined in numbers in recent years, possibly due to a lack of suitable old dead trees with holes for nesting and bare branches for perching.

Filip Verbelen

Distribution: Indonesian endemic. A generally uncommon resident on Seram and the nearby smaller islands of Ambon and Haruku. Vulnerable to global extinction.

CINNAMON-BANDED KINGFISHER

Halcyon australasia 21 cm F: Alcedinidae

Description: Unmistakable within its range, with its greenish cap and mantle, and blue primary wing feathers and tail.

Voice: Fairly quiet; sometimes a rapid weak descending trill.

Habits: A strictly arboreal kingfisher found in primary forest and closed secondary forest. Flies into forest edges near cultivation to feed, but always stays under cover. A low-density species, not numerous anywhere. Perches in the middle storey below the canopy, flying out to catch cicadas and other large invertebrates. Sometimes flies fairly low, but rarely lands on the ground. Usually spotted flying quickly among the forest trees.

Morten Strange

Distribution: Indonesian endemic. A generally scarce resident on Lombok, Sumba, Timor, Tanimbar and some smaller nearby islands within Nusa Tenggara.

SACRED KINGFISHER

Halcyon sancta 22 cm F: Alcedinidae

Description: Distinguished from the following species by its buff-coloured (not pure white) flanks and lores.

Voice: Similar to the voice of the Collared Kingfisher, a shrill *kee-kee-kee-kee*.

Habits: Usually found in Indonesia during the southern winter months (April–October) but can turn up any time of the year. Found along man-grove fringes, in open woodlands and along forest edges, and in scattered trees in fields near villages. Usually occurs in the coastal lowlands, but also inhabits hills inland. Found in West Papua to 2,400 m. Perches low and flies down to catch small prey on the ground.

Distribution: Australasia; southern population migrates north. A common southern winter visitor in West Papua and southern Wallacea; fairly common further north and west, including Java; uncommon in Kalimantan.

COLLARED KINGFISHER

Halcyon chloris 24 cm F: Alcedinidae

Description: Note turquoise upperparts with bright white underparts and collar.

Voice: A penetrating *krerk, krerk, krerk.*

Habits: This kingfisher is mainly associated with tidal habitats, from mangroves and mudflats to sandy beaches and coral reefs. Also found around fishing villages. In many areas it moves far inland, notably on Sumatra and in parts of Wallacea. Here it occurs at altitudes to 2,000 m, in open wood-lands and cultivation. This noisy and conspicuous bird sits on an open perch, often in resident pairs. Catches small animal prey on the mud or in grass.

Distribution: Oriental region and Australasia. A common resident throughout Indonesia; present on virtually all islands.

WHITE-RUMPED KINGFISHER

Caridonax fulgidus 30 cm F: Alcedinidae

Description: Note white under-parts that contrast with black head and dark blue wings and back. When it flies off, its white rump flashes brightly. A unique bird that has a *Halcyon*-like appearance, but has been placed in its own genus.

Voice: A characteristic series of yaps *kuff, kuff, kuff.*

Habits: An arboreal kingfisher found in closed forest and along forest edges. Often seen along trails and in villages near forest. Perches in the lower middle storey of large trees; also seen occasionally on roadside cables. Its peculiar call can be heard over a long distance in the early morning. Lands on the ground, presumably to catch small prey. The nest is built in a burrow in an earth bank.

Morten Strange

Distribution: Indonesian endemic. A locally fairly common resident on Lombok, Sumbawa, Flores and nearby Besar.

GREEN-BACKED KINGFISHER

Actenoides monachus 32 cm F: Alcedinidae

Description: Unmistakable. The photo shows a female from north Sulawesi. The male has a blue head. In the south of the island, the head is black.

Voice: A series of whistled notes; also a harsh alarm call.

Habits: An inconspicuous forest kingfisher found in primary and mature secondary rainforest, from sea level to 900 m. Usually sits quietly in the lower or low middle storey, in a large tree. From there it drops down to pick up prey from the leaf litter on the forest floor.

Sunarto

Distribution: Indonesian endemic. A generally scarce resident on Sulawesi.

COMMON PARADISE-KINGFISHER

Tanysiptera galatea 38 cm F: Alcedinidae

Description: Unmistakable within its range, except for the very similar, smaller Little Paradise-kingfisher, *T. hydrocharis*, of the Trans-Fly region. The only paradise-kingfisher west of New Guinea.

Voice: A soft, trilling whistle.

Habits: A forest kingfisher found in primary lowland rainforest and mature secondary growth, from the lowlands to 500 m. In Maluku occurs locally to 800 m. This bird is desperately shy and stays deep inside cover. Its call is quite often heard, but good views are rare. Sometimes seen flying across trail, long tail dangling behind. Perches fairly low, flying out to grab invertebrate prey.

Distribution: Indonesia, east through New Guinea; vagrant in northern Australia. A locally fairly common resident in Maluku and West Papua.

BIAK PARADISE-KINGFISHER

Tanysiptera riedelii 38 cm F: Alcedinidae

Description: Unmistakable on Biak. Included by Beehler et al. (1986) with previous species. Here follows Andrew (1992) who lists seven *Tanysiptera* kingfishers for Indonesia. Note light-blue head.

Voice: Similar to previous species.

Habits: A forest bird found in closed forest and along edges, where it perches in the middle storey (see photo). The partly disturbed forest around the village of Warafri, an hour's drive east of Biak Town, is a good place to see this bird, which is one of the five species endemic to Biak/Supiori. Including nearby Numfor and Meos Num, there are ten species endemic to the Geelvink Islands.

Distribution: Indonesian endemic. A generally scarce resident on Biak and its twin island of Supiori, in Geelvink Bay north of West Papua mainland.

CHESTNUT-HEADED BEE-EATER

Merops leschenaulti 20 cm F: Meropidae

Description: Look for full chestnut head and back, and fairly short, greenish tail.

Voice: A ringing trill *pruuip, pruuip* in flight.

Habits: Indonesia forms the southern limit of this bird's distribution. It prefers dry woodlands and savanna with scattered trees, and never inhabits closed forest. Often occurs on the coastal lowlands, although it is found on Sumatra to 900 m. On Bali usually seen at the Bali Barat National Park in the west. Perches fairly low and flies out to grab insects in the air. Not numerous.

Distribution: Oriental region. A widespread but generally scarce resident on Sumatra, Java and Bali.

BLUE-TAILED BEE-EATER

Merops philippinus 30 cm F: Meropidae

Description: Look for a diagnostic green head and neck. Mature breeding birds have elongated tail feathers.

Voice: A liquid ringing *be-rek, be-rek* in flight.

Habits: An open country bird seen mainly during the northern winter September–April. Resident birds breed April–November. This vocal and conspicuous bee-eater frequents fields and marshes with scattered trees and during migration forms dense flocks near the coast. Hawks for bees, wasps and butterflies with a characteristic flapping and gliding flight.

Distribution: Oriental region, east to New Guinea; partly migratory. A locally and seasonally common winter visitor in the Sunda subregion and Nusa Tenggara; resident on Sulawesi, Flores and in West Papua.

RAINBOW BEE-EATER

Merops ornatus 25 cm F: Meropidae

Morten Strange

Description: Distinguished from the previous species by its smaller size and black band across a greenish (not chestnut) upper breast. Also note rufous primaries in wing that show clearly in flight.

Voice: A frequent, short *prip, prip, prip,* especially in flight.

Habits: Habits much like other *Merops* bee-eaters. Found in open country, savanna and along edges of dense forest. Often seen around rivers, cultivated areas and gardens. Occurs from sea level to 1,600 m on Sulawesi and is seen rarely to 3,500 m in West Papua. Recorded during all months in Indonesia. Sits conspicuously on an open perch and sallies out for flying insects.

Distribution: Breeds in Australia and Papua New Guinea; migrates north-west into Indonesia. A locally and seasonally common non-breeding visitor throughout Wallacea and West Papua; rare on Bali.

BLUE-THROATED BEE-EATER

Merops viridis 28 cm F: Meropidae

Morten Strange

Description: Notice plain blue throat, overall turquoise appearance and very long tail.

Voice: Liquid notes in flight, like Blue-tailed Bee-eater.

Habits: Found in open country with some tree cover. Breeds in lowlands near water, but disperses widely after breeding into forest edges. Occurs occasionally to 900 m. Colonies gather in sandy beach woodland or along sandy river banks or islands. Burrows are dug in the ground, often many close together. Feeds by perching on a high branch, making short sallies for flying insects.

Distribution: Oriental region; nomadic outside breeding season. A locally fairly common resident in Sumatra and Kalimantan; rarer on Java.

RED-BEARDED BEE-EATER

Nyctyornis amictus 32 cm F: Meropidae

Description: Unmistakable; note pink forehead and red 'beard'.

Voice: A peculiar, harsh *aark, aark* and a growling alarm call; quite vocal.

Habits: A forest bird found only in closed rainforest, from the lowlands to 1,250 m. Very different from the *Merops* bee-eaters. This enigmatic bird perches high in large trees, usually concealed in the shade of the canopy. Sometimes seen near forest edges. Hawks for insects, although this is rarely observed. Nests in a burrow in the ground, but nesting records are very few.

Morten Strange

Distribution: Sunda subregion; sedentary. Resident on Sumatra, Bangka Island and Kalimantan.

PURPLE-BEARDED BEE-EATER

Meropogon forsteni 31 cm F: Meropidae

Description: Unmistakable; a unique bird. The only member of its genus.

Voice: A loud, high-pitched *wheep* and a softer *sip-sip*.

Habits: Found along the edges of tall forest, usually on sloping terrain in hills to 2,300 m elevation. Occurs in low densities in well-known national parks such as Lore Lindu and Dumoga-Bone, but not numerous anywhere. Sits quietly in the middle storey near a clearing in the forest and hawks from there for flying insects (see photo). Beats its prey on a branch to remove its sting before swallowing it, as do other bee-eaters. Nests inside a burrow in an earth bank, behaviour typical of the family.

John Warham

Distribution: Indonesian endemic. A generally scarce resident on Sulawesi, except in the south.

PURPLE-WINGED ROLLER
Coracias temminckii 32 cm F: Coraciidae

Description: Distinguished from following species by its bright turquoise cap; in flight distinguished by its turquoise rump and plain purple wings (no white patch).

Voice: A harsh *krark,* and loud chattering and barking notes.

Habits: Found in a variety of woodlands, from primary forest edges to savanna and nearby cultivation. Occurs mainly in the lowlands and inland to 1,100 m. Often seen on a prominent perch in a tree near a clearing or open area. Sometimes observed on a roadside wire or in denser forest. Pounces from its perch onto large invertebrates and small reptiles on the ground.

Alan OwYong

Distribution: Indonesian endemic. A locally fairly common resident on Sulawesi and some smaller nearby islands.

DOLLARBIRD (Common Dollarbird)
Eurystomus orientalis 30 cm F: Coraciidae

Description: Plumage may appear all black; note dark brown head and purple-greenish sheen on underparts. The white patch on wing (silver dollar) is visible in flight.

Voice: A harsh chatter *kack, kack* in flight.

Habits: Status on some islands is uncertain. Sedentary resident populations are augmented with Sunda subregion and Wallacea–West Papua migrants during certain months. Nowhere really numerous, but can be found along forest edges, where it perches high in a tree, alone or in resident pairs. Occasionally flies out to hawk for insects or displays with aerial acrobatics.

Morten Strange

Distribution: Eurasia, Oriental region and Australasia; northern populations migrate south; Australian birds migrate north. A widespread and locally fairly common resident and migrant throughout Indonesia.

WHITE-CROWNED HORNBILL

Berenicornis comatus 85 cm F: Bucerotidae

Description: Unmistakable; note diagnostic white head. Photo shows male; female has black underparts.

Voice: A hooting *hoo...hu-hu-hu*.

Habits: Occurs in lowland and lower montane rainforest to 1,000 m. Has been sighted recently in both Sumatra and Kalimantan, and in northern Sumatra feeding a juvenile. Generally a low-density species; rarely recorded. This hornbill stays in closed forest and flies within the canopies, feeding on fruits; also flies to the ground for animal prey.

Distribution: Sunda subregion. A local and rare resident in Sumatra and Kalimantan.

Morten Strange

BUSHY-CRESTED HORNBILL

Anorrhinus galeritus 70 cm F: Bucerotidae

Description: An all-dark hornbill; note dark casque and blue orbital skin; grey tail has black tip.

Voice: Excited chattering notes *klee-klee-klee*.

Habits: Similar to previous species. Found in lowland and lower montane rainforest. On Sumatra recorded to 1,800 m. Moves below or inside the canopy and makes short flights to the next tree. Regularly heard or glimpsed in small noisy groups during surveys, but generally a low-density species.

Distribution: Sunda subregion. An uncommon resident in Sumatra and Kalimantan.

Morten Strange

SULAWESI HORNBILL (Sulawesi Dwarf Hornbill)
Penelopides exarhatus 53 cmn F: Bucerotidae

Margaret Kinnaird

Description: Unmistakable; note small size and yellow face and throat (photo of male). Female's plumage is uniformly black, including face.

Voice: A series of braying and honking notes.

Habits: Found in closed lowland and hill rainforest, occasionally as high as 1,100 m. One of the middle storey hornbills; does not fly above the forest. Difficult to observe, since it stays within the canopy, flying from tree to tree in small groups, feeding on fruits.

Distribution: Indonesian endemic. Widespread and locally fairly common in Sulawesi.

WRINKLED HORNBILL
Rhyticeros corrugatus 81 cm F: Bucerotidae

Morten Strange

Description: Look for small red casque and pale neck in male (photo). The female is distinguished with some difficulty from the Wreathed Hornbill by its white throat and black tail base.

Voice: A short, loud *kak-kak*.

Habits: Mainly a lowland rainforest resident. Occurs on Kalimantan to 250 m and is found on Sumatra somewhat higher. Flocks of up to 14 birds have been reported in its preferred habitat of coastal swamp forest on Sumatra, while 75 have been reported at one roosting site on Kalimantan. Sometimes seen flying across the forest or visiting large fruiting trees, but is rather shy. The Indonesian population appears to be declining due to loss of habitat.

Distribution: Sunda subregion. A scarce resident in Sumatra and Kalimantan. Vulnerable to global extinction.

KNOBBED HORNBILL

Rhyticeros cassidix 104 cm F: Bucerotidae

Description: Unmistakable within its range; almost twice the size of the only other hornbill on Sulawesi. Photo shows male at nest; female has a black neck and smaller yellow casque.

Voice: A deep honking call: *wha-wha-wha*.

Habits: Occurs in primary rainforest, mainly in the lowlands up to 1,100 m; infrequently seen to 1,800 m. Also observed along forest edges and occasionally in nearby cultivated areas. A conspicuous and vocal species often reported by observers. Flies a fair distance, with slow, noisy wing-beats, and visits the tops of large fruiting trees. Also takes some animal prey. Can be quite approachable. Breeding and feeding are well documented.

Margaret Kinnaird

Distribution: Indonesian endemic. A widespread and generally common resident on Sulawesi.

WREATHED HORNBILL

Rhyticeros undulatus 100 cm F: Bucerotidae

Description: Note the white tail and diagnostic yellow gular pouch, with black stripe, of the male in photo. The female has a blue pouch.

Voice: A short, harsh *kuk-kwehk*.

Habits: Occurs in lowland rainforest, but is also found in lower montane forest on Sumatra, up to 2,000 m. Locally quite numerous in protected areas within its range. Often seen flying high between Baluran National Park on Java and Bali Barat National Park on Bali in flocks of up to 40 individuals. Breeds in large hardwood trees in primary forest, but roams widely into secondary forest and forest edges in search of fruiting trees.

Morten Strange

Distribution: Oriental region. A locally fairly common resident in Sumatra, Kalimantan, Java and Bali.

PLAIN-POUCHED HORNBILL

Rhyticeros subruficollis 90 cm F: Bucerotidae

Description: Distinguished with difficulty from the previous species by its smaller size and plain pouch (note lack of black stripe on this male).

Voice: Similar to, but pitched slightly higher than that of the Wreathed Hornbill.

Habits: Only recently recognised as a full species, so distribution and status are still under study. Observations from Sumatra could be juvenile Wreathed Hornbills. Habits presumed to be much like this species. Rare due to clearance of habitat. Regarded by BirdLife International as globally vulnerable to extinction.

Distribution: Southeast Asia. Status in Indonesia is uncertain; recorded in Sumatra; could also occur in Kalimantan.

BLYTH'S HORNBILL

Rhyticeros plicatus 85 cm F: Bucerotidae

Description: The only hornbill within its range. Male (left) has pale rufous head and neck. The female (right) has a black head and neck.

Voice: A variety of honking and grunting calls.

Habits: Occurs in lowland and lower montane rainforest, from sea level to 1,500 m. Also flies into forest edges to visit large fruiting trees. This conspicuous and quite approachable bird flies high over the forest, calling often. Its wings produce a whooshing sound. Often seen in resident pairs, although flocks of up to 50 have been reported.

Distribution: Australasia, from Indonesia east into the Solomon Islands. A locally fairly common resident in Maluku and West Papua.

SUMBA HORNBILL

Rhyticeros everetti 70 cm F: Bucerotidae

Description: Plumage and colours of soft parts are somewhat similar to those of the previous species, but note its black tail and the much smaller size of this male at nest.

Voice: Harsh, chuckling notes.

Habits: Breeds in primary drought deciduous forest typical of this part of Indonesia. However very little of this habitat is left on Sumba and the world population was estimated recently to be below 200 individuals. Also flies high and far, visiting forest edges and nearby cultivated areas, to feed in large fruiting trees. A flock of 70 birds has been recorded at a roosting site, although in general this species is rarely observed.

Margaret Kinnaird

Distribution: Indonesian endemic; an uncommon resident on the island of Sumba. Vulnerable to global extinction.

BLACK HORNBILL

Anthracoceros malayanus 75 cm F: Bucerotidae

Description: A fairly small, all-black hornbill. Note the white casque and nape on male (left). The female (right) has a black bill and casque.

Voice: Harsh, growling cries.

Habits: A lowland rainforest specialist found mainly in swamp forest and other wet primary forest. Occurs on Sumatra to 500 m. Flocks of 10–20 have been reported in prime protected habitat on Sumatra, but is usually seen in groups of 2–5 birds. Occurs on Kalimantan to 250 m, in lower densities. Nests in primary forest, but flies low into nearby mature logged forest, feeding in large fruiting trees.

Morten Strange

Distribution: Sunda subregion. An uncommon resident on Sumatra, including some eastern islands and in Kalimantan. Near-threatened with global extinction.

ASIAN PIED HORNBILL (Oriental Pied Hornbill)

Anthracoceros albirostris 70 cm   F: Bucerotidae

Description: Note white belly and large white casque of male. Female's casque is smaller and darker.

Voice: A peculiar cackle *yak-yak-yak*.

Habits: The only Indonesian hornbill that does not depend solely on primary closed forest. Seems to prefer forest edges and other broken habitats. Often found along rivers, in open coastal forest and nearby plantations. However it must have access to large, growing hardwood trees with cavities for nesting. This social and vocal bird is regularly seen, flapping and gliding low from tree to tree, searching for fruits and small prey.

Distribution: Oriental region. A widespread and fairly common resident on Sumatra and many nearby islands, and in Kalimantan; uncommon on Java and Bali.

RHINOCEROS HORNBILL

Buceros rhinoceros 110 cm   F: Bucerotidae

Description: Unmistakable. Note large size, red casque and black band in tail. Photo shows female; male has a dark red eye.

Voice: A characteristic goose-like honk *ga-rk, ga-rk,* before and after take-off.

Habits: Found in rainforest, mainly in primary growth, but also in nearby mature secondary forest. Occurs from the lowlands to 800 m. Still regularly encountered in protected areas, but this species requires vast expanses of territory. The Indonesian population is estimated to have declined to under 3,000 individuals. Seen flying high over the forest between roosting sites and large fruiting trees.

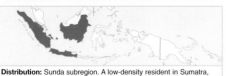

Distribution: Sunda subregion. A low-density resident in Sumatra, Kalimantan and Java.

GREAT HORNBILL
Buceros bicornis 125 cm F: Bucerotidae

Description: Unmistakable. Note massive size and yellow neck. In flight the yellow bar and white trailing edge in wing show clearly. Photo shows male at nest; female has a white iris.

Voice: A loud *ger-ok* during flight, like that of the previous species, but deeper and harsher.

Habits: Requires large expanses of primary rainforest. Occurs in the lowlands; in Sumatra reported to lower montane elevations at 1,000 m. Usually seen in resident pairs, never in flocks. Flies slowly, high above the forest, calling loudly. Lands in the tops of the tallest trees to feed on figs and other fruits.

Distribution: Oriental region. In Indonesia, resident only on Sumatra, where it is rarely reported.

HELMETED HORNBILL
Rhinoplax vigil 120 cm + tail F: Bucerotidae

Description: Unmistakable. The male near its nest has a rufous neck (top). The female has a pale blue neck. Note elongated tail, prominent in flight (bottom). A monotypic genus.

Voice: A characteristic series of loud honks, starting slowly, accelerating into bizarre laughter.

Habits: Mainly a lower hill species that roams widely, from the lowlands into foothills at 1,000 m. Its call and an occasional sighting are regularly reported from national parks. This conspicuous, low-density bird requires large expanses of primary forest. Feeds in the canopies of huge fruiting trees, often with other hornbills, barbets, pigeons and monkeys.

Distribution: Sunda subregion. A generally scarce resident in Sumatra and Kalimantan. Near-threatened with global extinction.

FIRE-TUFTED BARBET

Psilopogon pyrolophus 26 cm F: Megalaimidae

Description: Unmistakable. Note diagnostic facial pattern that includes red tufts at base of bill. A monotypic genus.

Voice: A loud, cicada-like buzz.

Habits: A strictly montane barbet found exclusively between 500 and 2,200 m. Locally numerous. Its buzzing call is often heard in the Sumatran mountain ranges. Can be difficult to spot, since it feeds in the canopy of medium-sized fruiting trees. Sometimes seen flying with cigar-shaped body and small, rapidly moving wings to the next tree. Its nest has been found in a hollow in a forest tree trunk.

Morten Strange

Distribution: Sumatra and Peninsular Malaysia. A locally common resident in the mountains of Sumatra.

LINEATED BARBET

Megalaima lineata 29 cm F: Megalaimidae

Description: Notice diagnostic whitish streaks on head combined with pale bill. Shown feeding on a banana palm in captivity.

Voice: A low-pitched, fluty *poo-poh, poo-poh*.

Habits: Unlike most other members of this family, this barbet avoids wet rainforest, preferring open monsoon forest, with scrub and long grass in between the trees, often just behind the coast. The national parks of Baluran in east Java and Bali Barat in west Bali provide the ideal habitat, and it is a common species in both places. Feeds on fruits fairly low in small trees. Nests in a cavity in a tree.

Morten Strange

Distribution: Oriental region. In Indonesia, occurs only on Java and Bali, where it is a locally fairly common resident.

GOLD-WHISKERED BARBET

Megalaima chrysopogon 30 cm F: Megalaimidae

Description: A large barbet. Look for large yellow cheek patch contrasting with narrow grey throat.

Voice: A deep, loud *kootook-ootook-ootook.*

Habits: Occurs in primary rainforest and mature secondary growth, with plenty of fruiting trees and dead stumps for nesting. In Kalimantan, it prefers the inland areas, from foothills to lower montane elevations. On Sumatra mainly recorded in coastal lowland and peat swamp forest, occasionally to 1,000 m. Inconspicuous; feeds high inside the canopy of large fig trees. Usually registered by call. Good views are rare.

Raymond Poon

Distribution: Sunda subregion. A locally fairly common resident in Sumatra and Kalimantan.

RED-CROWNED BARBET

Megalaima rafflesii 25 cm F: Megalaimidae

Description: Distinguished with difficulty from other barbets by its diagnostic full red crown.

Voice: A resonant *took-took,* then a pause followed by a longer series of notes.

Habits: A lowland rainforest bird. On Sumatra occurs perhaps up to 500 m. Lives in primary forest, in nearby disturbed forest and along forest edges. Previously numerous, but its numbers are now much reduced, mainly due to habitat clearance. Still recorded regularly in large forests and is usually located by call. Also sometimes seen high in fruiting fig trees, clambering about in the foliage, picking fruits.

Morten Strange

Distribution: Sunda subregion. A generally scarce resident on Sumatra, Bangka, the Belitung islands and Kalimantan. Near-threatened with global extinction.

RED-THROATED BARBET

Megalaima mystacophanos 23 cm F: Megalaimidae

Description: Male (photo) has bright red throat, which is diagnostic when present with blue breast patch; female has dull green head.

Voice: One to four slow *chok* notes, in a series of about one per second.

Habits: Sympatric with the previous species and has similar habitat preferences. Found mainly in closed primary forest or mature secondary forest. Occurs in lowland rainforest and lower montane forest up to 800 m. Moves high in trees, feeding mainly on figs and other fruits. Excavates a cavity in a decaying tree trunk to hold its nest.

Distribution: Sunda subregion. A generally scarce resident in Sumatra and Kalimantan..

BLACK-BROWED BARBET

Megalaima oorti 20 cm F: Megalaimidae

Description: Note the diagnostic combination of black eyebrow and yellow throat.

Voice: Loud staccato *tok-tr-trrrrrt.*

Habits: Strictly montane; this barbet can be found in rainforest on Sumatra between 600 and 2,000 m. Heard much more often than seen, its far-reaching call can be recognised in mountain forests all over the island. Frequents fruiting trees together with other frugivorous birds, squirrels and monkeys, but since it is small and green, this bird is not easy to see clearly.

Distribution: Oriental region. In Indonesia, a fairly common resident in montane parts of Sumatra.

BLUE-EARED BARBET

Megalaima australis 17 cm F: Megalaimidae

Description: Note its tiny size and its diagnostic blue, black and red head pattern. In the Javan subspecies, yellow replaces red. Captive photo.

Voice: A rapid, high-pitched and monotonous *tu-trruk, ku-trruk*.

Habits: Its call can be heard in lowland rainforest all through western Indonesia. Also occurs on Sumatra, in hills locally to 1,500 m. This green bird is not much bigger than a sparrow, but is very difficult to see clearly, since it stays high in dense canopies of massive fruiting trees. Will occasionally offer views when it comes lower or flies into cultivated areas near primary forest.

Distribution: Oriental region. A widespread and locally fairly common resident on Sumatra, Kalimantan, Java and Bali.

COPPERSMITH BARBET

Megalaima haemacephala 15 cm F: Megalaimidae

Description: Unmistakable; the smallest barbet. Note head pattern and streaked underparts. The Javan subspecies has red around its eye and throat instead of yellow.

Voice: A resonant *tonk, tonk* that goes on for minutes at a time, at a rate of 1–2 notes per second.

Habits: An adaptable and successful bird that is found in forest edges and open woodlands, never in closed forest. Occurs from coastal mangroves to lower montane villages and gardens. Visits trees with small fruits and berries; moves low and is quite approachable. Calls incessantly from a top branch, often late in the afternoon. The nest is in a hollow in a dead branch.

Distribution: Oriental region. A widespread and generally common resident on Sumatra, Java and Bali.

BROWN BARBET

Calorhamphus fuliginosus 18 cm F: Megalaimidae

Description: Unmistakable; the only brown barbet. Note its paler underparts and strong bill.

Voice: A thin, screaming *pseeoo,* unlike other barbets.

Habits: This peculiar bird is unique in appearance and behavior, and is the only member of its genus. Occurs in primary lowland rainforest and mature secondary growth and is sometimes seen in large trees along forest edges. This sociable bird climbs around large branches in small groups, exploring leaves and trunks carefully for insects, as a woodpecker or a tit would do. Also seen in fruiting trees, usually high up, but sometimes moves lower.

Morten Strange

Distribution: Sunda subregion. A locally fairly common resident in Sumatra and Kalimantan.

RUFOUS WOODPECKER

Celeus brachyurus 21 cm F: Picidae

Description: Note diagnostic black barring across rufous plumage. Photo shows a female; the male has a faint red spot behind its eye.

Voice: A descending series of loud notes *he, he, he.* Also drums on a hollow tree branch.

Habits: This adaptable woodpecker occurs in lowland rainforest and along forest edges. Also seen in adjacent villages and cultivated areas. Occurs at elevations up to 1,500 m in Sumatra. Hops upwards on tree trunks like other members of its family, but also ventures out onto thin branches near the ground in search of ants, its main source of food.

Morten Strange

Distribution: Oriental region. A widespread and locally fairly common resident in Sumatra and Kalimantan; uncommon on Java.

LACED WOODPECKER

Picus vittatus 30 cm F: Picidae

Description: Note green wings and faint streaks on lower underparts and along wing edges. Photo shows male; female has black crown.

Voice: A shrill, explosive *kweeck*.

Habits: In Indonesia this woodpecker is mainly coastal, occurring in open coastal forests, coconut groves and mangroves. Has not been recorded above 200 m and appears to be declining on Sumatra. Hops about, low in small trees, often landing on the ground to feed on ants and other invertebrates. Flies briefly to the next perch with an undulating flight pattern and a loud call.

Distribution: Oriental region. A generally uncommon resident on eastern Sumatra, Java and Bali.

Morten Strange

GREATER YELLOWNAPE

Picus flavinucha 34 cm F: Picidae

Description: Note the black-and-rufous flight feathers that always show in the folded wing. These flight feathers, together with plain grey underparts not visible in this photo, distinguish this species from the following one.

Voice: An explosive *kiyaep*.

Habits: Found in rainforest, along forest edges, in pine forest and in dense secondary growth. Occurs from 800 to 2,000 m. A large and conspicuous bird that is sometimes seen as it flies quickly between trees or across the trail. Often comes low to feed on ants and other invertebrate prey on or under the bark, gradually moving higher.

Distribution: Oriental region. In Indonesia, a fairly common resident in montane parts of Sumatra.

Morten Strange

LESSER YELLOWNAPE

Picus chlorolophus 26 cm F: Picidae

Description: Note barred flanks and thin, white cheek bar that distinguishes this species from the previous one. Photo shows female; male has full red crown and malar stripe.

Voice: A descending *peee-uu*.

Habits: Shares habitat and niche with the previous species, but this bird is quieter and more inconspicuous in behavior. Best seen when it moves through the forest with other insectivorous birds. These loosely connected, but sometimes large, mixed-species flocks, typical of tropical montane birdlife, are called bird waves.

Distribution: Oriental region. In Indonesia, a fairly common resident in montane parts of Sumatra.

CRIMSON-WINGED WOODPECKER

Picus puniceus 25 cm F: Picidae

Description: Note plain red wings and lack of barring, except for faint white spots on flanks. Photo shows female; male has a red malar stripe.

Voice: A distinctive *tiuik*.

Habits: Found in lowland rainforest, primary forest, closed secondary growth, and along forest edges. In Kalimantan, it occurs at lower montane elevations and in Sumatra is usually observed below 480 m, although it has been recorded to 900 m. A common bird, but never really numerous. Sometimes seen high in the trees. Comes out onto thin branches searching for ants and termites or feeds on plant sap.

Distribution: Sunda subregion. A locally fairly common resident in Sumatra (including nearby Nias and Bangka), Kalimantan and Java.

BANDED WOODPECKER

Picus miniaceus 23 cm F: Picidae

Description: Distinguished from the previous species by faint black barring on back and under-parts. Javan birds have reddish backs. Also note the reddish (not green) head.

Voice: A penetrating, descending *peew.*

Habits: Found in primary and secondary rainforest and along forest edges, mainly in the lowlands; occasionally recorded on Sumatra as high as 1,400 m. An adaptable species regularly reported during forest surveys; also seen in nearby plantations and sometimes gardens. Moves quite high on large branches, pecking the bark, mainly for ants. The nest hollow is excavated in a dead tree as shown in the photo.

Distribution: Sunda subregion. A locally fairly common resident in Sumatra and Kalimantan; uncommon on Java.

COMMON GOLDENBACK (Common Flameback)

Dinopium javanense 30 cm F: Picidae

Description: Distinguished with difficulty from the Greater Goldenback by its single (not double) black malar stripe and three toes. Photo of male; female has black crest with white dots.

Voice: A sharp *churrrr* and *klek-klek* in flight.

Habits: Prefers coastal areas; on Sumatra occurs locally inland up to 1,000 m. A noisy and conspic-uous woodpecker found in open coastal wood-lands, mangroves and around villages and cultivat-ed areas. Flies from tree to tree, landing low on the trunk. Searches the bark for ants and grubs, jumping upwards. Often seen in resident pairs.

Distribution: Oriental region. A widespread and locally fairly common resident in Sumatra, Kalimantan, Java and Bali.

BUFF-RUMPED WOODPECKER

Meiglyptes tristis 15 cm F: Picidae

Description: Thin white bars across all plumage including the head are diagnostic; its buff rump flashes in flight. Male (photo) has a faint red malar stripe.

Voice: A trilling *kiiiii;* also a sharp flight-note *chit*.

Habits: Restricted to lowland rainforest; in Sumatra occurs occasionally to 800 m. An adaptable species found in low densities in primary and mature secondary growth, forest edges and clearings. Also ventures into nearby scrub, flying and hopping about low in trees, picking ants from the thin branches and leaves as shown in the photo.

Distribution: Sunda subregion. A generally scarce resident in Sumatra and Kalimantan; rare on Java.

WHITE-BELLIED WOODPECKER

Dryocopus javensis 43 cm F: Picidae

Description: Unmistakable; note large size and diagnostic white lower belly and rump, only faintly visible in this photograph. Photo shows male; female has less red on head.

Voice: A characteristic, loud, single note: *keer;* also a noisy *kek-ek-ek* in flight.

Habits: Found in tall lowland rainforest, and often in coastal peat swamp forest and mangroves. Way Kambas National Park in southeast Sumatra is a good location for this species, but it usually occurs in low densities. Vocal, conspicuous and easy to observe at long distances. Flies high from tree to tree, mainly feeding on insects on large dead branches. Sometimes seen near the ground.

Distribution: Oriental region. A generally scarce resident on Sumatra and many nearby islands, and in Kalimantan; rare on Java and Bali.

FULVOUS-BREASTED WOODPECKER

Picoides macei 18 cm F: Picidae

Description: Note broad barring on wings contrasting with its pale (fulvous) underparts that are faintly streaked with black. Photo shows female; male has red cap.

Voice: An explosive *tchick*.

Habits: An open woodlands specialist found in dry savanna forest and adjacent gardens, mainly near the coast. Quite numerous in prime habitat. Flies from tree to tree in a fast, undulating manner typical of the family. Lands low on the tree and gradually jumps upwards, circling the small trunk while picking ants and termites from the bark.

Morten Strange

Distribution: Oriental region. In Indonesia only occurs on Java and Bali where it is a locally common resident; unconfirmed sighting records exist from east Sumatra.

BROWN-CAPPED WOODPECKER

Picoides moluccensis 13 cm F: Picidae

Description: A tiny woodpecker. Note heavy streaks on underparts.

Voice: A frequent, metallic trill; a vocal bird.

Habits: Mainly a mangrove bird, but sometimes found in secondary lowland forest and nearby cultivation. Mainly montane in Nusa Tenggara and occurs to 2,200 m on Lombok. Searches restlessly though the thin branches for minute prey, from eye level to the highest canopy. Seems to be increasing in number due to forest clearance, particularly in Sumatra. The similar Grey-capped Woodpecker, *D. canicapillus,* occurs in more dense inland forest and at higher elevations in Sumatra and Kalimantan.

Morten Strange

Distribution: Oriental region. A fairly common resident on Sumatra, Java, Lombok, Sumbawa, Flores and some smaller adjacent islands; rare on Bali and in Kalimantan.

ORANGE-BACKED GOLDENBACK

Reinwardtipicus validus 30 cm F: Picidae

Description: Female (photo) has a cream-colored back; male has reddish underparts and crown, and a striking orange back that flashes in flight. A unique, monotypic genus.

Voice: A sharp *kit, kit* and a trilling *ki-ik*.

Habits: Found mainly in primary forest and less often in mature secondary growth. Occurs from the lowlands to 2,000 m on Sumatra. A low-density species. Breeding has been recorded on Sumatra. Not numerous anywhere within its range. Sometimes encountered feeding high in large trees, usually on the main trunks.

Ong Kiem Sian

Distribution: Sunda subregion. A generally scarce resident in Sumatra, Kalimantan and Java.

GREATER GOLDENBACK (Greater Flameback)

Chrysocolaptes lucidus 33 cm F: Picidae

Description: Distinguished with difficulty from the Common Goldenback by its size and double black malar stripe. Note the white neck and broad eye-stripe extending down the neck of the female in photo. The male has a red cap.

Voice: A harsh, metallic *di-di-di-di;* also drums loudly.

Habits: Found in mangroves and coastal wood-lands with some large trees. Has recently been re-corded from east and south Sumatra, but its status is poorly documented. This shy bird can be difficult to distinguish from the apparently more numerous Common Goldenback in the field.

Morten Strange

Distribution: Oriental region. In Indonesia, a rarely recorded resident on Sumatra, Java and Bali; vagrant in Kalimantan.

DUSKY BROADBILL
Corydon sumatranus 27 cm F: Eurylaimidae

Description: Unmistakable; note broad red bill, pink throat and white spot in wing. This peculiar species is the only member of its genus.

Voice: A series of eerie screams *ky-ee, ky-ee*.

Habits: Found mainly in lowland primary rainforest, and in adjacent closed secondary growth. Extends to 1,000 m rarely. For some reason it is often spotted near water in swampy areas or along a forest stream. Can be observed as it moves through the tall canopies in noisy groups or when it sits passively in the upper storey.

Distribution: Southeast Asia. A generally scarce resident in Sumatra and Kalimantan.

BLACK-AND-RED BROADBILL
Cymbirhynchus macrorhynchus 25 cm F: Eurylaimidae

Description: Best distinguished from the following species by the white stripe in its wing. The only member of its genus.

Voice: A low, clear whistle followed by some harsher notes.

Habits: Found in lowland rainforest, often in disturbed areas, and almost always near water. Prefers coastal mangroves, flooded forests and inland rivers. Lives mainly at sea level, although in Sumatra it occurs to 900 m. Previously common on Sumatra, but in later years there have been very few field records, even from areas with prime habitat. Perches in the middle storey or lower, feeding on insects. The nest is a large pouch, suspended near or over water.

Distribution: Southeast Asia. A generally scarce resident in Sumatra, including the nearby Bangka and Belitung islands and Kalimantan.

BANDED BROADBILL

Eurylaimus javanicus 23 cm F: Eurylaimidae

Description: Note the diagnostic yellow stripe in wing. The distinct yellow blotches on the lower back and rump are characteristic.

Voice: A single, whistled *yeow* followed by a cicada-like, buzzing trill.

Habits: Occurs in primary and mature secondary lowland rainforest; rarely seen in open patches. Occurs mainly in the lowlands. On Sumatra recorded to 1,000 m; on Java to 1,500 m. Seen fairly regularly at prime forest locations, but is generally a low-density species and difficult to find. Usually seen sitting passively below the canopy, occasionally moving out onto thin branches to catch insects.

Ong Kiem Sian

Distribution: Southeast Asia. A scarce resident on Sumatra, including nearby Riau, Bangka and the Belitung islands, Kalimantan and Java.

BLACK-AND-YELLOW BROADBILL

Eurylaimus ochromalus 15 cm F: Eurylaimidae

Description: Unmistakable; note small size, broad bill, and yellow on wings and back; pinkish underparts show in front view.

Voice: An accelerating trill, 7–11 seconds long.

Habits: Found in primary and mature secondary lowland rainforest. Occurs up to 900 m on Sumatra. Not often seen because of its small size. Feeds mainly on insects, high in the middle and upper storeys of the forest. Possibly more numerous than sightings suggest. Once its call is learned, this species may be recorded more often.

Morten Strange

Distribution: Sunda subregion. A generally scarce resident on Sumatra and many adjacent islands, and Kalimantan.

SILVER-BREASTED BROADBILL

Serilophus lunatus 15 cm F: Eurylaimidae

Description: Unmistakable; underparts are silvery. The female has a narrow, white band across its breast. A unique bird; the only member of its genus.

Voice: A short whistle *ki-uu*.

Habits: A forest bird found in primary rainforest and along forest edges, where it occupies the middle storey. Strictly montane; on Sumatra found from 850 to 1,500 m. Not particularly shy. This individual is carrying nesting material. The nest is a large pouch with a side entrance, suspended from a branch, often near water.

Allen Jeyarajasingam

Distribution: Oriental region. In Indonesia, found only on Sumatra, where it is an uncommon montane resident.

LONG-TAILED BROADBILL

Psarisomus dalhousiae 28 cm F: Eurylaimidae

Description: Unmistakable and unique, the only member of its genus. Captive photo.

Voice: A distinctive series of 5–8 shrill notes *pseew, pseew*.

Habits: This strictly montane bird is found in rainforest from 700 to 1,500 m; occurs on Mt. Kerinci to 2,500 m. Located by call or seen when it moves through the middle storey, perching on open branches just below the canopy. Sometimes seen in company with other insectivorous species in bird waves.

Morten Strange

Distribution: Oriental region. In Indonesia found on Sumatra, where it is a scarce montane resident; recently recorded in Kalimantan.

GREEN BROADBILL

Calyptomena viridis 18 cm F: Eurylaimidae

Distribution: Sunda subregion. In Sumatra and Kalimantan a locally fairly common resident.

Description: Unmistakable, apart from the rarer Hose's Broadbill, *C. hosii*, which has a blue belly and is found in Kalimantan. Photo shows male; female lacks black spots on neck and wings.

Voice: A soft trill *tui, tui, trrrr*.

Habits: Difficult to observe, but probably quite numerous in prime habitat, which is closed lowland rainforest. Moves occasionally into lower montane elevations. Takes more fruits than other broadbills, often feeding high in large fig trees. Its camouflaged plumage makes it almost impossible to detect. Sometimes sits motionless inside the canopy and flies quickly on rapidly moving wings to a new tree when disturbed.

BANDED PITTA

Pitta guajana 23 cm F: Pittidae

Distribution: Sunda subregion. A locally fairly common resident on Sumatra, Java and Bali; uncommon in Kalimantan.

Description: Unmistakable; especially note the diagnostic bars across its underparts. Photo shows captive male of the Borneo race; the female is duller. Sumatran birds have blue (not yellow) underparts.

Voice: A falling whistle *pouw;* also a soft *kirr.*

Habits: Indonesia is a good place to hear and see this shy Sunda endemic. It is locally numerous in protected areas, especially on Sumatra and Java, where it is a lowland forest species. On Kalimantan it is predominantly submontane, reported mainly from 600 to 1,200 m. Found in closed rainforest, where it hops on the ground or perches on fallen logs and low branches.

BLUE-BREASTED PITTA (Red-bellied Pitta)

Pitta erythrogaster 17 cm F: Pittidae

Description: Unmistakable within its range. Head patterns vary somewhat with location and subspecies, but the blue breast separated from red belly by a black band is always distinctive.

Voice: A drawn-out, two-note whistle *hoooo-hooooh*.

Habits: Inhabits primary rainforest and mature secondary growth with a closed canopy and an open forest floor, where it can hop about and feed in leaf litter. Occasionally flies up and calls from a branch in the middle storey. Found mainly in the lowlands, but occurs to 900 m on Sumatra and in West Papua to 1,200 m. During the wet season, calls are fairly common, but good views are rare.

Distribution: Occurs from the Philippines into Cape York Peninsula (Australia); possibly somewhat nomadic. A locally fairly numerous but usually uncommon resident in Sulawesi, Maluku and West Papua.

GARNET PITTA

Pitta granatina 17 cm F: Pittidae

Description: Upperparts are dark purple. Photo shows the north Borneo race, *P. g. ussheri*, which has a black (not red) cap. The Sumatra subspecies has a red cap and a black mottled belly. The montane population on Sumatra has an all-black head and back and is treated by Andrew (1992) and M&P (1993) as a separate species, the Black-crowned Pitta, *P. venusta*.

Voice: A monotonous whistle.

Habits: Restricted to primary forest. Often occurs in flat, wet areas, in the extreme lowlands below 400 m. On Sumatra, the allospecies Black-crowned Pitta replaces this one from 400 to 1,400 m. Skulks on the forest floor feeding on insects and grubs in the leaf litter.

Distribution: Sunda subregion. A local and rare resident in Sumatra and Kalimantan.

HOODED PITTA
Pitta sordida 18 cm F: Pittidae

Description: Unmistakable; note all-green plumage with black head and short tail. A white spot in wing is distinct in flight. Captive photo.

Voice: A monosyllabic whistle *pih-pih*.

Habits: Found mainly in closed lowland forest, but also in nearby cultivated areas. Occurs on West Papua in lower montane elevations. Good views are difficult to obtain of this shy bird. Hops on the ground, turning over fallen leaves to flush out invertebrate prey. Flies off low and fast when disturbed. The nest is a large ball of vegetation, with a side entrance on or near the ground.

Distribution: Oriental region and Australasia; partly migratory. A widespread but generally scarce resident in Indonesia; also a winter visitor in the Sunda subregion

IVORY-BREASTED PITTA
Pitta maxima 25 cm F: Pittidae

Description: Unmistakable. A large bird. Note green in wing and red centre on belly.

Voice: A penetrating wolf-whistle repeated regularly for several minutes.

Habits: This very vocal bird's characteristic call can be heard in primary forest and nearby disturbed areas throughout most of the day, sometimes even at night. May respond somewhat to imitation and come closer, but good views are difficult. More arboreal than other pittas; often perches on branches in the middle storey of the forest as shown in the photo. Also seen flying heavily over the ground on small, rapidly moving wings. Otherwise little studied.

Distribution: Indonesia endemic. A locally common resident on Halmahera; less common on adjacent Bacan, Obi, Kasiruta and Morotai.

BLUE-WINGED PITTA
Pitta moluccensis 20 cm F: Pittidae

Description: Unmistakable within its range, except for the Mangrove Pitta, *P. megarhyncha*, which overlaps with this species on eastern Sumatra. Recognised by its pale coronal band and smaller bill (see Strange 2000). Captive photo.

Voice: A fluty *tu-teew*.

Habits: Essentially a forest bird, but in winter quarters also often found in open woodlands and scrub, usually near the coast. Occurs inland on Sumatra to 1,000 m, from September to May. Feeds on invertebrate prey, while hopping along on the ground. Also perches on low branches and makes quick low flights from branch to branch. Its short tail and small wings give it a stocky appearance.

Distribution: Oriental region. A widespread and seasonally fairly common winter visitor in Sumatra and Kalimantan; vagrant on Java and Sulawesi.

SINGING BUSH-LARK (Australasian Lark)
Mirafra javanica 15 cm F: Alaudidae

Description: The only member of the lark family Alaudidae in Indonesia.

Voice: A melodic, whistling song.

Habits: Strictly an open country bird that occurs in short grass areas, on dry fields and cleared areas near villages. Found mainly in the coastal lowlands, but has been recorded at 1,200 m on Flores and New Guinea. Sings from the ground or while fluttering in the air. Flies off low when disturbed and quickly drops back onto the ground. Feeds on insects and also some seeds.

Distribution: Africa, Oriental region and Australasia. A locally fairly common resident in south Kalimantan, Java, Bali and parts of Nusa Tenggara and West Papua.

BARN SWALLOW

Hirundo rustica 15 cm F: Hirundinidae

Description: Distinguished from the following species by a black band across its chest that contrasts with its white belly. Note also its longer, very forked tail.

Voice: A high-pitched, chattering *twit, twit*.

Habits: Found in open country. Observed mainly in the coastal lowlands during migration, but has been recorded up to 1,200 m. Most numerous from August to May, but can occur anytime. Flutters about low, catching small insects; perches on wires, buildings or branches between raids. Birds spread out while feeding, but congregate at roosting sites during the evening.

Distribution: Breeds worldwide in the Northern Hemisphere; winters to the south. A common passage migrant and winter visitor throughout Indonesia; abundant in the west; less numerous further east.

Morten Strange

PACIFIC SWALLOW

Hirundo tahitica 14 cm F: Hirundinidae

Description: Distinguished from the previous species by its uniformly dusky underparts and shorter, less forked tail.

Voice: Like that of the Barn Swallow.

Habits: This common Indonesian swallow is found in all types of open country habitat, from the coast and inland, to lower montane elevations, often near water, but not exclusively. During winter it mixes with the migratory Barn Swallows, but does not form dense flocks. Usually seen in pairs or small groups. The nest is made of mud pellets, built under a cliff overhang, underneath a roof or inside a building, as shown in the photo.

Morten Strange

Distribution: Oriental region and Australasia; sedentary. A widespread and common resident throughout Indonesia.

STRIATED SWALLOW

Hirundo striolata 20 cm F: Hirundinidae

Description: Note its chunky build and long forked tail. The heavy streaks on its underparts are diagnostic. Sometimes considered conspecific with the Red-rumped Swallow, *H. duarica*, of Eurasia.

Voice: Sometimes a loud *tjuw-tjuw*; usually quiet.

Habits: Much like other swallows. Seems to prefer more remote hilly terrain, from the coast to lower montane elevations. Often found near forest edges and around villages, nesting on buildings. Sometimes turns up in open country. Usually seen in resident pairs or in small groups. Associates with other swallows, but is easily picked out as its flight pattern is much more leisurely. Often flies low near the ground.

Distribution: Oriental region; somewhat nomadic. In Indonesia, resident in small numbers on Java, Bali and parts of Nusa Tenggara; vagrant in Sumatra, Kalimantan and West Papua.

FOREST WAGTAIL

Dendronanthus indicus 18 cm F: Motacillidae

Description: Note prominent and diagnostic black-and-white pattern on wings and breast. A unique, monotypic genus.

Voice: A soft *pink*.

Habits: Largely arboreal, unlike other members of this family. During migration found in a variety of wooded habitats, from lowland rainforest and tidal mangroves to nearby scrub and plantations. On Sumatra occurs inland to 900 m. Recorded from September to May. Usually solitary and not numerous anywhere. Sometimes encountered walking on the ground on a trail in or near forest. Flies up into a tree when disturbed, swaying its body slowly from side to side.

Distribution: Breeds in East Asia; winters in the Oriental region. A generally scarce winter visitor on Sumatra and Java.

YELLOW WAGTAIL

Motacilla flava 18 cm F: Motacillidae

Morten Strange

Description: Distinguished from the following species by its yellow (not white) throat, an olive (not grey) mantle, and lack of wing band in flight.

Voice: A loud *tswe-ep* in flight.

Habits: During peak migration this species is locally abundant. A flock of 4,000 has been recorded in Sulawesi; smaller flocks of 50–100 at roosting sites are not unusual. Seen during northern winter months, from September to April, mainly near coastal fields. Also recorded inland at other short grass areas, usually near water. Occurs locally to 2,000 m. Feeds on insects while walking briskly along the ground. Flies off with an undulating flight pattern.

Distribution: Breeds in Eurasia and Alaska; winters in tropics, into northern Australia. A widespread and common passage migrant and winter visitor throughout Indonesia.

GREY WAGTAIL

Motacilla cinerea 19 cm F: Motacillidae

Morten Strange

Description: In winter plumage, this bird is distinguished from other wagtails by its grey (not olive-brownish) mantle in combination with a white throat and pale yellow underparts.

Voice: A disyllabic *tzi-zick* on take-off.

Habits: Favours montane habitat, from the lowlands to 3,500 m. Prefers wooded terrain near a stream, but can turn up almost anywhere, near stagnant water, in a clearing or on a roadside. There it can be seen running forward, grabbing minute prey and wagging its tail. Occurs from August to May and is usually seen alone, never in flocks. Never mixes with the previous species.

Distribution: Breeds in temperate Eurasia; winters in tropical regions, into northern Australia. A widespread and generally fairly common winter visitor throughout Indonesia.

RICHARD'S PIPIT (Common Pipit)
Anthus novaeseelandiae 17 cm F: Motacillidae

Description: Note its diagnostic long legs and posture. This resident subspecies is considered a separate species, the Paddyfield Pipit, *A. rufulus,* by Sibley & Monroe (1990). Northern migrants could also occur.

Voice: A loud *chip* on take-off.

Habits: A typical open country bird found in fields and short grass areas, from coastal plains to montane elevations. Often seen on airstrips and sport fields. In West Papua found at mainly lower montane elevations. Replaced at alpine altitudes by the following species. Always feeds on the ground, but sometimes flies up onto a low perch.

Morten Strange

Distribution: East Asia, Oriental region and Australasia. A common resident in the Sunda subregion; uncommon in parts of Wallacea and West Papua.

ALPINE PIPIT
Anthus gutturalis 18 cm F: Motacillidae

Description: Unmistakable; the only pipit within its range and elevation.

Voice: A faint *tsip* on take-off; also a clear whistle.

Habits: This upper montane specialist is only found at the tree limit and upwards, from 3,200 to 4,500 m. In cleared areas it has been recorded down to 2,600 m. Frequents alpine meadows and grasslands with scattered trees and bushes, where it sometimes perches and surveys the terrain, chipping softly. Quite confiding. Flies out low and lands on the ground among rocks and short grass to feed on insects and seeds.

Morten Strange

Distribution: New Guinea. A locally fairly common resident in upper montane parts of central West Papua.

WALLACEAN CUCKOO-SHRIKE
Coracina personata 33 cm F: Campephagidae

Description: A large cuckoo-shrike with a long tail. Photo shows female; male has a full black face and throat.

Voice: A drawn-out, whistled *weeer*.

Habits: This arboreal bird requires primary forest or mature secondary growth with large trees. Found from coastal lowlands to lower montane elevations; recorded on Timor to 2,200 m. In prime habitat it is seen quite regularly, but is not really numerous anywhere. Two or three birds might gather together, calling. Usually seen moving about, high in the canopies. Little else is known about this bird's habits.

Distribution: Indonesian endemic. A widespread but generally scarce resident in Nusa Tenggara, from Sumbawa east, to the Kai Islands in Maluku.

BLACK-FACED CUCKOO-SHRIKE
Coracina novaehollandiae 30 cm F: Campephagidae

Description: Distinguished from other cuckoo-shrikes by its diffuse black mask and pale belly. The sexes are similar. The resident subspecies in the Sunda subregion is treated by Andrew (1992) and M&P (1993) as a separate species, the Malaysian Cuckoo-shrike, *C. javensis*.

Voice: A far-carrying, ringing *kle-eeep*, often heard as it flies high over the trees.

Habits: Found in savanna, open woodlands, along forest edges and near villages. Occurs from the coast up to 1,500 m. In the east, migratory birds from southeast New Guinea and Australia visit from April to November. Seen flying high between trees, especially in early morning and late evening. Generally scarce.

Distribution: Oriental region and Australasia. An uncommon resident on Java and Bali; visitor during southern winter to Wallacea and West Papua; locally common on Flores.

MOLUCCAN CUCKOO-SHRIKE

Coracina atriceps 33 cm F: Campephagidae

Description: Distinguished from the Halmahera Cuckoo-shrike by larger size, full slate-coloured head and pale underparts. Male shown in photo; the female's head is somewhat paler.

Voice: A harsh chatter.

Habits: An adaptable species found in all kinds of wooded habitat, from disturbed coastal woodlands to primary forest in the hills up to 1,200 m. Conspicuous and easy to observe as it flies about and perches in large trees. Feeds on invertebrate prey caught in the canopies and is sometimes seen low in the trees. Otherwise little studied.

Morten Strange

Distribution: Indonesian endemic. A locally common resident on Halmahera, Ternate, Bacan, Kasiruta and Seram.

STOUT-BILLED CUCKOO-SHRIKE

Coracina caeruleogrisea 33 cm F: Campephagidae

Description: Note black mask, heavy bill and uniformly blue-grey plumage of male (top), at nest. The female (bottom) is similar to the sympatric Boyer's Cuckoo-shrike, *C. boyeri*, except for its larger size and stronger bill.

Voice: A variety of harsh, chirping, mewing calls.

Habits: Found in primary rainforest, from the lowlands into lower montane elevations up to 1,600 m; rarely occurs at 2,100 m. Also found in nearby secondary growth and edges with tall trees. Moves high in the canopies, catching large insects as shown in the photo on the right. The nest is a small cup built high in a large forest tree.

Morten Strange

Distribution: New Guinea. A locally fairly common resident in West Papua; Yapen and the Aru Islands.

CAERULEAN CUCKOO-SHRIKE

Coracina temminckii 30 cm F: Campephagidae

Description: Sexes are similar; note uniformly bluish-grey plumage and distinct white iris.

Voice: A characteristic, very harsh, abrupt call and high-pitched whistles.

Habits: Found in primary rainforest and forest edges. Recorded from 100 to 2,200 m, but most numerous at the lower montane elevations above 500 m. Moves through the upper and middle storey of the forest, usually in small vocal groups. Gleans invertebrates from the foliage and occasionally rests on tall, exposed branches.

B. Van Elegem

Distribution: Indonesian endemic. A locally fairly common resident on Sulawesi only.

YELLOW-EYED CUCKOO-SHRIKE

Coracina lineata 23 cm F: Campephagidae

Description: Yellow iris is diagnostic. Photo shows female; male is a uniform dark grey and lacks barring on belly.

Voice: A high-pitched whistle *whee-uuu*.

Habits: Occurs in forest, from primary rainforest to edges, and is occasionally seen in nearby cultivated areas. Prefers the foothills and lower montane elevations from 600 to 1,500 m; also recorded close to sea level. Moves restlessly through the canopies or just below, often in pairs or small groups, sometimes in company with other species. Feeds on fruits and small insectivorous prey.

Morten Strange

Distribution: Australasia, from New Guinea into eastern Australia. A generally scarce resident in West Papua and the nearby smaller Waigeo and Numfor islands.

HALMAHERA CUCKOO-SHRIKE

Coracina parvula 25 cm F: Campephagidae

Description: Sexes similar; distinguished from the male Common Cicadabird by its darker blue-grey plumage and dark throat.

Voice: A series of staccato, chattering notes.

Habits: Found in primary rainforest and forest edges; also seen in secondary forest with large trees. Usually occurs from 100 to 900 m, mainly in the hills. Seen flying conspicuously about, calling and sallying for insects; often perches in the open on a dead branch as shown in the photo. Often a resident pair interacts together. Otherwise little studied.

Morten Strange

Distribution: Indonesian endemic. A local and generally scarce resident on Halmahera.

COMMON CICADABIRD

Coracina tenuirostris 23 cm F: Campephagidae

Description: Photo shows unmistakable female. The male is distinguished with some difficulty from the previous species by its paler plumage and throat.

Voice: A cicada-like *ch-ch-ch*.

Habits: Found in primary and secondary forest, and in forest edges. Occurs mainly in the lowlands; recorded on Seram to 1,000 m. Moves about within the cover of the dense canopies of large trees, where it catches invertebrate prey. Good views are difficult, although its buzzing call sometimes gives it away.

Morten Strange

Distribution: Australasia; partly migratory. A locally common but generally scarce resident in the Wallacea and southwest West Papua. Migrants from Australia reach West Papua during southern winter.

PALE-SHOULDERED CICADABIRD (Sumba Cicadabird)
Coracina dohertyi 24 cm F: Campephagidae

Description: Note the diagnostic light-grey wing coverts that create a pale patch in wing of this male; face and throat is black. Female has underparts that are finely barred from throat to vent.

Voice: Not very vocal; a harsh call has been reported from Flores.

Habits: Found in primary forest and mature secondary growth with large trees. Also seen along forest edges and roadsides. Prefers the foothills and lower montane elevations from 200 to 1,700 m. This quiet and inconspicuous, low-density bird can be spotted occasionally as it moves from tree to tree, just below the canopy. Often seen in resident pairs.

Distribution: Indonesian endemic. A generally scarce resident on Sumbawa, Flores and Sumba. Near-threatened with global extinction.

BLACK-BELLIED CUCKOO-SHRIKE
Coracina montana 24 cm F: Campephagidae

Description: Black belly contrasting with grey upperparts of male (photo) is distinct and diagnostic. Female is a nondescript blue-grey, but look for diagnostic black tail.

Voice: Vocal; a frequent whistling and buzzing chatter.

Habits: Found in montane primary rainforest, from 800 to 2,400 m. Moves about high in the dense and humid moss forest. Calls while flying from tree to tree, often in pairs or in small groups. Clambers about in the thin branches, feeding on invertebrates.

Distribution: New Guinea. A generally scarce resident in montane parts of West Papua.

BLACK-BREASTED FRUIT-HUNTER
Chlamydochaera jefferyi 21 cm F: Campephagidae

Description: Unmistakable; photo shows male; female has grey on belly and mantle replaced with brown. A monotypic genus. Placed with thrushes Turdidae by M&P (1993) and Strange (2000).

Voice: No information.

Habits: Occurs in montane parts of Kalimantan; reported down to the Schwaner Mountains in the centre of the province, and in Gunung Niut near the border with Sarawak. Few recent records. Appears to be a low-density forest bird. Has been observed feeding in fruiting trees. More studies of this unique restricted-range species are needed.

Chua Ee Kiam

Distribution: Borneo endemic. A rare resident in montane parts of Kalimantan only.

PIED TRILLER
Lalage nigra 16 cm F: Campephagidae

Description: Female similar to immature bird (photo), with less streaks on underparts. Male has white underparts with black upperparts and a large white patch in wings.

Voice: A trilling *tre-tre-tre*.

Habits: Occurs in lightly wooded areas, from mangroves and coastal casuarina groves to forest edges and cultivated areas up to 1,000 m. In spite of habitat preference, good views are surprisingly difficult. Usually moves in trees catching insects on the thin branches. As soon as approached, it flies with a characteristic lethargic flight to another tree.

Morten Strange

Distribution: Southeast Asia. A widespread and fairly common resident in Sumatra, Kalimantan and west Java.

WHITE-SHOULDERED TRILLER

Lalage sueurii 17 cm F: Campephagidae

Description: Distinguished from the previous species by its white shoulder (not full white wing patch).

Voice: A rich, whistling song; also a harsher, rapid series of notes.

Habits: Frequents open woodlands, savanna and often plantations and gardens in villages. Occurs from the beach to lower montane elevations. Often seen flying quickly from tree to tree. Also flies down from a low perch to catch insects on the ground.

Distribution: Indonesian endemic. A locally common resident on east Java, Bali, Nusa Tenggara and south Sulawesi.

RUFOUS-BELLIED TRILLER

Lalage aurea 19 cm F: Campephagidae

Description: Unmistakable; note rufous underparts. Photo shows female. Male has a black (not grey) crown and back.

Voice: A series of staccato, piping notes.

Habits: An adaptable species found in primary rainforest, secondary forest and along forest edges, as well as in mangroves, cultivated areas and village gardens. Moves about at the upper storey level or lower in small trees, gleaning insects from the foliage. Otherwise little information is available on feeding and nesting habits.

Distribution: Indonesian endemic. A fairly common resident on Halmahera and adjacent islands.

BLACK-BROWED TRILLER

Lalage atrovirens 18 cm F: Campephagidae

Description: Unmistakable; the only *Lalage* triller within its range. Photo shows female; male has all-white underparts (lacks black barring on flanks). The Tanimbar population may be treated as a separate endemic species, the Tanimbar Triller, *L. moesta* (see *Kukila*, Volume 10).

Voice: A whistling series of soft notes *twee-twee-twee* and *teweet-teweet*.

Habits: Found in forest and forest edges, and in nearby scrub and cultivated areas. Occurs mainly in the coastal lowlands; in West Papua, inland up to 1,200 m. Moves around in the tops of smaller trees, often in pairs or small groups, flying from perch to perch. Feeds on small fruits and insects.

Morten Strange

Distribution: Indonesia and northwestern Papua New Guinea. A fairly common resident in northern parts of West Papua and nearby islands; common on Yamdena, Tanimbar Islands.

SMALL MINIVET

Pericrocotus cinnamomeus 15 cm F: Campephagidae

Description: Small bird. Photo shows female; male has orange breast and belly. On Sumatra and Kalimantan it is replaced by the Fiery Minivet, *P. igneus*. The male of this species has red (not orange) underparts and the female has yellow (not grey) underparts.

Voice: A thin, whistled *tsee-tsee*.

Habits: A restless bird, constantly on the move through open woodlands, mangroves and plantations, usually in small groups. Flutters about from tree to tree calling softly, its long tail dangling behind. Rests briefly on the thin branches. Gleans insects and larvae from the foliage, while perched or while hovering near the stems.

Morten Strange

Distribution: Oriental region. In Indonesia, found only on Java and Bali, where it is a locally fairly common resident.

LITTLE MINIVET (Flores Minivet)
Pericrocotus lansbergei 17 cm F: Campephagidae

Description: Unmistakable; the only minivet within its range. Male (bottom) has black face and throat, and a red breast. Female (top) has a white breast.

Voice: A soft, trilling whistle.

Habits: This elegant, attractive bird is found in primary rainforest and more open deciduous woodlands with large trees. Typical of its genus, it flutters about in the thin outer branches of the canopy, hovering and perching briefly while gleaning small invertebrates from the foliage. Usually seen in pairs or small groups, sometimes near flycatchers, warblers and other insectivorous birds.

Morten Strange

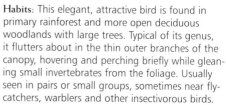

Distribution: Indonesian endemic. A locally fairly common resident on Sumbawa and Flores only.

GREY-CHINNED MINIVET
Pericrocotus solaris 17 cm F: Campephagidae

Description: The female is distinguished with difficulty from the following species by its grey (not yellowish) head. The male is similar to the following species, except for its grey (not black) throat.

Voice: A diagnostic, thin *tsee-sip*.

Habits: A strictly montane minivet that occurs exclusively at altitudes between 900 and 2,400 m, mainly from 1,200 to 1,600 m. Found in primary rainforest and along forest edges, and is often seen from roads and logging trails. Flutters high on the outside of the canopy, in a constant search for insects.

Morten Strange

Distribution: Oriental region. A locally fairly common resident in montane parts of Sumatra and Kalimantan.

SCARLET MINIVET

Pericrocotus flammeus 20 cm F: Campephagidae

Description: Note its scarlet underparts and black head of male (photo); female has yellow face, and red is replaced with yellow.

Voice: A soft but penetrating high-pitched *tweep, tweep*.

Habits: A forest bird found in small densities, predominantly in primary lowland rainforest and in disturbed habitats nearby. Occurs from the lowlands locally up to 1,500 m. A neck-straining bird to watch; usually seen in small groups, flitting about high in the canopies of large trees, balancing briefly in the outer branches and moving quickly to the next tree.

Morten Strange

Distribution: Oriental region. A generally scarce resident in Sumatra, Kalimantan, Java and Bali; rare on Lombok.

LARGE WOOD-SHRIKE

Tephrodornis gularis 18 cm F: Campephagidae

Description: Unmistakable within its range; the only wood-shrike in Indonesia. Note distinct black mask contrasting with pale underparts.

Voice: A variety of fairly loud, harsh whistles.

Habits: A forest bird found mainly in lowland primary rainforest; on Java recorded up to 1,500 m. Turns up in the middle storey, below the canopy, Usually seen in open patches near denser forest, where it hunts for insects. Previously regarded as a frequently seen bird in Sumatra and Borneo, occurs in most major reserves. However, there have been few recent records, therefore it is listed here as rarely seen.

Alan Ow Yong

Distribution: Oriental region. A generally rare resident in Sumatra, Kalimantan and Java.

STRAW-HEADED BULBUL

Pycnonotus zeylanicus 28 cm F: Pycnonotidae

Distribution: Sunda subregion. A rare resident in Sumatra, Kalimantan and west Java. Vulnerable to global extinction.

Description: Unmistakable; its large size and orange cap are diagnostic. Captive photo.

Voice: A loud and bubbling song, sometimes in duet; sounds more like a thrush than a bulbul.

Habits: Prefers forest edges near waterways such as streams, large rivers and tidal mangroves. Occurs mainly in the coastal lowlands; on Sumatra found up to 1,600 m locally. Shy and retiring, but vocal and highly territorial, so is easy to catch. Previously common, but now numbers are much reduced mainly due to the bird trade. Few sightings in Indonesia since 1985; in fact the species might be locally extinct in the wild (*Kukila*, Volume 8, p. 35).

BLACK-HEADED BULBUL

Pycnonotus atriceps 18 cm F: Pycnonotidae

Distribution: Oriental region. A locally fairly common resident in Sumatra, Kalimantan and Java, uncommon on Bali.

Description: Distinguished from the following species by its olive-yellow plumage, black wings and lack of crest.

Voice: Weak, tuneless, sharp chirps.

Habits: Found in rainforest, along forest edges and especially in mature secondary forest. Occurs from the lowlands to lower montane altitudes; on Sumatra occurs locally to 1,200 m. Moves in the middle storey and sometimes down to eye level. Often seen together with other bulbuls in fruiting trees. Also takes some small animal prey.

BLACK-CRESTED BULBUL

Pycnonotus melanicterus 19 cm F: Pycnonotidae

Description: Distinguished from the previous species by long crest, white eye and brighter yellow belly; Sumatran subspecies has a red throat.

Voice: A slurred whistle.

Habits: A forest bird found in rainforest, often along forest edges and in mature secondary growth with fruiting trees. Occurs on Sumatra from sea level to 1,000 m; on Kalimantan only in the interior mountains. Frequents large trees, and is often seen together with other bulbuls, calling and picking small fruits; also takes some insects.

Distribution: Oriental region. A locally fairly common resident in Sumatra, Kalimantan and west Java; uncommon on east Java and Bali.

SCALY-BREASTED BULBUL

Pycnonotus squamatus 16 cm F: Pycnonotidae

Description: A small bird. Unmistakable; note diagnostic scaly underparts and white throat; upperparts are olive-yellow.

Voice: A series of sharp notes *wit-wit*.

Habits: Found in primary rainforest, usually at lower montane elevations. Occurs in Sumatra from 400 to 700 m, and has been found breeding there at 500 m. A low-density species often missed during surveys. Moves high in the forest, at canopy or middle storey levels, feeding in fruiting trees with other bulbuls.

Distribution: Sunda subregion. A rarely recorded resident in Sumatra and Kalimantan; seen in 1993 on Mt. Kawi (east Java).

GREY-BELLIED BULBUL

Pycnonotus cyaniventris 16 cm F: Pycnonotidae

Description: Look for diagnostic dark grey head and underparts.

Voice: A typical bulbul-like whistle *pi-pi-pi-pi*.

Habits: This low-density rainforest specialist is found mainly in primary rainforest, but also in tall secondary growth and in forest edges. It can be seen from the lowlands to lower montane elevations, and in Sumatra has been recorded at 1,000 m. Feeds in the canopies, sometimes lower, most often seen visiting fruiting trees with other bulbuls.

Morten Strange

Distribution: Sunda subregion. A scarce resident in Sumatra and Kalimantan.

SOOTY-HEADED BULBUL

Pycnonotus aurigaster 20 cm F: Pycnonotidae

Description: Note black head contrasting with pale neck and underparts; pale rump flashes in flight.

Voice: A soft chatter with whistling and harsher notes.

Habits: A successful and adaptable species found in open country with scattered bushes and trees. Also seen in cultivated areas and gardens, often near rural villages. A vocal and conspicuous bird that moves about in small flocks, low in the trees. Expansion on Sumatra, Sulawesi and recently Borneo and Timor has been attributed to escaped cage birds.

Morten Strange

Distribution: Oriental region. A widespread and common resident on Java and Bali; introduced on Sumatra and south Sulawesi, where now well established; recently recorded in south Kalimantan and Timor.

PUFF-BACKED BULBUL

Pycnonotus eutilotus 23 cm F: Pycnonotidae

Description: Distinguished with difficulty from other similar bulbuls by a tufty crest in combination with dark brown (not olive or greyish) wings.

Voice: A typical bulbul-like whistle *tju-lip*.

Habits: A lowland rainforest specialist that is found in both primary forest and nearby secondary growth and edges. On Sumatra it has been recorded to 400 m. Usually moves in the middle storey of the forest. A low-density species that is sometimes seen with other bulbuls in fruiting trees, but is often overlooked during surveys. There are no nesting records of this bird.

Distribution: Sunda subregion. A scarce resident in Sumatra and Kalimantan.

ORANGE-SPOTTED BULBUL

Pycnonotus bimaculatus 20 cm F: Pycnonotidae

Description: Look for brown spotted chest contrasting with pale belly, and diagnostic yellow-orange lores. Captive photo.

Voice: A loud *tuk-tuk-turuk*.

Habits: A strictly montane bulbul found in forest edges, clearings, cultivated areas and scrub at altitudes from 800 to 3,000 m. Especially numerous at higher montane elevations, especially in stunted alpine growth, where it can be seen moving about in small vocal parties. Otherwise a little-studied species.

Distribution: Indonesian endemic. A locally fairly common resident in montane parts of Sumatra, Java and Bali.

FLAVESCENT BULBUL

Pycnonotus flavescens 20 cm F: Pycnonotidae

Description: Distinguished from the following species by its olive-greyish (not cream) underparts and a uniformly greyish head.

Voice: A harsh *tcherrp*.

Habits: A montane specialist found in rainforest, forest edges and nearby scrub. On Borneo occurs at elevations between 1,000 and 3,000 m. Its presence in Indonesian Borneo (Kalimantan) was confirmed in 1993, when this bird was reported in moss forest at 1,900 m on Mt. Lunjut, and again in 1996, when a pair was observed. More studies are needed to determine status. Moves in the upper and middle storey of the forest, sometimes at eye-level, feeding mainly on fruits.

Distribution: Oriental region. Occurs in montane parts of Kalimantan but status is uncertain.

YELLOW-VENTED BULBUL

Pycnonotus goiavier 20 cm F: Pycnonotidae

Description: Look for prominent white supercilium contrasting with dark crown; also note yellow vent.

Voice: A bubbling, chattering song; also a harsh alarm call *tweit-tweit*.

Habits: One of the most numerous birds throughout its range. This is an adaptable species that has invaded disturbed habitats, from its original haunts of forest edges and coastal woodlands. Today this predominantly garden bird is found in every west Indonesian village, from the lowlands locally to 1,500 m. This attractive, active and vocal bird feeds on all edible matter, from small fruits high in the trees, to insects on the ground.

Distribution: Southeast Asia. A common resident in Sumatra, Kalimantan, Java and Bali; also on Lombok and south Sulawesi, where presumably introduced; locally abundant.

OLIVE-WINGED BULBUL

Pycnonotus plumosus 20 cm F: Pycnonotidae

Description: Fairly nondescript, but look for diagnostic olive flight feathers in the closed wing of this singing individual.

Voice: A subdued, chattering song; more squeaky than that of the Yellow-vented Bulbul.

Habits: Although this forest bird is only found in the wet Sunda subregion rainforest, it seems to avoid closed primary forest. Prefers forest edges, secondary growth, mangroves, even nearby scrub, but not villages. Occurs mainly in the lowlands; has been recorded on Sumatra to 300 m. Moves low at the edge of the vegetation, but is elusive and tries to stay under cover. Sings from a concealed location.

Distribution: Sunda subregion. A fairly common resident in Sumatra, Kalimantan, and west and central Java.

Morten Strange

CREAM-VENTED BULBUL

Pycnonotus simplex 17 cm F: Pycnonotidae

Description: On Sumatra look for diagnostic white eyes. On Kalimantan and Java (where the local race has orange-brown eyes) this bird is distinguished from other similar species by its slender build and pale belly and vent.

Voice: A short *clip-clip*.

Habits: Has a preference for tall primary rainforest, but can also be found in mature secondary growth and along forest edges. Occurs from the lowlands to 600 m. Smaller and faster than other bulbuls, it flits about, often together with other bulbuls, high in large, fruiting trees. Also takes insects.

Morten Strange

Distribution: Sunda subregion. A fairly common resident in Sumatra and Kalimantan; local and uncommon on south Java.

RED-EYED BULBUL

Pycnonotus brunneus 18 cm F: Pycnonotidae

Description: Note red eye and a generally dark appearance, including brownish underparts. Sympatric with the Spectacled Bulbul, *P. erythrophalmos* (see Strange 2000) which is paler and has an orange eye-ring.

Voice: A high-pitched, trilling whistle.

Habits: This forest bird is found in primary and mature secondary forest and on forest edges. Occurs from the lowland into lower montane elevations; on Sumatra recorded at 900 m. Often seen in prime habitat, feeding actively with other bulbuls at canopy and middle storey levels. Otherwise little studied; no nesting records from Indonesia of this locally numerous bird.

Distribution: Sunda subregion. A locally fairly common resident in Sumatra and Kalimantan.

OCHRACEOUS BULBUL

Criniger ochraceus 23 cm F: Pycnonotidae

Description: Look for bright white throat contrasting with brown upperparts; also notice crest.

Voice: Whistling calls and a noisy chatter *chi-wau*.

Habits: This rainforest specialist occurs in low densities, mainly in lower montane primary forest; also found in forest edges and nearby scrub. Recorded from foothills at 300 m to lower montane elevations at 1,000 m; occurs on Sumatra to 1,400 m. Stays under cover more than other bulbuls; often moves about at eye-level and lands on the ground. This vocal and active bird feeds on small berries and insects.

Distribution: Southeast Asia. A generally scarce resident in Sumatra and Kalimantan.

YELLOW-BELLIED BULBUL

Criniger phaeocephalus 20 cm   F: Pycnonotidae

Description: Similar to the Grey-cheeked Bulbul, *C. bres*, of the Sunda subregion, including Java and Bali, which also has a yellow belly, but is less bright and has a brown (not grey) crown and small crest.

Voice: A harsh alarm call *cree-cree*.

Habits: Prefers primary rainforest; found less often in secondary growth and edges. Occurs mainly in the lowlands; on Sumatra to 800 m. Quite predictable in the right habitat; often seen in the open space below the canopy, where it flies conspicuously around among the trees, calling loudly. Feeds on small fruits and insects.

Morten Strange

Distribution: Sunda subregion. A locally fairly common resident in Sumatra and Kalimantan.

BUFF-VENTED BULBUL

Hypsipetes charlottae 20 cm   F: Pycnonotidae

Description: A nondescript bulbul. Its best feature is a brown crown that contrasts with buff face, that shows well in the photo. Also look for slender shape and buff underparts.

Voice: A typical bulbul-like *whee-it*.

Habits: Found in lowland rainforest, in primary forest, nearby secondary growth and in forest edges. Usually seen feeding high in large trees at canopy or middle storey level, often together with other bulbuls. In Indonesia there are no local nesting records of this low-density bird.

Morten Strange

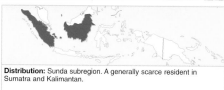

Distribution: Sunda subregion. A generally scarce resident in Sumatra and Kalimantan.

HAIRY-BACKED BULBUL

Hypsipetes criniger 17 cm F: Pycnonotidae

Description: Note the diagnostic yellow patch around eye, contrasting with olive-brown crown; small and stocky build.

Voice: A short chatter with whistling notes.

Habits: Found in primary and mature secondary rainforest, mainly in the lowlands; occurs on Sumatra to 1,000 m. Moves quietly at the edge of the forest, picking up small fruits or chasing insects, sometimes in small groups, near other bulbuls.

Morten Strange

Distribution: Sunda subregion. A locally fairly common resident in Sumatra and Kalimantan.

GOLDEN BULBUL

Hypsipetes affinis 23 cm F: Pycnonotidae

Description: Unmistakable; the only bulbul within its range.

Voice: A whistling chatter, typical of the bulbul.

Habits: An adaptable species found in all kinds of wooded habitat, from primary forest to secondary growth and nearby cultivated areas and gardens. Recorded from the lowlands into lower montane elevations and occurs locally to 1,500 m. Seen moving low in the middle storey and in small trees, often in small groups and sometimes with insectivorous birds in bird waves. Otherwise little studied.

Morten Strange

Distribution: Indonesian endemic. A widespread and generally common resident in Maluku and some nearby islands.

STREAKED BULBUL (Common Streaked Bulbul)

Hypsipetes malaccensis 23 cm F: Pycnonotidae

Description: Unmistakable in the lowlands; note the diagnostic grey-streaked breast. The Sunda Streaked Bulbul, *Hypsipetes virescens*, endemic to Sumatra and Java, is strictly montane, and may in fact be conspecific with the Mountain Bulbul, *H. mcclellandii* (see Strange (2000)).

Voice: A loud, metallic rattle.

Habits: A low-density species restricted to primary rainforest or mature secondary growth with large trees. Occurs mainly in the lowlands; on Sumatra to 900 m. This canopy bird is often overlooked during surveys, maybe because it does not descend to the lower storeys.

Morten Strange

Distribution: Sunda subregion. A generally scarce resident in Sumatra and Kalimantan.

ASHY BULBUL

Hypsipetes flavala 20 cm F: Pycnonotidae

Description: Look for pale underparts contrasting with dark face and crest; Sumatran subspecies lacks the green streak in wing shown here.

Voice: A variety of short, harsh and ringing notes.

Habits: A lower montane specialist. On Sumatra occurs in primary forest at altitudes between 500 and 1,000 m, but there are few recent records from this island. Recorded on Kalimantan at higher altitudes. Prefers tall primary forest, but is also seen at forest edges, coming out to feed on small fruits alone or in small groups; often seen together with other bulbuls.

Morten Strange

Distribution: Oriental region. In Indonesia, a locally fairly common but generally scarce resident in Kalimantan; uncommon on Sumatra.

COMMON IORA

Aegithina tiphia 15 cm   F: Irenidae

Description: Underparts are bright yellow. Photo shows female at nest; male has darker upperparts. Ioras and leafbirds are placed in the family Chloropseidae by M&P (1993) and Strange (2000).

Voice: A soft, musical whistling.

Habits: This adaptable species originates from the open coastal woodlands and mangroves, but has taken readily to disturbed habitats including cultivated areas, villages and gardens. Occurs mainly in the lowlands; on Sumatra to 1,000 m. Inconspicuous, but once its pleasant call is learned, it can be found in many places. Hops and climbs around in small trees and bushes, gleaning invertebrates from the leaves.

Distribution: Oriental region. A widespread and common resident in Sumatra, Kalimantan, Java and Bali.

GREEN IORA

Aegithina viridissima 14 cm   F: Irenidae

Description: Male (photo) distinguished from the previous species by its uniformly green plumage and yellow eye-ring. Female has paler underparts and the same distinct eye-ring.

Voice: Like previous species.

Habits: This species replaces the previous one in rainforest habitat. Occurs in primary rainforest and closed secondary growth; on Sumatra found mainly in the coastal lowlands, from sea level to 600 m. Way Kampas National Park in Sumatra is a good location for this species, but even here it only occurs in low densities. Hops about, high inside the canopies or lower at forest edges, in a constant and restless search for invertebrates.

Distribution: Sunda subregion. A widespread but generally scarce resident on Sumatra and some nearby islands, and Kalimantan.

GREATER GREEN LEAFBIRD
Chloropsis sonnerati 21 cm F: Irenidae

Description: Distinguished with difficulty from the Lesser Green Leafbird, *C. cyanopogon*, see Strange (2000), by its powerful bill, yellow throat and eye-ring. Photo of captive female; male has black throat (so does the male Lesser, but with a yellow border).

Voice: A loud, ascending whistle *chee-zi-chee*.

Habits: A low-density rainforest specialist found in tall primary forest and mature secondary growth with large trees. Occurs mainly in the lowlands; on Sumatra to 1,000 m. Moves high at canopy level, but is fairly easy to observe, as it often climbs about on the outside branches of fruiting trees. Flies into another tree with a characteristic undulating flight.

Morten Strange

Distribution: Sunda subregion. A generally scarce resident in Sumatra, Kalimantan and Java.

BLUE-WINGED LEAFBIRD
Chloropsis cochinchinensis 19 cm F: Irenidae

Description: Look for diagnostic blue stripe in wing. Photo shows male; female lacks black throat. Montain subspecies female has black throat.

Voice: A liquid whistle *chee-cheerup*.

Habits: Although essentially a forest bird, this somewhat adaptable species is found in primary forest as well as disturbed forest edges. Moves in all strata of the rainforest, from the tallest canopies to bushes near the ground along the trails. Feeds by clambering along the outer branches like a warbler, calling softly and picking up fruits and small insects.

Morten Strange

Distribution: Oriental region. A widespread and fairly common resident in Sumatra, Kalimantan and Java.

GOLDEN-FRONTED LEAFBIRD

Chloropsis aurifrons 20 cm F: Irenidae

Description: Sexes are alike. Distinguished from other leafbirds by orange forecrown and blue patch on throat. Captive photo.

Voice: A soft, whistling song.

Habits: Found in forest at foothills and lower montane elevations between 500 and 1,500 m. Occurs mainly in primary forest and in large trees nearby; also flies into cultivated areas to feed. Unlike most other leafbirds, this species is mainly insectivorous (note the thin bill) and does not take much fruit. Climbs on the thin branches of tall trees, gleaning insects and grubs.

Distribution: Oriental region. In Indonesia, found only on Sumatra, where it is a locally fairly common montane resident.

ASIAN FAIRY BLUEBIRD

Irena puella 25 cm F: Irenidae

Description: Unmistakable; male (top photo); female (bottom photo). This species is placed with the orioles (Oriolidae) by M&P (1993).

Voice: A loud, liquid whistle *whee-eet*.

Habits: Although this forest bird is found mainly in primary rainforest, it can be a quite predictable and locally numerous bird. It occasionally ventures into adjacent secondary growth if large trees are left standing. On Sumatra it has been recorded at altitudes up to 1,000 m. Moves high at canopy level. Usually spotted in fruiting trees or while flying high between the canopies, calling with a penetrating whistle.

Distribution: Oriental region. A locally fairly common resident in Sumatra and Kalimantan; uncommon on Java.

TIGER SHRIKE

Lanius tigrinus 19 cm F: Laniidae

Description: Distinguished from the following species by its strong bill, fairly short tail and some black barring across its back. Immature bird (photo) has white eye-ring; adult has black mask and grey crown.

Voice: A harsh chatter, often from inside cover.

Habits: Indonesia constitutes the southern limit for this species, which can only be found from September to April. This shrike is more arboreal than others and during migration it turns up in forest edges and nearby scrub, from the coast to 900 m. Less obvious than the two following species; prefers to stay inside cover.

Distribution: Breeds in northern East Asia; winters in Southeast Asia. On Sumatra can be seasonally fairly common, but is a generally scarce winter visitor to Sumatra and Kalimantan; rare on Java and Bali; one record from Sulawesi.

BROWN SHRIKE

Lanius cristatus 20 cm F: Laniidae

Description: Photo shows immature bird; adult lacks scales in plumage and has a black mask.

Voice: A harsh *chak-chak-chak*.

Habits: Strictly an open country bird found on cleared land, roadsides, in cultivated areas, and sometimes in villages and gardens. Occurs only during the northern winter, from September to May. In winter quarters it stakes out a claim to a certain perch, a pole or a wire. From there it drops down into the grass below, to pick up small prey.

Distribution: Breeds in East Asia; winters in the Oriental region reaching Indonesia. A locally common winter visitor in Sumatra and northern Kalimantan; uncommon on Java and Bali; rare in Wallacea; one record from West Papua.

LONG-TAILED SHRIKE

Lanius schach 25 cm F: Laniidae

Description: Look for long black tail and black wings.

Voice: A low, squeaky song, also a harsh *keep*.

Habits: An open country species found in open fields and scrub, often near rural roads and villages. Occurs in the lowlands and at lower montane elevations; on Sumatra to 1,800 m. Very conspicuous; can be spotted a long way off, perching in the open over long grass. Pounces from its perch onto small prey below. Flies low across the fields to the next perch when disturbed.

Morten Strange

Distribution: Oriental region, east into Papua New Guinea. A locally common resident on Sumatra, Java and Bali; uncommon in parts of Kalimantan and Nusa Tenggara.

WHITE-BROWED SHORTWING

Brachypteryx montana 15 cm F: Turdidae

Description: Male (top photo) is dark blue, with a distinct white eye-brow; female (bottom photo) is brown.

Voice: A short, warbling song; also an abrupt alarm call *tack*.

Habits: A strictly upper montane species. Occurs on Sumatra at altitudes from 1,400 to 3,000 m; on Java found above 1,500 m; on Flores mainly from 1,200 to 1,900 m and occasionally down to 600 m. Fairly predictable in the right habitat, but never numerous. A shy and skulking bird that moves on or near the ground, more like a babbler (Timaliidae) than a thrush (Turdidae). Often seen near a small stream.

Morten Strange

Distribution: Oriental region. A locally fairly common resident in montane parts of Sumatra, Kalimantan, Java and Flores.

ORIENTAL MAGPIE-ROBIN (Magpie Robin)
Copsychus saularis 23 cm F: Turdidae

Description: Unmistakable; top photo shows male; female has a slaty-grey colour where male has black. Bottom photo shows the east Java and Bali subspecies male, with all-black underparts.

Voice: A clear, melodious song; also a rasping alarm call.

Habits: Still common, although much reduced in numbers throughout western Indonesia. This adaptable species has invaded cultivated areas and villages from its original habitat of forest edges and mangroves. Sings from a branch or a rooftop in the morning. Finds most of its food on the ground. Its flimsy nest is placed low in a bush.

Distribution: Oriental region. A widespread and locally common resident on Sumatra and most adjacent islands, Kalimantan, Java and Bali.

WHITE-RUMPED SHAMA
Copsychus malabaricus 28 cm F: Turdidae

Description: Note long tail and rufous belly; its diagnostic white rump flashes in flight.

Voice: A rich, melodious, nightingale-like song; also a harsh alarm call.

Habits: Similar to the previous species. This attractive bird is much reduced in the field, since it is easy to trap (using a singing decoy) and is popular in the bird trade. Still numerous in remote or protected areas, from lowland rainforest to secondary growth in the lowlands. On Sumatra occurs locally to 1,500 m. Shy and elusive; more often heard than seen.

Distribution: Oriental region. A locally fairly common resident in Sumatra and Kalimantan, rare on Java.

LESSER FORKTAIL (Sunda Forktail)

Enicurus velatus 16 cm F: Turdidae

Description: Note the greyish (not chestnut) mantle; breast and belly are white.

Voice: A shrill *hie-tie-tie*.

Habits: Found in montane primary forest locations from 600 to 2,000 m elevation. A fairly predictable species at well-known national parks like Gunung Kerinci in Sumatra, and Gunung Gede in Java. Shy and elusive; best observed early in the morning at fast-flowing, forested streams. Similar to the following species in habits. This is an active bird that runs along the ground near the water's edge, or on nearby trails and open patches, to pick up small insects.

Distribution: Indonesian endemic. A locally fairly common resident in montane parts of Sumatra and Java.

CHESTNUT-NAPED FORKTAIL

Enicurus ruficapillus 20 cm F: Turdidae

Description: Distinguished from the previous species by its chestnut (not grey) mantle and scaly, black (not white) chest.

Voice: Piercing, shrill whistles.

Habits: A low-density forest bird that is sometimes encountered along forested rivers and small streams, often deep inside the forest. Found mainly in the lowlands; occurs on Sumatra up to 800 m, where it is replaced by the previous species. Shy and restless, but can be located by its high-pitched and penetrating call. Feeds on insects that it catches by running along and flying low above the gravel banks and boulders. Otherwise a little-studied species; few nesting records exist.

Distribution: Sunda subregion. A scarce resident in Sumatra and Kalimantan.

PIED BUSH-CHAT (Pied Chat)
Saxicola caprata 14 cm F: Turdidae

Description: Unmistakable; male (left photo) has faint white patch in wing and white rump; female (right photo) is dark brown with a rusty-coloured rump. The Sulawesi subspecies' rump is a streaky grey.

Voice: A short, weak song; also faint alarm call *chack chack*.

Habits: An open country species that seems to have benefited from widespread forest clearance. Found in cultivated areas and savanna grasslands with scattered trees. Occurs in the lowlands and often into montane elevations. Recorded on West Papua to 2,850 m. Sits on a low exposed perch and flies down to grab insects on the ground.

Distribution: Middle East Asia through the Oriental region, and east to New Guinea. A locally common resident in Java, Bali and parts of Wallacea and West Papua; a single sighting from south Sumatra.

WHITE-BELLIED BUSH-CHAT (White-bellied Chat)
Saxicola gutturalis 16 cm F: Turdidae

Description: Male (left photo) is unmistakable; female (right photo) is dull brown, with paler underparts.

Voice: Four whistling notes.

Habits: Found in low drought deciduous forest, often at the edge of open woodland with some undergrowth. Occurs from sea level to 1,200 m. Sits upright in the middle storey, sometimes near the ground, often in resident pairs. Male sings softly from a high perch. Sallies out and searches the foliage for insects, occasionally landing on the ground. Also visits flowers in trees, presumably for nectar. Otherwise little known.

Distribution: Indonesian endemic. A locally fairly common resident on Timor and the nearby smaller Roti and Semau islands.

SUNDA WHISTLING-THRUSH

Myiophoneus glaucinus 25 cm F: Turdidae

Distribution: Sunda subregion (except the Malay Peninsula). A generally scarce resident in Sumatra, Kalimantan and Java; rare on Bali.

Description: Distinguished from the Shiny Whistling-thrush, *M. melanurus*, endemic to high mountains on Sumatra, by a lack of white spots in its variable blue/brown plumage. Photo shows all-blue male from Java.

Voice: A variety of loud, ringing calls.

Habits: Found in dense montane forest, where it moves low, often near a stream or a steep rocky ravine. This low-density bird is a fairly regular resident in national parks like Gunung Gede on Java (where this photo was taken) and in Gunung Kerinci, where it overlaps with the Shiny Whistling-thrush.

BLUE WHISTLING-THRUSH

Myiophoneus caeruleus 32 cm F: Turdidae

Distribution: Oriental region. A generally rare resident on Sumatra and Java.

Description: Look for large size and diagnostic yellow bill. Captive photo.

Voice: A rich, whistling song; also a harsh *scree*.

Habits: Found along forest rivers, streams and rocky patches. Occurs mainly in the lowlands, but has been recorded occasionally to 1,250 m. Is never found at higher altitudes, where it is replaced by the previous species. A shy and retiring bird that is sometimes spotted on or near the ground.

CHESTNUT-CAPPED THRUSH

Zoothera interpres 17 cm F: Turdidae

Description: Unmistakable in the Sunda subregion. Distinguished from the Chestnut-backed Thrush, *Z. dohertyi,* by its slaty-grey (not chestnut) back and rump. Captive photo.

Voice: A melodious song that has been compared to the White-rumped Shama's, but is higher pitched.

Habits: A low-density, lowland rainforest bird apparently restricted to primary forest. In Nusa Tenggara appears to be more adaptable and is also reported from degraded habitats and even villages. This shy bird usually moves on or near the ground, feeding on fallen fruits; is also seen high in fruiting trees.

Morten Strange

Distribution: Southeast Asia. Within the region, a rare resident in Sumatra, Kalimantan and Java; locally fairly common on Enggano, Lombok, Sumbawa and Flores.

ORANGE-SIDED THRUSH (Orange-banded Thrush)

Zoothera peronii 21 cm F: Turdidae

Description: Unmistakable, except on Timor where it overlaps with the Chestnut-backed Thrush, *Z. dohertyi*, which has a black throat and black-spotted chest.

Voice: A rich, whistled song with clear and harsher notes mixed.

Habits: This arboreal thrush is found in dry, deciduous wood-lands, from sea level to wetter lower montane forest reaching 1,200 m. Comes down to the ground in early morning to feed. Moves low in the trees and flies higher when disturbed. Also visits fruiting trees. Good views of this shy, skulking bird are difficult, but its call is often heard, so it may be numerous in right habitat.

Morten Strange

Distribution: Indonesian endemic. A locally fairly common resident on Timor and the nearby smaller Roti, Wetar, Babar, Romang and Damar islands.

SIBERIAN THRUSH

Zoothera sibirica 24 cm F: Turdidae

Description: Female (photo) distinguished from the rarer montane resident Scaly Thrush, *Z. dauma*, 28 cm, by its smaller size and smooth upperparts. The male is unmistakable, with slaty-dark plumage and a white eye-brow.

Voice: A quiet *chit* during migration.

Habits: Indonesia constitutes the southern limit for the distribution of this species; which can only be found here from November to April. Can be locally numerous then and flocks of 40 have been reported from Sumatra. Seems to prefer the montane habitat, with low trees and pine forests that resemble those in its northern breeding grounds. Seen on the ground and high in fruiting trees, but is generally shy and retiring.

Distribution: Breeds in northeast Asia; winters in Southeast Asia, reaching Indonesia. A fairly common winter visitor in Sumatra; rarer further east in Java and Bali.

ISLAND THRUSH

Turdus poliocephalus 22 cm F: Turdidae

Description: Unmistakable. The Seram subspecies has a pale head and underparts.

Voice: A clear, melodious song, typical of the genus; also a rattling alarm call.

Habits: In Indonesia, a strictly montane bird found at altitudes from 400 to 4,100 m, usually above 2,000 m. Moves low in the stunted montane forest and alpine grasslands, often dropping down to feed on the ground. Somewhat skulking in habit, but can be confiding and approachable.

Distribution: Oriental region and Pacific islands. A locally fairly common resident in upper montane Sumatra, Java, Sulawesi, Seram, Timor and West Papua.

EYE-BROWED THRUSH

Turdus obscurus 23 cm F: Turdidae

Description: Look for diagnostic white supercilium with orangy chest and flanks. Also note whitish lower belly and vent.

Voice: Just a thin contact call *tseep* during winter.

Habits: Indonesia constitutes the southern limit for this bird; only found here from November to March. In winter quarters, it settles mainly in montane forest from 1,000 to 2,000 m. Flocks of over 100 individuals have been reported from Gunung Kerinci in Sumatra during February. Mainly arboreal; often visits fruiting trees.

Morten Strange

Distribution: Breeds in northern Siberia; winters in the Oriental region, reaching Indonesia. A locally common winter visitor on Sumatra; uncommon on Java and Bali; vagrant on Sulawesi and Flores.

BLUE JEWEL-BABBLER

Ptilorrhoa caerulescens 22 cm F: Orthonychidae

Description: Blue upperparts are diagnostic. Photo shows female; male lacks thin white eyebrow. This species and two montane species are the only members of this genus.

Voice: An alarm call *chew-chik-chik* and a high, whistling song.

Habits: Found in primary rainforest, where it scuttles along on the ground. Occurs from sea level to 800 m, where it is replaced by the Chestnut-backed Jewel-babbler, *P. castanonotus*, which has a chestnut mantle. This species occurs from 900 to 1,500 m, where it is replaced in turn by the Spotted Jewel-babbler, *P. leucosticta*, which has white spots on black wings. This species occurs from 1,500 to 2,500 m.

Brian J. Coates

Distribution: New Guinea. Locally common in Papua New Guinea, but reported less often from Indonesia. A generally scarce resident in West Papua and nearby Misool island.

BLACK-CAPPED BABBLER

Pellorneum capistratum 17 cm F: Timaliidae

Description: Note its warm rufous plumage and black cap contrasting with white eyebrow; underparts are a paler rufous colour. Its throat is white.

Voice: A descending, whistled *pi-uu*.

Habits: Found in rainforest, mainly in primary lowland forest. Occurs from the lowlands to foothills at 700 m. This terrestrial bird walks along the ground and makes a short flight up to a low perch when disturbed. Feeds on small invertebrates in the leaf litter. Here it is shown holding a cricket. A fairly regular bird in lowland forest locations such as Way Kambas on Sumatra, and Carita near Bogor on Java, but good views of this low-density skulker are rare.

B. Van Elegem

Distribution: Sunda subregion. A generally scarce resident in Sumatra and nearby Bangka and Belitung, Kalimantan and Java.

SHORT-TAILED BABBLER

Trichastoma malaccense 14 cm F: Timaliidae

Description: Distinguished with difficulty from other babblers by a short tail and a white throat and chest that contrasts with its grey head and brown crown. Its call is diagnostic.

Voice: Often calls at dawn; 4–5 clear, slowly descending notes.

Habits: A rainforest bird that inhabits primary and mature secondary forest. Can be found near the forest edge, but always under cover. Occurs mainly in the lowlands; on Sumatra to 900 m. Hops about on the ground and on low sticks and fallen logs like a small mammal. Never flies far. Can sometimes be attracted by mimicking its call.

Morten Strange

Distribution: Sunda subregion. A locally fairly common resident in Sumatra and Kalimantan.

WHITE-CHESTED BABBLER
Trichastoma rostratum 15 cm F: Timaliidae

Description: Note the bright white underparts contrasting with uniformly brown upperparts. Its call is diagnostic.

Voice: A powerful, whistled *chee-swee-phew.*

Habits: Mainly found near water in wet lowland rainforest, in peat swamps, near streams and sometimes behind tidal mangroves. The river at Way Kambas National Park on Sumatra is a good place to view this bird. Secretive and shy, it moves low on or near the ground, often in resident pairs. Calls early in the morning from a hidden perch.

Distribution: Sunda subregion. A generally scarce resident in Sumatra and Kalimantan.

HORSFIELD'S BABBLER
Trichastoma sepiarium 14 cm F: Timaliidae

Description: Distinguished with difficulty from other babblers by its thick bill, buff underparts and a grey face. Its call is diagnostic.

Voice: A loud *pee-oo-weet*, at early dawn.

Habits: This babbler seems to prefer slightly elevated forest at altitudes from 300 to 1,400 m. In Kalimantan it has been recorded at only 3 locations in recent years. Usually found in low hills. On Java present at both Gunung Gede and lowland locations, but absent from Way Kambas on Sumatra. Found in primary forest and along forest edges, often near rivers and streams, where it moves through the lower middle storey, hopping along low branches and creepers.

Distribution: Sunda subregion. In Indonesia, a widespread but generally scarce resident in Sumatra, Kalimantan, Java and Bali.

ABBOTT'S BABBLER

Trichastoma abbotti 16 cm F: Timaliidae

Description: Distinguished with difficulty from other babblers by its pale throat in combination with a buff belly and fairly long tail. Its call is diagnostic.

Voice: A clear, whistled 3–4 notes. The last note is always sharply higher.

Habits: In Indonesia, this low-density rainforest bird is found mainly in primary lowland rainforest, swamp forest and along forest edges. Restricted to lowlands below 300 m. This skulker hops through dense undergrowth near the ground and calls in the dim light of dusk and dawn. Will come out to investigate if its call is played back or mimicked.

Distribution: Oriental region. A generally scarce resident in Sumatra, Belitung, Kalimantan and Bawean.

MOUSTACHED BABBLER

Malacopteron magnirostre 16 cm F: Timaliidae

Description: Distinguished with difficulty from the following species by a faint black stripe that separates the white throat and grey head.

Voice: A rich whistle of 4–5 descending notes.

Habits: Occurs in primary rainforest, forest edges and closed secondary growth. Found mainly in the lowlands. Occurs on Sumatra to 800 m. Has a patchy distribution. Although it is locally numerous on the Malay Peninsula, there are few recent records from Indonesia. Moves through the forest at eye-level or slightly higher, restlessly flying from branch to branch.

Distribution: Sunda subregion. A generally rare resident on Sumatra, including the nearby Riau and Lingga islands, and Kalimantan.

SOOTY-CAPPED BABBLER

Malacopteron affine 17 cm F: Timaliidae

Description: Look for a dark slaty-coloured crown and greyish (not brown) upperparts.

Voice: A pretty song of about 8 whistling tones, on an undulating scale.

Habits: A rainforest bird found in primary forest and nearby secondary growth and edges. Occurs predominantly in the lowlands. On Sumatra observed occasionally up to 700 m. Fairly numerous in many forest reserves. Moves from eye-level to slightly higher in the forest, resting briefly on twigs and creepers as shown in the photo. Gleans invertebrates from the foliage on its rounds.

Distribution: Sunda subregion. A locally common resident in Sumatra and Kalimantan.

SCALY-CROWNED BABBLER

Malacopteron cinereum 17 cm F: Timaliidae

Description: A slender bird, distinguished from the following species by its pink legs and pale chest. Scales on its rufous crown are sometimes visible.

Voice: A whistled 5–6 notes, ascending slowly.

Habits: A forest bird found in primary rainforest and mature secondary forest, mainly in the lowlands. Occurs on Sumatra locally to 1,200 m. Fairly numerous in prime habitat. Inhabits the lower storey of the forest, hopping steadily along inside the undergrowth. Occasionally moves up into the middle storey. Often seen with other insectivorous species in moving flocks called bird waves.

Distribution: Southeast Asia. A locally common resident on Sumatra, including many nearby islands and Kalimantan; local and uncommon on south Java.

RUFOUS-CROWNED BABBLER

Malacopteron magnum 18 cm   F: Timaliidae

Description: A fairly chunky bird distinguished from the previous species by its size, grey (not pink) legs, grey streaks on chest, and 'clean' rufous-black crown.

Voice: Similar to that of the Sooty-capped Babbler, but more varied. Up to 12 clear, undulating whistles, rising at the end.

Habits: Similar to the previous species, but does not venture into montane forest; on Sumatra recorded to 800 m. Often seen moving through the forest at eye-level and sometimes in the middle storey. Never ventures onto the ground. Jumps and flies sluggishly from perch to perch, but does not rest for long. Often seen in bird waves.

Distribution: Sunda subregion. A locally fairly common resident in Sumatra and Kalimantan.

Morten Strange

RUSTY-BREASTED WREN-BABBLER

Napothera rufipectus 18 cm   F: Timaliidae

Description: Distinguished from the Large Wren-babbler, *N. macrodactyla*, of lowland Sumatra, Java and the Malay Peninsula, by its rufous (not grey) underparts. Possibly conspecific with this species.

Voice: Loud whistles, sometimes in duet.

Habits: A strictly montane species found in primary rainforest at altitudes from 900 to 2,500 m. Moves near the ground inside cover, but can be lured forward with a playback of its call. Occurs in all montane areas of Sumatra, including isolated mountain tops. The Gunung Kerinci area is a good place to look for this bird. Its nest has never been found.

Distribution: Indonesian endemic. A locally fairly common resident in montane parts of Sumatra.

Filip Verbelen

PYGMY WREN-BABBLER

Pnoepyga pusilla 9 cm F: Timaliidae

Description: Distinguished from other wren-babblers by its small size. Note almost complete lack of tail. This is the only Timaliidae east of Wallace's Line, apart from the three species endemic to Sulawesi.

Voice: A sharp, whistled 2–3 notes, descending slowly.

Habits: Strictly montane; found only in closed forest from 900 to 3,000 m. This tiny bird is difficult to see clearly as it scuttles along the dark forest floor. However, once its penetrating call is learned, it appears to be quite numerous in the right habitat. This individual is on the way to its nest, a ball of vegetation built into a damp embankment near a trail through primary montane forest.

Morten Strange

Distribution: Oriental region. A locally fairly common resident in montane parts of Sumatra, Java and Flores; rare on Timor.

GOLDEN BABBLER

Stachyris chrysaea 13 cm F: Timaliidae

Description: Unmistakable. Its bright yellow underparts with slightly darker upperparts and some faint black streaks on head (not visible from this angle) are diagnostic.

Voice: A soft whistled *pi-pi-pi-pi*, trailing off.

Habits: Restricted to closed montane forest and forest edges from 800 to 3,000 m. Seems numerous in this habitat. Inevitably turns up in small flocks or with other species in bird waves. This small, restless bird is always on the move, fluttering through thickets, just off the ground or at eye-level, constantly going over the foliage for small insects as shown in the photo.

Morten Strange

Distribution: Oriental region. In Indonesia, occurs only on Sumatra, where it is a locally common montane resident.

GREY-THROATED BABBLER

Stachyris nigriceps 15 cm   F: Timaliidae

Description: Distinguished with difficulty from other babblers by its pale malar patch contrasting with grey throat.

Voice: A high-pitched, rattling whistle *pree-pree-eee*.

Habits: Mainly a montane species, usually seen at elevations around 500 m, but may occur at lower altitudes. One of the most common babblers on Sumatra and Kalimantan, usually found in the lower montane forest from 900 to 1,700 m. On Sumatra recorded to 2,300 m. This typical skulker moves restlessly through the lower storey in primary forest or forest edges, often mixing with other species. Stays under cover and good views are difficult.

Distribution: Oriental region. A locally common resident mainly in montane parts of Sumatra, the Lingga islands and Kalimantan.

CHESTNUT-RUMPED BABBLER

Stachyris maculata 17 cm   F: Timaliidae

Description: Look for chunky size and streaks on its breast and forehead. Chestnut rump area is noticeable when it flies off.

Voice: A loud series of hooting notes *who-hoop who-hoop*.

Habits: Found in primary rainforest, mature secondary forest and along forest edges. Occurs mainly in lowland forest and forested swamps. On Sumatra recorded to 700 m. Shy and skulking, but will respond to a playback of its call. Occasionally small flocks engage in excited displays. Then members fly about, call loudly, land on branches and tree trunks, and bob their heads. Otherwise little studied; few nesting records.

Distribution: Sunda subregion. A locally fairly common resident in Sumatra and Kalimantan.

CHESTNUT-WINGED BABBLER
Stachyris erythroptera 14 cm F: Timaliidae

Description: Distinguished with difficulty from other babblers by a blue orbital ring in combination with a lack of streaks on forehead and throat. Also note chestnut wings contrasting with grey underparts.

Voice: A rapid series of low, hooting whistles *hoop-hoop-hoop*.

Habits: This rainforest bird is found in primary and mature secondary forest and along forest edges, mainly in lowland forest. Occurs on Sumatra to 700 m. In the right habitat it is quite a predictable bird, but good views are difficult since it is constantly on the move under very low cover. Its call is easy to mimic and sometimes that can lure it forward.

Ong Kiem Sian

Distribution: Sunda subregion. A locally fairly common resident in Sumatra and Kalimantan.

STRIPED TIT-BABBLER
Macronous gularis 13 cm F: Timaliidae

Description: Note diagnostic broad streaks on yellowish throat and chest.

Voice: A resonant, monotonous *chuck chuck chuck* repeated incessantly. Also a harsh churring rattle while feeding.

Habits: An adaptable species found along edges of primary rainforest, in nearby low scrub and overgrown cultivated areas, and even dense gardens. Occurs from the lowlands into lower montane elevations. On Sumatra recorded to 1,000 m. Always seen in small groups, hopping about inside cover, searching for insects and grubs, churring quietly and flying only briefly.

Morten Strange

Distribution: Oriental region. A widespread and common resident in Sumatra, Kalimantan and many adjacent islands; local in west and central Java only.

FLUFFY-BACKED TIT-BABBLER

Macronous ptilosus 15 cm F: Timaliidae

Description: Note its very dark brown plumage. The blue orbital ring and black throat contrasting with chestnut cap are diagnostic.

Voice: A loud, hollow *poop-poop-poop*.

Habits: Found in primary forest, but often comes out into forest edges and clearings with thick re-growth. Occurs in lowland rainforest, often near swampy areas. On Sumatra recorded to 700 m. Always moves low at eye-level or just off the ground. Flies quickly across open areas into the next cover and never perches in the open. Usually seen in resident pairs or a family group.

Distribution: Sunda subregion. A locally fairly common resident in Sumatra and Kalimantan.

SUNDA LAUGHINGTHRUSH

Garrulax palliatus 27 cm F: Timaliidae

Description: Unmistakable; note grey head and breast, and prominent pale blue orbital skin. Captive photo.

Voice: A variety of whistling and harsher notes.

Habits: Occurs in closed forest in the montane belt between 850 and 2,200 m. Not really numerous anywhere, but is spotted quite regularly in the right habitat. Always seen in small groups. Moves low through the forest, often with other species in bird waves. This vocal, active bird hops and flies briefly from branch to branch, and can be quite approachable. Otherwise little studied; there are few nesting records.

Distribution: Endemic to Sumatra and Borneo. In Indonesia a locally fairly common resident in montane parts of Sumatra and Kalimantan.

WHITE-CRESTED LAUGHINGTHRUSH

Garrulax leucolophus 30 cm F: Timaliidae

Description: Unmistakable; no other *Garrulax* babbler has a similar striking head pattern. Captive photo.

Voice: A peculiar laughing chatter that carries a long way.

Habits: Found in primary forest and forest edges, from 750 to 2,000 m elevation. Often flies into nearby open woodlands and cultivated areas, roaming through the terrain in small noisy flocks. Always on the go, jumping around and making brief, gliding flights into the next tree. Perches in the lower and middle storey, but often drops down onto the ground to feed.

Morten Strange

Distribution: Oriental region. In Indonesia occurs only on Sumatra, where it is a generally scarce resident in montane parts of the island.

BLACK LAUGHINGTHRUSH

Garrulax lugubris 26 cm F: Timaliidae

Description: Unmistakable; note all-black plumage and reddish bill, contrasting with its blue orbital skin.

Voice: A variety of clear *hoopoop* notes, mixed with a harsher 'laughing' call.

Habits: On Sumatra it inhabits primary rainforest and is occasionally found along forest edges in the lower montane range between 500 and 1,600 m. Although it can be found in north Borneo, there are still no records from Kalimantan. Moves in small vocal groups through the lower and middle storeys of the forest, sometimes with other species in bird waves. This low-density species is shy and rarely seen clearly. Little studied; its nest has never been found.

Morten Strange

Distribution: Sunda subregion. In Indonesia, a generally rare resident in montane parts of Sumatra only.

CHESTNUT-CAPPED LAUGHINGTHRUSH

Garrulax mitratus 25 cm F: Timaliidae

Description: Unmistakable; note chestnut head contrasting with grey body. The white patch in wing shows well in flight; Sumatra subspecies has a white (not yellow) eye-patch.

Voice: A varied song of slurred whistles.

Habits: A lower montane specialist found between 700 and 2,000 m on Sumatra. In Kalimantan occurs locally down to 300 m in the foothills. At these elevations it is one of the most numerous birds in the rainforest. Also ventures into forest edges and nearby cultivation. Often seen in small groups, moving through the middle and lower storeys of the forest, feeding on fruits and insects.

Distribution: Sunda subregion. A locally common resident in montane parts of Sumatra and Kalimantan.

SILVER-EARED MESIA

Leiothrix argentauris 18 cm F: Timaliidae

Description: Unmistakable. The underparts of the Sumatra subspecies are a brighter red than this individual's.

Voice: A slurred song mixed with clear whistles; also a low chattering while feeding.

Habits: A strictly montane bird found in rainforest from 600 to 2,200 m. In the right habitat, it is a numerous bird, seen daily in small vocal feeding parties, moving through primary forest. Often comes out near trails and roadsides. Usually stays low at eye-level, but is also sometimes observed higher in the middle storey, feeding on insects, berries and nectar.

Distribution: Oriental region. In Indonesia, occurs only on Sumatra, where it is a locally common resident in montane parts of the island.

WHITE-BROWED SHRIKE-BABBLER

Pteruthius flaviscapis 13 cm   F: Timaliidae

Description: Unmistakable; the chestnut patch in its wing is partly obstructed in this photo of a male. The female has the same pattern but is a duller colour.

Voice: A 4–note whistle *chi-chewp, chi-chewp*.

Habits: This montane bird is found in low densities in closed forest from 1,000 to 2,300 m. Moves high just below the canopy in large trees, often crawling along the main branches somewhat like a nuthatch (Sittidae), searching for insects on the trunk. Also seen briefly with other birds in bird waves.

Distribution: Oriental region. A generally scarce resident in montane parts of Sumatra, Kalimantan and Java.

BROWN FULVETTA

Alcippe brunneicauda 15 cm   F: Timaliidae

Description: A nondescript bird. Note pale underparts and a lack of markings on its uniformly greyish head.

Voice: Sometimes a series of descending, high-pitched whistles *pi-pi-pi-pi*; mostly quiet.

Habits: This rainforest specialist is found in primary and mature secondary forest. Occurs in the lowlands, but is often seen in the foothills; recorded on Sumatra to 1,000 m. A low-density species often missed during surveys, perhaps due to its inconspicuous looks and habits. Moves through the lower and sometimes middle storey of the forest, feeding mainly on invertebrates, often as part of mixed-species flocks.

Distribution: Sunda subregion. A generally scarce resident in Sumatra and Kalimantan.

LONG-TAILED SIBIA

Heterophasia picaoides 30 cm F: Timaliidae

Description: Unmistakable; unlike any other member of the babbler family.

Voice: A single, ringing note repeated incessantly *tsiip-tsiip-tsiip*.

Habits: A montane species occurring exclusively from 600 to 3,000 m. Lives in primary forest and along forest edges and is numerous in the prime locations such as Gunung Leuser or Gunung Kerinci. Never seen alone; always travels in small vocal flocks, feeding on insects, high in small montane trees. Flies quickly from tree to tree, its long tail dangling behind.

Distribution: Oriental region. In Indonesia, found only in Sumatra, where it is a locally common resident in montane parts of the island.

CHESTNUT-CRESTED YUHINA

Yuhina everetti 14 cm F: Timaliidae

Description: Unmistakable; note its grey upperparts and chestnut cap raised into a crest. Underparts are whitish.

Voice: A low *chit-chit*.

Habits: Mainly a montane species, but it has also been recorded in the lowlands, e.g. at Kutai National Park. Occurs in the lower montane forest, from the foothills up to 1,800 m. Always seen in small chattering flocks, sometimes numbering as many as 20. Moves high through the forest, restlessly searching the thin branches for tiny invertebrates.

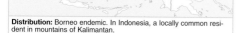

Distribution: Borneo endemic. In Indonesia, a locally common resident in mountains of Kalimantan.

WHITE-BELLIED YUHINA

Yuhina zantholeuca 12 cm   F: Timaliidae

Description: Note its warbler-like appearance. Its most outstanding features are its distinct crest and uniformly olive upperparts with pale underparts.

Voice: A high-pitched *si-si-si*.

Habits: In tropical Indonesia this species is scarce, although numerous in other parts of its range. Occurs in closed forest at lowland and lower montane altitudes, predominantly from 300 to 1,500 m. Moves restlessly through the middle storey and canopy, often with other species in bird waves.

Distribution: Oriental region. In Indonesia, found only in Kalimantan, where it is a scarce resident. There is one record from Sumatra, where it is possibly a rare resident.

Morten Strange

JAVAN TESIA

Tesia superciliaris 7 cm   F: Sylviidae

Description: Unmistakable. This species and the Russet-capped Tesia, *T. everetti*, endemic to Sumbawa and Flores, are the only members of this genus in Indonesia.

Voice: A loud and musical song.

Habits: This peculiar, tiny warbler is restricted to montane rainforest at altitudes between 1,000 and 3,000 m. This photograph was taken at Gunung Gede, a place where this bird is regularly seen, but it usually occurs in low densities. Moves on or just off the ground in dense undergrowth, a behaviour typical of its genus. Good views of this babbler-like skulker are difficult to obtain, but it might respond to a mimic of its call.

Distribution: Indonesian endemic. A generally scarce resident in montane parts of Java.

B. Van Elegem

SUNDA BUSH-WARBLER
Cettia vulcania 13 cm F: Sylviidae

Description: A nondescript, all-brown warbler with pale underparts. Distinguished from similar babblers by its whitish supercilium and fairly long, thin tail.

Voice: A loud, clear whistle *chee-tyi-weee*; also a harsh *trrrik* in alarm.

Habits: Mainly an upper montane species; occurs on Sumatra from 2,100 m up to the tree limit at 3,400 m. On other islands found mainly above 1,500 m. On Timor also occurs locally down to sea level. This babbler-like bird skulks low in the dense undergrowth of stunted montane moss forest. Often seen among ferns and never flies far. Quite confiding and can be lured forward by an imitation of its call.

Distribution: Sunda subregion into Nusa Tenggara. In Indonesia, a locally fairly common resident in montane parts of Sumatra, Kalimantan, Java, Bali, Lombok, Sumbawa and Timor.

CLAMOROUS REED-WARBLER
Acrocephalus stentoreus 18 cm F: Sylviidae

Description: Distinguished with great difficulty from the following species by the lack of streaks on breast.

Voice: Vocal; a loud, warbling song and some harsher call notes.

Habits: Always lives near water, usually around extensive lakes, rivers and marshlands with large reed beds. Also found in nearby wet fields. Usually seen alone or in resident pairs. This secretive and skulking bird is best seen during the breeding season, when it will emerge and sing from an open perch, often on a reed stem as shown in this photo.

Distribution: North Africa east across the Oriental region into southern Australia; mainly sedentary. A locally common resident on some islands in Wallacea; uncommon in the Sunda subregion and West Papua.

ORIENTAL REED-WARBLER

Acrocephalus orientalis 18 cm F: Sylviidae

Description: Distinguished with difficulty from the previous species by its greyish (not brown) upperparts and faint streaks on breast.

Voice: During migration, a penetrating alarm call: *chack*.

Habits: Indonesia is the southern limit of this bird's distribution. Only a few make it this far during the northern winter, from September to May. In winter quarters, mainly found in mangroves and marshlands along the coast. Occurs inland to 200 m. Skulks in tall grasses, bushes and small trees, but its characteristic alarm call gives it away.

Distribution: Breeds in East Asia; winters in Southeast Asia, reaching Indonesia. A widespread but generally scarce winter visitor throughout the Sunda subregion and parts of Wallacea; vagrant in West Papua.

ZITTING CISTICOLA

Cisticola juncidis 11 cm F: Sylviidae

Description: Distinguished from the following species by its plain head and neck, and white tip in tail.

Voice: A metallic *zitt-zitt*, sometimes uttered during display flights.

Habits: An open country species that has become locally numerous following forest clearance in the country. Seen in fields and grasslands, often near swampy areas. Occurs from the coast, inland to lower montane elevations; on Sumatra recently recorded at 1,400 m. During the breeding season, it sings incessantly, but is otherwise inconspicuous and easy to miss, since it usually stays under cover in tall grasses.

Distribution: Africa and Eurasia into northern Australia. In Indonesia, a widespread and common resident on Sumatra, Java, Bali and parts of Wallacea and West Papua.

THE BIRDS OF INDONESIA 273

GOLDEN-HEADED CISTICOLA (Bright-capped Cisticola)
Cisticola exilis 11 cm F: Sylviidae

Description: Breeding male (photo) is unmistakable. The non-breeding male is distinguished with difficulty from the previous species by a rufous wash on neck and flanks.

Voice: A characteristic buzzing and more liquid call.

Habits: Found in open country, fields and grasslands, much like the previous species, only generally in the drier areas. Occurs locally to 1,800 m. Best viewed when singing from a low open perch or in song-flight. Its flight is fluttering and bouncy, but short, and then the warbler quickly drops back into cover.

Distribution: Oriental region and Australasia. A widespread and locally common resident throughout much of Indonesia; recorded from Kalimantan, but status there is uncertain.

HILL PRINIA
Prinia atrogularis 16 cm F: Sylviidae

Description: Distinguished from other prinias by its long tail and black streaks on breast.

Voice: A liquid but somewhat monotonous song: *cho-eep, cho-eep*.

Habits: Restricted to montane habitat from 600 to 2000 m and occasionally found at lower altitudes. Often seen in open country with some tree cover such as along forest edges, roadsides and around plantations and villages. Sometimes sings loudly from an open perch. Flies low between small trees and bushes, feeding on insects.

Distribution: Oriental region. In Indonesia, found only on Sumatra where it is a fairly common montane resident.

BAR-WINGED PRINIA

Prinia familiaris 13 cm F: Sylviidae

Description: Distinguished from other prinias by two bars in wings.

Voice: An explosive and high-pitched *twee-wee-wee*.

Habits: An open country species that has readily invaded the garden niche. In many places within its range, it is the common village and garden bird. On Bali it feeds on rice in the family temples. Its original habitats were mangroves and forest edges, but it is now also found in open woodlands, scrub and cultivated areas. Occurs on Sumatra to 2,000 m. Sings from an open perch as shown in the photo. The nest is a ball of vegetation with a side entrance, built low in a bush.

Morten Strange

Distribution: Indonesian endemic. A widespread and common resident on Java and Bali; fairly common on Sumatra.

YELLOW-BELLIED PRINIA

Prinia flaviventris 13 cm F: Sylviidae

Description: Distinguished from other prinias by its bright yellow lower belly.

Voice: A short, bubbling song, often sung from an exposed perch.

Habits: An open country species found in cultivated fields, along roadsides and in scrub with long grasses. Often seen around marshy areas. Occurs mainly in the coastal lowlands; on Sumatra occasionally recorded to 900 m. Seen clearly when it sings from an open perch or flies briefly across the grass. Has a wobbly, top-heavy flight pattern that is typical of the genus.

Morten Strange

Distribution: Oriental region. A widespread and fairly common resident in Sumatra and Kalimantan; uncommon on west Java.

PLAIN PRINIA (Tawny-flanked Prinia)
Prinia inornata 15 cm F: Sylviidae

Description: Distinguished from the Brown Prinia, *P. polychroa*, of the Oriental region (also occurs on Java), by its shorter tail, paler plumage and prominent white supercilium.

Voice: A buzzing *jirt-jirt*.

Habits: Found in scrub, cultivated fields and in open country with long grasses. Often seen near marshes. Occurs at higher elevations in drier areas and has been recorded on Java to 1,500 m. An active bird often seen flying across the grass or singing from a low, exposed perch.

Distribution: Africa and the Oriental region. In Indonesia, found only on Java, where it is a fairly common resident.

MOUNTAIN TAILORBIRD
Orthotomus cuculatus 12 cm F: Sylviidae

Description: Look for slender build, long bill and yellow lower belly and vent.

Voice: A high-pitched whistle of 4–6 thin notes; also a short trill.

Habits: A strictly montane tailorbird found from 1,000 to 2,500 m. In Wallacea occurs locally down to 500 m. Frequents primary forest and forest edges, where it moves inside dense bamboos thickets and creepers, often with other species in bird waves. Cryptic to observe, but its call gives it away. Does not stitch leaves together for its nest as do other members of this genus.

Distribution: Oriental region. A locally fairly common resident in montane parts of Sumatra, Kalimantan, Java, Bali, Sulawesi, Sula, Bacan, Buru, Seram and Flores.

COMMON TAILORBIRD

Orthotomus sutorius 10 cm F: Sylviidae

Description: Distinguished from the Olive-backed Tailorbird by its rufous forecrown and white underparts, including vent.

Voice: A loud, repetitive *chee-rup, chee-rup*.

Habits: Indonesia is the southern limit for this species, and it is quite scarce. Can be found along the edges of secondary forest, in scrub and around villages, from the coastal lowlands into lower montane elevations at 1,500 m. This restless and vocal bird hops low through scrub and ornamental plants catching insects.

Distribution: Oriental region. In Indonesia found only on Java, where it is a widespread but uncommon resident; also recently recorded on the Riau Islands, Sumatra.

DARK-NECKED TAILORBIRD

Orthotomus atrogularis 11 cm F: Sylviidae

Description: Distinguished with difficulty from the previous species by its yellowish (not white) undertail coverts showing clearly here. The male (photo) has black streaks on neck.

Voice: A loud, repetitive *trii-ip*, more high-pitched and trilling than the Common Tailorbird's call.

Habits: Habits and behaviour are much like that of the previous species. In Indonesia these species only overlap on the Riau Islands, so confusion is unlikely. Prefers slightly more wooded habitat than the Common Tailorbird, but is never found in closed forest. Occurs along forest edges, in scrub and near roads and villages. On Sumatra has recently expanded to an altitude of 1,550 m.

Distribution: Oriental region. In Indonesia, a widespread and fairly common resident on Sumatra, including many islands and Kalimantan.

RUFOUS-TAILED TAILORBIRD
Orthotomus sericeus 11 cm F: Sylviidae

Description: Note red crown combined with dark grey upperparts and white underparts; also look for rufous tail.

Voice: A powerful series of *tee-cher, tee-cher*.

Habits: Found in lowland rainforest edges and nearby scrub. Often seen in scrub behind mangroves and in sea level woodlands. Occurs in Sumatra to 700 m. Avoids closed forest, but is often seen in disturbed patches of re-growth and wooded rural areas. Not as numerous as other tailorbirds, but in the right habitat can be quite predictable. Skulks low inside dense scrub, but during the breeding season it is very territorial and will respond strongly to an imitation of its call.

Distribution: Sunda subregion. A widespread and locally fairly common resident on Sumatra and the nearby islands of Riau, Lingga and Belitung; also Kalimantan.

ASHY TAILORBIRD
Orthotomus ruficeps 10 cm F: Sylviidae

Description: Note ashy grey body and red face. Photo shows female; male has darker underparts.

Voice: A penetrating *trill treee-chip*.

Habits: Often found in tidal mangroves, but in Kalimantan and Sumatra has also been recorded far inland in scrub and cultivated areas. and along forest edges. Occurs on Sumatra to 900 m. An active and restless species that hops through the low bushes, or higher in small trees, constantly chasing insects and calling loudly.

Distribution: Sunda subregion. A widespread and generally fairly common resident in Sumatra and Kalimantan; on Java found only in northern mangroves.

OLIVE-BACKED TAILORBIRD

Orthotomus sepium 10 cm F: Sylviidae

Description: Formerly considered conspecific with the previous species; similar in appearance but duller and paler.

Voice: A variety of trilling and chipping calls: *chew-chew* and *turr-turr*.

Habits: Found in open woodlands, along forest edges and in cultivated areas. Also a frequent visitor to villages and gardens—even enters houses to pick up nesting material. Occurs from the coast inland up to 1,500 m; on Lombok (where the Mountain Tailorbird is absent) it occurs to 1,875 m. Restless and skulking, but not shy. The nest is built inside a leaf that is folded and sewn together, a habit typical of the genus.

Distribution: Indonesian endemic. A locally common resident on Java, Bali and Lombok.

ARCTIC WARBLER (Arctic Leaf-warbler)

Phylloscopus borealis 12 cm F: Sylviidae

Description: Note the combination of slender shape, fairly dark olive plumage, white supercilium and one faint wing bar.

Voice: A sharp *zik* during migration.

Habits: Indonesia is the southern limit for this species, but from September to May it can be quite numerous in wooded areas. Occurs mainly along the coast and locally inland to 1,600 m. In winter quarters it settles in all kinds of wooded terrain, from the canopies of huge trees in primary forest to scattered trees and bushes behind the coast. Seen constantly hopping and flying from branch to branch, catching insects.

Distribution: Breeds in arctic and subarctic Eurasia; winters in the tropics reaching Indonesia. A widespread and locally fairly common winter visitor throughout the Sunda subregion and Wallacea.

TIMOR LEAF-WARBLER (Timor Warbler)

Phylloscopus presbytes 11 cm   F: Sylviidae

Description: Within its small range can only be confused with the previous species. Note its much yellower (not grey) underparts and lack of wing bar.

Voice: A soft, short, warbling whistle.

Habits: Found in primary forest and along edges near clearings and trails. Restricted on Flores to montane forest. Locally abundant from 1,200 to 1,800 m; also recorded from 1,000 to 2,100 m. Occurs on Timor from near sea level to 2,300 m, but is less numerous near the coast. This confiding and easily observed bird moves actively through the forest, often in small groups or mixing with other species. Does not respond well to call playback.

Distribution: Indonesian endemic. A common resident on Flores and fairly common on Timor.

YELLOW-BREASTED WARBLER

Seicercus montis 10 cm   F: Sylviidae

Description: A small bird. Note its lemon-yellow underparts and olive upperparts in combination with a rufous head.

Voice: A thin, high-pitched song that undulates up and down the scale.

Habits: Found in lower and upper montane rainforest between 1,000 and 2,200 m on Sumatra. Occurs in Nusa Tenggara between 1,200 and 2,300 m. At these elevations it can be quite numerous and is often seen mixing with other species in moving flocks. Moves quickly and restlessly through the thin branches of the middle and upper storeys, gleaning insects and larvae from the leaves.

Distribution: Southeast Asia. A locally fairly common resident in montane parts of Sumatra, Kalimantan, Flores and Timor.

WHITE-RUMPED WARBLER (Sunda Warbler)

Seicercus grammiceps 10 cm F: Sylviidae

Description: Distinguished from the Chestnut-crowned Warbler, *S. castaniceps* of the Oriental region (see Strange (2000)), by its slate-coloured (not olive-green) wings, full rufous head, and white (not grey) breast.

Voice: A high-pitched *chee-chee*.

Habits: A strictly montane species found between 1,400 and 2,200 m on Sumatra; on Java and Bali occurs between 800 and 2,500 m. Moves through the lower and middle storey of primary forest and sometimes along forest edges. Often seen with other insectivorous birds in mixed-species flocks. Otherwise not much is known about this little-studied warbler.

Distribution: Indonesian endemic. A locally common resident in montane parts of Sumatra, Java and Bali.

Alan OwYong

RUSSET-BACKED JUNGLE-FLYCATCHER

Rhinomyias oscillans 14 cm F: Muscicapidae

Description: On Flores distinguished with some difficulty from the female Little Pied Flycatcher by its rufous wings and tail. Also note its broad bill.

Voice: A soft, high-pitched warbling song; also a quiet alarm call: *tak*.

Habits: Found in primary rainforest and along forest edges, mainly in elevated areas. Occurs on Sumbawa from 500 to 650 m; on Flores from 400 to 1,500 m; on Sumba from the lowlands to 1,000 m. This inconspicuous bird sits quietly in the lower middle storey, as shown in the photo, and comes and goes so fast that its change in location is not noticed. Will respond to an imitation of its call. Sallies for insects and also takes some fruits.

Distribution: Indonesian endemic. A generally scarce resident on Sumbawa, Flores and Sumba only.

Morten Strange

GREY-CHESTED FLYCATCHER

Rhinomyias umbratilis 15 cm F: Muscicapidae

Description: Note brown upper-parts contrasting with white throat and belly; brownish-grey band across chest is diagnostic.

Voice: A liquid song of 2-6 rising notes.

Habits: Found in primary and adjacent mature secondary rain-forest, also wet patches and peat swamp forest. Occurs mainly in the lowlands; on Sumatra to 1,000 m. Inconspicuous; stays inside closed forest and does not come to the forest edges. Little studied, but is sometimes spotted perching low and flying out occa-sionally to grab insects in the air or on the thin branches in the undergrowth.

Distribution: Sunda subregion. A generally scarce resident in Sumatra and Kalimantan.

ASIAN BROWN FLYCATCHER

Muscicapa dauurica 12 cm F: Muscicapidae

Description: Distinguished with difficulty from the rarer Dark-sided Flycatcher, *M. sibirica,* by its grey-ish plumage, longer tail and bill, and lack of dis-tinct streaks on underparts.

Voice: Usually quiet; sometimes a sibilant *tit-tit-tit.*

Habits: Indonesia is the southern limit of this species' distribution; occurs in the Sunda only from September to March. The resident Sumba sub-species, *M. d. segregata,* is possibly a different species. In winter quarters it turns up in all kinds of wooded areas, from coastal mangroves and gar-dens to montane forest edges at 1,000 m. Sits qui-etly at middle storey level, occasionally flying out to grab tiny insects in the air, returning swiftly.

Distribution: East Asia and the Oriental region; migratory. A wide-spread and seasonally fairly common winter visitor to the Sunda sub-region; an uncommon resident on Sumba Island.

FERRUGINOUS FLYCATCHER

Muscicapa ferruginea 13 cm F: Muscicapidae

Description: Note its diagnostic reddish brown wings, back and rump that contrast with its greyish head. Has a distinct eye-ring.

Voice: Usually quiet during migration.

Habits: Indonesia constitutes the southern limit for this bird. Few come this far south, but those that do can be found from November to March. Mainly settles at lower montane elevations between 500 and 1,500 m. Usually solitary. Perches low inside closed forest and flies out to catch small insects in the air, returning to the same branch.

Distribution: Oriental region; migratory. In Indonesia, found only on Sumatra and west Java, where it is a generally rare winter visitor.

VERDITER FLYCATCHER

Eumyias thalassina 16 cm F: Muscicapidae

Description: Distinguished from other blue flycatchers by its uniformly greenish-blue plumage, pale scales on vent and erect stance. The male in the photo is brighter than the female, and has black lores.

Voice: A soft, penetrating, melodious warble.

Habits: A forest bird found in primary forest and along disturbed edges with large trees. Occurs in the lowlands, but seems to have a preference for somewhat elevated hills. Occurs locally on Sumatra to 1,400 m. This fairly conspicuous bird perches high in the open, as shown in the photo, singing and flying out to catch insects in the air.

Distribution: Oriental region. A generally scarce resident in Sumatra and Kalimantan.

INDIGO FLYCATCHER

Eumyias indigo 14 cm F: Muscicapidae

Description: Distinguished with difficulty from other blue flycatchers by its comparatively small size, deep indigo-blue plumage, and characteristic black face contrasting with whitish forehead.

Voice: A ringing, squeaky call.

Habits: A strictly montane species found between 1,500 and 2,400 m, and occasionally down to 900 m. A regular bird at major montane destinations such as Gunung Kerinci on Sumatra and Gunung Gede on Java. Spotted in closed forest and along the trails. Sits quietly on a low perch, hawking for insects. Also seen with other species in bird waves.

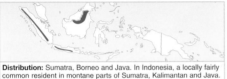

Distribution: Sumatra, Borneo and Java. In Indonesia, a locally fairly common resident in montane parts of Sumatra, Kalimantan and Java.

SNOWY-BROWED FLYCATCHER

Ficedula hyperythra 11 cm F: Muscicapidae

Description: In the Sunda subregion and Sulawesi, the male (photo) is distinguished from the migratory Mugimaki Flycatcher, *F. mugimaki*, by the lack of bar in wing. Female is dull brownish with a buff-coloured breast.

Voice: Song is a soft, high-pitched series of 3–4 whistled notes.

Habits: A strictly montane forest species that occurs mainly in the upper montane zone from 1,200 to 2,800 m; seen occasionally down to 600 m. Common, confiding and easy to observe in Sumatra; less numerous on other islands. This inconspicuous bird perches low in dense moss forest and often drops onto the ground to pick up insects and grubs.

Distribution: Oriental region. In Indonesia, a widespread and locally common resident in upper montane parts of the Sunda and Wallacea subregions.

RUFOUS-CHESTED FLYCATCHER

Ficedula dumetoria 11 cm F: Muscicapidae

Description: The immature bird (photo) is similar to the female, but has faint streaks on breast. Note diagnostic contrasting rufous chest and white belly. The male is similar to the migratory Mugimaki Flycatcher, *F. mugimaki,* with black upperparts, and white supercilium and wing bar.

Voice: A weak, high-pitched 1–3 note song: *tsst tsst.*

Habits: A rainforest bird found in the Indonesian part of the Sunda subregion. Occurs mainly in the hills and lower montane elevations, from 600 to 1,500 m; in the Wallacea, recorded from 300 to 1,900 m. In Tanimbar also found in the lowlands. Shy, inconspicuous and easily overlooked. Sometimes spotted perching low in the undergrowth.

Morten Strange

Distribution: Sunda subregion into eastern Indonesia. A generally scarce resident in Sumatra, Kalimantan, Java, Lombok, Sumbawa, Flores and Tanimbar islands.

LITTLE PIED FLYCATCHER

Ficedula westermanni 11 cm F: Muscicapidae

Description: The male, shown in photo, is unmistakable. Note its prominent white supercilium. Female is a nondescript grey-brown colour, with paler underparts.

Voice: Quite vocal, with a thin *pi-pi-pi.*

Habits: This strictly montane flycatcher is found in forest from 1,000 to 2,500 m; occurs on Sulawesi down to 800 m. Found mainly in closed, undisturbed forest, but also along forest edges and roads. Sits quietly on an exposed branch in the upper or middle storey and flies out to catch insects in the air. The nest is a finely constructed cup, built high in a forest tree.

Morten Strange

Distribution: Oriental region. A fairly common resident in montane parts of Sumatra, Kalimantan, Java, Bali, Lombok, Sumbawa, Flores, Alor, Timor, Wetar, Sulawesi, Sula, Bacan and Seram.

LARGE NILTAVA

Niltava grandis 21 cm F: Muscicapidae

Description: The female (photo) is distinguished from the female Rufous-vented Niltava, *N. sumatrana* (that also occurs in montane Sumatra), by its size and brown (not grey) underparts. The male is blue with paler crown and shoulder patch.

Voice: A clear whistle of 3–4 ascending notes.

Habits: A strictly montane flycatcher found in closed forest, from 900 to 2,500 m. Sits lethargically in the middle storey. Moves about unnoticed, somewhat like a trogon, and is often seen in resident pairs. May occasionally fly out from the vegetation or drop down onto the forest floor to catch small invertebrate prey.

Distribution: Oriental region. In Indonesia, occurs only on Sumatra, where it is a generally scarce montane resident.

TIMOR BLUE FLYCATCHER

Cyornis hyacinthinus 16 cm F: Muscicapidae

Description: Unmistakable within its range. The male (top) has a blackish face and dark blue upperparts. The female (bottom) has a bluish tail.

Voice: A soft, bubbling song.

Habits: This forest bird is found in undisturbed forest and along forest edges, from sea level to 2,000 m. Widely distributed, but not numerous anywhere. Not shy, but is quiet and unobtrusive; usually solitary and easy to overlook. Sits in the lower middle storey or near the ground and sallies out for flying insects. Flies low and moves to a new location very quickly.

Distribution: Indonesian endemic. A generally scarce resident on Timor and the smaller nearby islands of Roti, Semau and Wetar.

BLUE-FRONTED FLYCATCHER

Cyornis hoevelli 15 cm F: Muscicapidae

Description: The male, shown in photo, is distinguished from the Mangrove Blue Flycatcher by its blue throat. The female has blue replaced with a greyish colour on head, and its throat is a pale grey-buff colour.

Voice: A loud, thrush-like song.

Habits: A strictly montane species found in forest at altitudes between 1,400 and 2,300 m. Lore Lindu National Park is a good place to find this bird, which can be lured forward with an imitation of its characteristic call. Perches in the lower middle stories where it gleans insects from the foliage.

B. Van Elegem

Distribution: Indonesian endemic. A locally fairly common resident in central and southeastern parts of Sulawesi.

MALAYSIAN BLUE FLYCATCHER

Cyornis turcosus 13 cm F: Muscicapidae

Description: The female, shown in photo, is distinguished with difficulty from other small blue flycatchers by its pale shoulder and forehead together with a cream-coloured throat. The male has a blue throat.

Voice: A soft, whistling song, very weak and barely audible.

Habits: This lowland specialist is found mainly in sea level rainforest, where it prefers swampy places and forested rivers and streams. Occurs below 100 m elevation on Sumatra. Recorded in Kalimantan to 500 m. The river at Way Kambas National Park is a well-known haunt of this low-density bird. Here it flies quickly about, between the river bank and nearby bamboo and scrub, perching low as shown in photo.

Morten Strange

Distribution: Sunda subregion. A local and uncommon resident in Sumatra and Kalimantan.

MANGROVE BLUE FLYCATCHER

Cyornis rufigastra 15 cm   F: Muscicapidae

Description: Male, shown in photo, is distinguished with difficulty from other *Cyornis* flycatchers by its uniformly dark blue upperparts and black lores and chin. The female has white lores.

Voice: A clear, melodious trill.

Habits: In the Sunda subregion, this is strictly a coastal bird found in low densities in tidal mangroves and nearby scrub. Peculiarly, on Sulawesi it occupies the montane niche and is locally numerous in forest and along the edges from 500 to 1,200 m. Occurs locally to 2,300 m. Perches low, in shady areas of the vegetation, flying out to catch tiny insects.

Distribution: Southeast Asia. An uncommon resident in coastal Sumatra and Kalimantan; rare on Java and Bali; locally common on Sulawesi.

GREY-HEADED FLYCATCHER

Culicicapa ceylonensis 12 cm   F: Muscicapidae

Description: Unmistakable. Note diagnostic yellow belly that contrasts with grey head and breast. Placed by Coates et al. (1997) in Petroicidae family.

Voice: A fine, rising three-note whistle; also a metallic rattle.

Habits: This flycatcher prefers closed submontane forest between 600 and 1,600 m, but can be found across a wide range of altitudes, from the lowlands to 2,200 m. Often seen mixing with other insectivorous species in moving feeding parties (bird waves). This restless and vocal bird flits about in the open space below the canopy, catching flying insects.

Distribution: Oriental region. A widespread and fairly common resident in Sumatra, Kalimantan, Java, Bali, Lombok, Flores and Sumba.

ORANGE-CROWNED FAIRY-WREN

Clytomyias insignis 15 cm F: Maluridae

Description: Unmistakable. Note its characteristic orange head contrasting with pale throat; also note its long tail.

Voice: Vocal; a soft, chattering call and an abrupt *jib, jib.*

Habits: This upper montane specialist is found between 2,000 and 2,700 m. Rarely observed down to 1,400 m. Moves low in the undergrowth and thickets near trails and clearings in montane moss forest. Skulks under cover, but will emerge briefly into the open, lifting its tail and scolding the observer.

Distribution: New Guinea. A generally scarce resident in montane parts of West Papua.

WHITE-SHOULDERED FAIRY-WREN

Malurus alboscapulatus 11 cm F: Maluridae

Description: Distinguished from the male of the sympatric Pied Bush-chat (Turdidae) by its much smaller size and black (not white) rump, which shows best in flight.

Voice: Vocal; a frequent, soft twitter and chattering.

Habits: Found in savanna grassland, cleared forest, cultivated fields and along overgrown roadsides. Usually occurs from sea level to lower montane plateaus. Recorded to 3,000 m. This restless skulker sometimes perches briefly on an open twig while calling. The universal habit of hunting and stone throwing in West Papua has made all the birds near villages extremely wary and difficult to approach, even this abundant species.

Distribution: New Guinea. A widespread and common resident throughout West Papua.

BECCARI'S SCRUB-WREN

Sericornis beccarii 11 cm F: Acanthizidae

Description: Distinguished with difficulty from the sympatric Large Scrub-wren, *S. nouhuysi,* by spots on flanks seen well from this angle. Photo shows the montane subspecies that is treated by Beehler (1986) as a separate species, the Perplexing Scrub-wren, *S. virgatus.*

Voice: A high-pitched short song and a dry chip while feeding.

Habits: A peculiar member of this heterogeneous family that lives in the Trans-Fly region, in extreme lowland rainforest, often near rivers. In the Vogelkop and Snow Mountains, it is a lower montane bird found in wet moss forest from 600 to 1,500 m elevation. Feeds somewhat like a nuthatch by moving slowly along, low on tree trunks and creepers.

Distribution: From New Guinea into Cape York Peninsula, Australia. A widespread but generally scarce resident in West Papua, including Aru and Yapen islands.

VOGELKOP SCRUB-WREN

Sericornis rufescens 10 cm F: Acanthizidae

Description: Distinguished from other scrub-wrens by its tiny size and pale olive (not brown) plumage; also note pale eye-ring.

Voice: Vocal; a thin, whistling song and a frequent *chee-chee* while feeding.

Habits: Recorded from the Arfak, Tamrau and Kumawa mountains on the Vogelkop peninsula, where it is restricted to altitudes between 1,300 and 1,800 m. It is quite numerous within this small area. Moves through primary forest in small groups, often mixing with other species in bird waves. Feeds restlessly, searching the leaves and thin branches in the lower canopy and middle storey for insects and larvae.

Distribution: Indonesian endemic. A locally fairly common resident in the Vogelkop region of West Papua only.

PAPUAN SCRUB-WREN

Sericornis papuensis 11 cm F: Acanthizidae

Description: Distinguished with difficulty from other scrub-wrens by its greyish cheeks contrasting with a buff crown.

Voice: A loud chipping series.

Habits: This is a strictly montane forest bird found mainly in the upper montane zone, from 2,100 m upwards to the tree limit at 3,500 m. Observed occasionally down to 1,700 m. Moves low through primary forest and along forest edges, gleaning insects from small leaves and stems. Always on the go. Unrestricted views are rare.

Morten Strange

Distribution: New Guinea. A fairly common resident in the upper montane parts of central West Papua.

GREEN-BACKED GERYGONE

Gerygone chloronotus 9 cm F: Acanthizidae

Description: The distinctive combination of a grey head and greenish back is diagnostic.

Voice: A thin, trilling song of 4–6 ascending notes.

Habits: A forest bird found in the lowland and lower montane forest. In the southern part of its range, in riverine forest and drought deciduous coastal woodlands, it often occurs near water. Further north it is found mainly in tall primary rainforest and forest edges. This small bird moves high in the canopies of large trees and good views are difficult. It sometimes comes lower near clearings and edges, where it hops among the outer branches searching through the foliage for small invertebrates.

Morten Strange

Distribution: New Guinea into northern Australia. A widespread but scarce resident in West Papua, including Waigeo and Aru Islands.

FLYEATER (Golden-bellied Gerygone)

Gerygone sulphurea 9 cm F: Acanthizidae

Distribution: Southeast Asia. A widespread and generally common resident in Sumatra, Kalimantan, Java, Bali, Flores, Alor and Sulawesi.

Description: Yellow breast and throat, and contrasting grey face are distinctive. Taxonomic dispute over family: C&B (1997) uses family Pardalotidae; M&P (1993) family Sylviidae; here follows Andrew (1992).

Voice: Vocal; a frequent, wheezy song, usually a descending *zwee-zwee-zwee*.

Habits: Found in a variety of wooded habitats, from mangroves, open coastal woodlands, roadsides and parks to closed forest. Occurs mainly in the lowlands—on Sumatra to 1,000 m and on Sulawesi to 2,300 m. Moves through the upper and middle storeys, picking invertebrates from the thin branches.

PLAIN GERYGONE (Plain Fairy Warbler)

Gerygone inornatus 10 cm F: Acanthizidae

Distribution: Indonesian endemic. A widespread and locally fairly common resident on Timor and nearby smaller islands of Sawu, Roti and Wetar.

Description: Dark greyish upperparts contrast sharply with white underparts. Its yellow iris is also distinctive.

Voice: Vocal; a distinctive series of 16–18 descending, whistling notes.

Habits: A forest bird that is found in the mangroves and drought deciduous coastal woodlands typical of this region, as well as in the wetter montane forest. Occurs from sea level inland to 2,500 m. Moves in the canopies and middle storey of large trees and also in nearby scrub. Never numerous, but once its call is learned, it is quickly recognised as one of the characteristic sounds of the Timor forest habitat.

BROWN-BREASTED GERYGONE

Gerygone ruficollis 10 cm F: Acanthizidae

Description: Distinguished from the sympatric Grey Gerygone, *G. cinerea*, by its brown (not grey) upperparts and brown (not white) breast.

Voice: A high-pitched series of descending, then whistling notes.

Habits: Habits: Found in tall lower montane rainforest and in stunted upper montane growth, up to the last bushes before the tree line at 3,500 m. Here it is usually the most numerous small song bird. (The Grey Gerygone reaches only 2,700 m.) Extends down to 1,400 m, and is occasionally seen at 1,000 m. Skulks low in isolated bushes in alpine patches; also frequents canopies in tall forest, forest edges, and nearby scrub and cultivated areas.

Morten Strange

Distribution: New Guinea. A locally fairly common resident in montane parts of West Papua.

RUFOUS-WINGED FLYCATCHER

Philentoma pyrhopterum 18 cm F: Monarchidae

Description: Note pale blue head, chest and mantle of the male shown in photo. The female has rufous wings and tail.

Voice: A soft, two-note whistle; also a harsher alarm call.

Habits: A forest bird found in primary forest and closed mature secondary forest. Occurs mainly in the lowlands, although observed occasionally up to 900 m in Sumatra and 1,500 m in Kalimantan. A regular species in the right habitat, but occurs in small numbers. Usually spotted in the middle storey, flying out to catch insects in the open space below the canopy. Often seen in resident pairs.

Morten Strange

Distribution: Sunda subregion. A generally scarce resident in Sumatra and Kalimantan.

BLACK-NAPED MONARCH

Hypothymis azurea 16 cm m F: Monarchidae

Description: Note the bright blue upperparts with black stripe across chest, and small black spot on top of head of this male. The female is duller and lacks black markings.

Voice: A ringing *pwee-pwee-pwee*.

Habits: Frequents a variety of wooded habitats, from wet primary rainforest in the Sunda subregion to deciduous forest and secondary growth in eastern Indonesia. Found from the coast into lower montane elevations at 1,200 m. Moves quickly from perch to perch in the lower to lower middle storey, often with other insectivorous species in bird waves.

Distribution: Oriental region. A widespread and locally fairly common resident in Sumatra, Kalimantan, Java, Bali, Lombok, Sumbawa, Flores, Alor, Sulawesi, Banggai, Sula and many smaller adjacent islands.

ASIAN PARADISE-FLYCATCHER

Terpsiphone paradisi 22 cm + tail F: Monarchidae

Description: Unmistakable in Indonesia. Photo shows female; male has elongated tail (20-25 cm). Some males have a white body and tail.

Voice: A whistling song and a loud *chee-tew* call.

Habits: Found in all kinds of arboreal habitats, from primary lowland rainforest to more open deciduous monsoon forest in eastern Indonesia. Perches in the middle storey or at the edge of the forest and sallies out for flying insects. The flying white morph male, with elongated tail, gives a peculiar, small ghost-like appearance.

Distribution: Central and East Asia, and the Oriental region. A locally fairly common resident in Sumatra, Kalimantan, Java, Sumbawa, Flores, Alor and Sumba.

WHITE-NAPED MONARCH

Monarcha pileatus 15 cm F: Monarchidae

Description: Note the diagnostic white side of head with black eye-stripe. Black wings have a broad white band.

Voice: A series of chattering and harsher notes.

Habits: A forest bird found in primary forest as well as disturbed forest and edges. Occurs mainly in the lowlands and locally up to 700 m. Moves steadily along, fairly high in the trees, gleaning insects. Often seen together with other species in mixed flocks. Otherwise little studied.

Distribution: Indonesian endemic. A locally fairly common resident on Halmahera, Buru and the Tanimbar islands.

Morten Strange

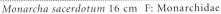

FLORES MONARCH

Monarcha sacerdotum 16 cm F: Monarchidae

Description: Very similar to the following species, but the rufous colour on breast is replaced with white.

Voice: A single, distinctive, clear, ascending whistle; also some soft, harsher notes.

Habits: Found in primary rainforest, in a narrow zone from 400 to 1,000 m; occurs mainly from 700 to 900 m. For many years (since discovery in 1971) it was only known to occur in the remote Tanjung Kerita Mese forest in southwest Flores. During field surveys in 1998, it was also recorded from the Puarldo Tele Tower forest. Skulks in the lower middle storey of closed forest, but does respond to an imitation of its call.

Distribution: Indonesian endemic. A generally scarce resident on Flores only. Endangered with global extinction.

Morten Strange

SPECTACLED MONARCH

Monarcha trivirgatus 16 cm F: Monarchidae

Description: Note diagnostic black mask and throat.

Voice: A series of rasping notes.

Habits: An arboreal bird found in primary and logged forest, from the lowlands locally on some islands into lower montane elevations. Actively moves through the middle or lower storeys of the forest, gleaning insects from the foliage, sometimes alone and sometimes with other species in bird waves.

Distribution: Australasia. A locally fairly common resident in parts of Wallacea; migrants from Australia reach West Papua.

SHINING FLYCATCHER

Piezorhynchus alecto 17 cm F: Monarchidae

Description: The male, shown in photo, is the only black flycatcher throughout most of its range. The female has rufous upperparts and tail, and white underparts.

Voice: A variety of whistling and harsher notes.

Habits: An arboreal bird found in lowland rainforest and drought deciduous woodlands. Occurs often at sea level, in mangroves and coastal and riverine forest, and inland to 500 m. Seen rarely up to 1,200 m. Moves low, catching flying insects in the middle storey or lower. Sometimes drops down onto the mud to pick up prey.

Distribution: New Guinea into northern Australia. A widespread but generally scarce resident in West Papua and on most nearby islands.

BLACK-BREASTED BOATBILL

Machaerirhynchus nigripectus 14 cm F: Monarchidae

Description: Unmistakable; the similar Yellow-breasted Boatbill, *M. flaviventer*, lacks black spot on breast and replaces this species below 800 m elevation. Together they form their own genus.

Voice: A buzzing, descending *swe bzzbzzbzz*.

Habits: A strictly montane species found in primary forest at altitudes from 1,300 to 3,000 m. The Yellow-breasted Boatbill is less common in lowland forest and found on islands. Both move through the middle storey in tall forest, darting out to grab small insects. They also come lower into thickets near trails and clearings, sometimes raising their tails while fluttering restlessly about.

Distribution: New Guinea. A locally fairly common resident in montane parts of West Papua.

LOWLAND PELTOPS

Peltops blainvillii 19 cm F: Monarchidae

Description: Almost identical to the Mountain Peltops, *P. montanus*. Best distinguished by call. Together they form a separate genus. Beehler et al. (1986) place it under F: Cracticidae.

Voice: A series of sharp clicks lasting 4–5 seconds. The montane species has a very different musical whistle: *tit tit tit*.

Habits: Both species are found in tall rainforest, often perching high at the edge of primary forest near an opening, road or river bank. This species occurs from sea level to 600 m, and the Mountain Peltops occurs from 600 to 3,000 m, but they might overlap. This conspicuous bird flies out from an exposed branch to catch flying insects. The montane species may be more numerous.

Distribution: New Guinea. A generally uncommon resident in West Papua and nearby Misool, Salawati and Waigeo islands.

RUFOUS-TAILED FANTAIL
Rhipidura phoenicura 18 cm F: Rhipiduridae

Distribution: Indonesian endemic. A locally fairly common resident in montane parts of Java only.

Description: Note the diagnostic rufous tail, lower back and vent. Andrew (1992) places the fantails with Monarchidae; M&P (1993) with Muscicapidae. Here they are placed in their own family: Rhipiduridae, following Beehler (1986) and C&B (1997).

Voice: A squeaky whistle.

Habits: A montane species found only in forest at altitudes from 1,000 to 2,500 m. Moves fairly low in the thick undergrowth of primary forest and along forest edges, fluttering restlessly about and fanning its tail. Gunung Gede National Park, where this rare photograph was taken, is a good place to find it. Note the delicately constructed nesting cup typical of the family.

WHITE-THROATED FANTAIL
Rhipidura albicollis 19 cm F: Rhipiduridae

Distribution: Oriental region. A common resident in montane parts of Sumatra and Kalimantan.

Description: Distinguished from other fantails by its black underparts that contrast with a white throat. The similar White-bellied Fantail, *R. euryura*, replaces this species as an uncommon montane endemic on Java.

Voice: A whistling, descending song; also frequently a harsh *cheet*.

Habits: Strictly montane. Found in forest between 900 and 2,400 m. A restless and vocal bird that flutters through the middle storey, often fanning its tail and never staying long in one spot. Numerous in the right location and an inevitable member of montane bird waves.

PIED FANTAIL

Rhipidura javanica 18 cm F: Rhipiduridae

Description: Distinguished from the White-bellied Fantail, *R. euryura*, by its white (not dark) throat and dark grey chest band separating its white belly.

Voice: A penetrating, metallic squeak.

Habits: Found in a variety of coastal woodland habitats, from mangroves and forest edges to scrub and rural gardens. On Sumatra occurs inland to 900 m. Jumps restlessly through the lower storey of the vegetation, calling and fanning its tail. Makes short flights into the next cover. Easily agitated and often seen chasing other birds from its territory.

Morten Strange

Distribution: Southeast Asia. A widespread and common resident in Sumatra, Kalimantan, Java and Bali; one record from Lombok.

WILLIE WAGTAIL

Rhipidura leucophrys 20 cm F: Rhipiduridae

Description: Unmistakable. Note the black upperparts contrasting with white belly and prominent supercilium.

Voice: A squeaky, irregular, whistling chatter.

Habits: Found in disturbed woodlands and open country, usually near a river or swampy area. Occurs mainly near the coast at sea level; occasionally inland up to 1,200 m. This tolerant species is often found near villages and road sides, where it flutters about on or near the ground. In spite of its name, it is in no way related to pipits and wagtails. Sways its tail constantly and deliberately from side to side, unlike the other members of its family, which fan their tails.

Morten Strange

Distribution: Australasia; occurs from eastern Indonesia into all of Australia. A generally fairly common resident in Maluku and West Papua and nearby islands.

NORTHERN FANTAIL
Rhipidura rufiventris 18 cm F: Rhipiduridae

Description: A fairly nondescript brownish-grey fantail. Its plumage is somewhat variable; some birds have a dark breast band. Photo shows Timor subspecies.

Voice: A varied series of melodious, high-pitched whistles.

Habits: An adaptable species found in both primary forest and forest edges. Also moves into nearby scrub and wooded cultivated areas, from the lowlands to 1,500 m in West Papua; occurs to 2,000 m on Timor. Numerous in some areas, less so in others. Moves though the middle storey, sometimes dropping down to eye-level. Generally more lethargic than other members of its family.

Distribution: Australasia, from eastern Indonesia into northern Australia. A widespread and locally common resident in eastern Maluku, Nusa Tenggara, and West Papua and nearby islands.

BROWN-CAPPED FANTAIL
Rhipidura diluta 17 cm F: Rhipiduridae

Description: Unmistakable on Sumbawa where it is the only fantail. On Flores, it is distinguished from the Rufous Fantail by a lack of breast band.

Voice: A series of soft and scratchy whistling notes.

Habits: Found in the semi-deciduous primary forest typical of these islands. Also seen along forest edges and occasionally in nearby scrub. Occurs mainly in hill forest; on Flores primarily from 1,000 to 2,100 m elevation. Moves in the low canopies and sometimes drops down near the ground to feed on insects, as shown in the photo.

Distribution: Indonesian endemic. A locally common resident on Sumbawa, Flores and nearby smaller Lomblen.

CINNAMON-TAILED FANTAIL

Rhipidura fuscorufa 18 cm F: Rhipiduridae

Description: Distinguished from the less common Long-tailed Fantail, *R. opistherythra,* endemic to Tanimbar, by its dark (not pale) brown head and mantle, dark belly, and distinct rufous stripe in wing.

Voice: Soft whistling notes.

Habits: Found in forest, along forest edges, in mangroves and near habitation. Typically moves in the middle storey, but also flies into canopies and low to the ground, hawking for flying insects in the air and gleaning them from the foliage. Sometimes seen with other species in bird waves.

Filip Verbelen

Distribution: Indonesian endemic. A locally fairly common resident on Babar and Tanimbar Islands.

FRIENDLY FANTAIL

Rhipidura albolimbata 15 cm F: Rhipiduridae

Description: Distinguished from the male of the sympatric Black Fantail, *R. atra*, by white patches on its wings, belly and throat.

Voice: A series of rising and falling whistling notes.

Habits: A strictly montane fantail found from 1,750 m up to the end of the vegetation in the Snow Mountains. Occurs on the Vogelkop Peninsula down to 1,400 m. Locally numerous at the higher elevations. Moves through the middle storey of primary forest and lower at the edges of stunted moss forest and alpine bushes. An attractive and confiding species that often sits on the same perch, sallying out for insects.

Morten Strange

Distribution: New Guinea. A common resident in montane parts of West Papua.

DIMORPHIC FANTAIL

Rhipidura brachyrhyncha 16 cm F: Rhipiduridae

Description: Distinguished with some difficulty from the female of the sympatric Black Fantail, *R. atra*, by its grey-brown (not bright rufous) underparts and all-rufous tip of tail (lacks black centre feathers).

Voice: A squeaky, tinkling whistle.

Habits: Found mainly in tall dense primary forest from 1,700 to 3,000 m. Occurs occasionally down to 1,400 m. Moves through the lower middle storey and is extremely restless, never seeming to stay in one place for more than a few seconds. Drops its wings and fans its tail as it flutters about, stirring up and catching tiny insects.

Distribution: New Guinea. A fairly common resident in montane parts of West Papua.

RUFOUS FANTAIL

Rhipidura rufifrons 16 cm F: Rhipiduridae

Description: The distinctive black upper breast band and contrasting white throat are diagnostic within its range. Its rufous rump flashes as it flies away.

Voice: A series of high-pitched, descending notes.

Habits: Occurs in a variety of wooded habitats and is especially numerous in coastal forest and mangroves on smaller offshore islands. Also found inland on larger islands, to montane elevations of 2,000 m, but in lower densities. Prefers low forest with dense undergrowth and scrub, where it hops restlessly about, often close to the ground. Can suddenly fly high into a nearby canopy.

Distribution: Australasia; occurs from eastern Indonesia into southern Australia; Australian birds migrate north reaching Trans-Fly region in West Papua. A widespread and locally fairly common resident in Maluku and Nusa Tenggara.

LEMON-BELLIED FLYCATCHER
Microeca flavigaster 12 cm F: Petroicidae

Description: Distinguished from the similar Olive Flycatcher, *M. flavovirescens,* that occurs in dense rainforest, by its pale throat and habits.

Voice: A melodious, varied song with repeated phrases. Sometimes performs a distinctive circling song-flight.

Habits: Occurs in the open lowland savanna woodlands typical of the Trans-Fly region, mainly in coastal areas or near water. Sometimes moves into nearby cultivated areas. Perches in the middle storey of open trees and flies out to catch insects in the air.

Martin Hale

Distribution: New Guinea into northern Australia. A widespread and locally fairly common resident in southern parts of West Papua.

CANARY FLYCATCHER (Canary Fly-robin)
Microeca papuana 12 cm F: Petroicidae

Description: Distinguished with some difficulty from the sympatric Yellow-legged Flycatcher, *M. griseoceps*, by its yellow (not whitish) throat, and olive (not greyish) head and mantle.

Voice: A tinkling, descending warble; also a weak *tseet* call note.

Habits: This strictly montane bird is found in upper montane rainforest, from 1,750 m up to the tree line at 3,500 m; rarer to 1,400 m. Fairly inconspicuous. Moves about high in the canopies or in the middle storey of primary forest near clearings. Sometimes seen lower. Flies out into the clearing or open space below the canopy to hawk for insects. Sometimes sits on a high perch singing softly.

Morten Strange

Distribution: New Guinea. A fairly common resident in montane parts of West Papua.

GARNET ROBIN
Eugerygone rubra 11 cm F: Petroicidae

Description: Unmistakable; a unique, monotypic genus. Photo shows female; male has red (not olive green) upperparts.

Voice: A rising and falling series of high notes.

Habits: Found only in primary rainforest between 1,400 and 3,600 m, mainly in the rich upper montane zone between 1,800 and 2,500 m. Appears to be a low-density species. Occasionally located by its call. Moves from ground level into the lower middle storey. Usually flits about, inside cover like a warbler, pausing briefly then quickly shifting to another perch. Often seen near other birds, but is shy and elusive; good views are difficult.

Distribution: New Guinea. A generally scarce resident in montane parts of West Papua.

MOUNTAIN ROBIN (Alpine Robin)
Petroica bivittata 11 cm F: Petroicidae

Description: Distinguished from the next species by its white belly and lack of white in wing.

Voice: A loud, chirping note.

Habits: Restricted to tall upper montane moss forest and stunted alpine growth at the tree limit from 2,700 to 3,500 m. Perches in the middle storey or near the ground, often in resident pairs. This somewhat lethargic species sits in one place for long periods at a time, eventually darting out to catch small insects.

Distribution: New Guinea. A locally fairly common resident in the central mountain ranges of West Papua.

WHITE-WINGED ROBIN

Peneothello sigillatus 14 cm F: Petroicidae

Description: Note its diagnostic white wing patch; Papua New Guinea birds do not have the white shoulder patch.

Voice: A trilling whistle.

Habits: A strictly upper montane bird that occurs in the high parts of the Snow and Star Mountains, from 2,500 m up to the tree limit, and occasionally down to 2,100 m. Found low inside the tall moss forest or further up in the stunted alpine growth; sometimes moves out onto the ground in nearby meadows to catch insects. Usually flies quickly from one low perch to the next, grabbing insects; sometimes sits briefly on tree trunks and rocks.

Morten Strange

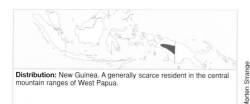

Distribution: New Guinea. A generally scarce resident in the central mountain ranges of West Papua.

BLUE-GREY ROBIN

Peneothello cyanus 15 cm F: Petroicidae

Description: Distinguished from the dark whistlers and pitohuis by its small size and thin bill. In the Vogelkop area, distinguished from the Indonesian endemic, the Smoky Robin, *P. cryptoleucus*, by its uniformly bluish black plumage. (The Smoky Robin has a slaty-grey plumage with pale underparts.)

Voice: A loud and penetrating *teeder teeder teeder*; also some trilling, musical notes.

Habits: This forest bird is found in primary tall moss forest and nearby edges. Occurs in the montane zone between 1,000 and 2,700 m, but is seen mainly between 1,500 and 2,200 m. This low-density species is extremely shy and prefers to stay in dense cover in the lower or lower middle storey.

Morten Strange

Distribution: New Guinea. A generally scarce resident in montane parts of West Papua.

YELLOW-FLANKED WHISTLER (Olive-flanked Whistler)

Hylocitrea bonensis 16 cm F: Pachycephalidae

Description: Note the dark olive plumage and yellow flanks of this male. The female has heavy yellowish streaks on throat. The sympatric, rarer Maroon-backer Whistler, *Corocornis raveni*, is brown (female) and black with maroon wings (male).

Voice: Often quiet; sometimes a thin, buzzing song and a louder, piping call.

Habits: A montane forest bird found from 1,200 m to the highest summits of the island at around 3,500 m. Most numerous at the higher elevations above 2,000 m. Moves inconspicuously through the middle storey of the forest, often with other birds in bird waves, feeding on small berries and invertebrates.

B. Van Eliegem

Distribution: Indonesian endemic. A locally fairly common resident on Sulawesi only.

RUFOUS-NAPED WHISTLER

Pachycephala rufinucha 17 cm F: Pachycephalidae

Description: Note rufous head and yellowish underparts. Sometimes placed in the monotypic genus *Aleadryas*.

Voice: A distinctive, harsh *shhhk*; also a clear, whistling song.

Habits: A strictly montane bird found in primary forest between 1,400 and 3,500 m, mainly in the upper montane zone from 1,800 to 2,600 m. Also seen along forest edges and near trails and clearings. Has the peculiar habit (for an arboreal forest bird) of dropping down onto the ground and hopping about like a finch. Also perches high in the middle storey or at canopy level. Feeds on both insects and small fruits.

Morten Strange

Distribution: New Guinea. A generally scarce resident in montane parts of West Papua.

BORNEAN WHISTLER

Pachycephala hypoxantha 16 cm F: Pachycephalidae

Description: Unmistakable; note its chunky build, and olive upperparts. Underparts are bright yellow.

Voice: An intermittent, loud song.

Habits: A strictly montane forest bird found in rainforest from 900 to 2,000 m. Occurs mainly in closed undisturbed forest, but is also occasionally seen along forest edges. Perches in the middle storey and flies out to glean invertebrates from the foliage. Often seen mixing with other species in bird waves.

Morten Strange

Distribution: Borneo endemic. In Indonesia, a locally fairly common resident in montane parts of Kalimantan.

YELLOW-VENTED WHISTLER (Sulphur-bellied Whistler)

Pachycephala sulfuriventer 15 cm F: Pachycephalidae

Description: Note the diagnostic pale underparts and yellow vent seen well from this angle.

Voice: A short series of rapid whistles, with an emphasised ending.

Habits: Found in forest, mainly at lower montane elevations from 800 to 2,000 m; rarely observed at sea level and occasionally to 2,500 m. Moves fairly elaborately through the middle storey below the canopies and is sometimes seen at eye-level. Hops about from branch to branch, often with other birds, frequently calling and generally quite easy to observe.

B. Van Elegem

Distribution: Indonesian endemic. A generally fairly common resident on Sulawesi only.

VOGELKOP WHISTLER

Pachycephala meyeri 15 cm F: Pachycephalidae

Description: Note pale grey breast patch contrasting with white throat. The female sympatric Sclater's Whistler, *P. soror*, has a dark breast band. The female Regent Whistler, *P. schlegelii*, is similar, but has a dark breast and occurs at higher altitudes.

Voice: A descending series of soft, clear whistles with an abrupt ending.

Habits: Found in dense montane rainforest, in a narrow range between 1,000 and 1,500 m. This small distribution species hops about inconspicuously in the middle storey, or lower around clearings and edges, gleaning insects from the foliage. In the right habitat can be quite predictable, but in general only seems to occur in low densities.

Morten Strange

Distribution: Indonesian endemic. A locally fairly common resident in montane parts of the Vogelkop Peninsula of West Papua only. Near-threatened with global extinction.

FAWN-BREASTED WHISTLER

Pachycephala orpheus 14 cm F: Pachycephalidae

Description: Unmistakable, except for the next distinct species, the only whistler within its range.

Voice: A series of 10–16 clear, whistling notes that terminate abruptly.

Habits: Found in coastal wooded areas and in drought decidous forest, in primary undisturbed areas and at forest edges near roads and clearings. Occurs from the lowlands into lower montane elevations at 1,200 m. Moves in the middle storey, but is also often seen lower near eye-level, hopping sluggishly around the undergrowth, picking up invertebrates. Easy to observe.

Morten Strange

Distribution: Indonesian endemic. A widespread and locally common resident on Timor and the nearby smaller Semau, Jaco and Wetar islands. Near-threatened with global extinction.

COMMON GOLDEN WHISTLER (Golden Whistler)
Pachycephala pectoralis 16 cm F: Pachycephalidae

Description: The male, shown in photo, is unmistakable within its range. The female is a nondescript brownish colour with whitish underparts.

Voice: Three to four clear and penetrating whistling notes. The male sings loudly from a hidden perch.

Habits: An adaptable bird with many subspecies. Found in a variety of wooded habitats, from primary forest to dry woodlands and cultivated areas. Occurs from the lowlands to lower montane elevations; on Timor recorded at 2,100 m. Occasionally seen moving through the forest, low or in the middle storey, sometimes with other birds in mixed flocks.

Distribution: Australasia, from east Java into south Australia. A local and uncommon resident on Java and Bali; widespread and fairly common in parts of Wallacea; local in montane parts of West Papua.

BARE-THROATED WHISTLER
Pachycephala nudigula 19 cm F: Pachycephalidae

Description: Unmistakable. The male (top) has a bare red throat; the female (bottom) has a grey head, bright white throat and pale yellowish breast and belly.

Voice: An unmistakable, powerful song of nightingale quality that carries for a kilometre.

Habits: Found in elevated forested areas between 200 and 2,000 m. Especially numerous from 1,200 to 1,800 m. The Ruteng and Kali Mutu areas in Flores are good places to find this bird. Each morning from 6 to 7 am, many males call from all directions. At other times this bird is inconspicuous and more difficult to find, as it moves quietly though the middle storey of dense forest.

Distribution: Indonesian endemic. A locally common resident on Sumbawa and Flores only.

LORENTZ'S WHISTLER

Pachycephala lorentzi 16 cm F: Pachycephalidae

Description: Note the diagnostic full pale grey throat and breast seen well from this angle.

Voice: A small series of clear whistles.

Habits: Found only in upper montane forest between 1,800 and 3,500 m, in tall moss forest and high stunted alpine vegetation near the tree limit. Seems to be a low-density species. Moves through the middle storey. Seems somewhat more agile and active than some other members of this family.

Distribution: New Guinea. A generally scarce resident in the central mountain ranges of the Snow and Star mountains of West Papua.

LITTLE SHRIKE-THRUSH

Colluricincla megarhyncha 18 cm F: Pachycephalidae

Description: Plumage somewhat variable; most birds are a nondescript brown as shown here, although the birds in the northwest are greyer. Distinguished with difficulty from the Rusty Pitohui, *Pitohui ferrugineus*, by its dark iris and pale bill.

Voice: A low *too-ee, what-what-what*; also a distinctive *dyoong* call note.

Habits: Occurs in forest and along forest edges, from coastal lowlands up to 1,400 m. Seen rarely to 2,100 m. Moves across the entire strata of the forest, from the ground to the canopy. Numerous in some areas, but rarely seen in others. Generally shy and skulking, so good views are difficult.

Distribution: New Guinea into northern Australasia. A widespread and locally fairly common resident in West Papua.

GREAT TIT

Parus major 13 cm F: Paridae

Description: Unmistakable. The only member of its family in Indonesia. Note the white cheeks contrasting with black head and chest.

Voice: A high-pitched, penetrating *chee-wit*.

Habits: In Kalimantan this bird is restricted to coastal mangroves and prefers tidal areas facing the sea front. In the rest of Indonesia it occurs in open woodlands and along forest edges inland to 2,700 m on Sumatra and to 2,400 m on Lombok. Seen in small trees, from the canopy down to eye-level, constantly clambering about on the thin branches feeding on insects and small fruits and seeds.

Morten Strange

Distribution: Eurasia and the Oriental region. A widespread and fairly common resident on Sumatra, Java and Bali; locally common in south Kalimantan only and parts of Nusa Tenggara.

VELVET-FRONTED NUTHATCH

Sitta frontalis 12 cm F: Sittidae

Description: Unmistakable in Indonesia. The male has a black eye-brow that is missing in the female shown in the photo.

Voice: A sharp, ringing *chih-chih*.

Habits: Found in low densities in rainforest, from the lowlands to lower montane elevations; on Sumatra recorded at 1,500 m. Prefers closed forest with large trees, but also feeds in nearby cultivation. A very agile climber that runs up and down branches and trunks with amazing speed and ease, gleaning insects from the bark as shown in the photo. Flies quickly to the next tree. Often seen with other insectivorous birds in bird waves.

Morten Strange

Distribution: Oriental region. A widespread but generally scarce resident in Sumatra, Kalimantan and Java.

BLUE NUTHATCH

Sitta azrea 13 cm F: Sittidae

Description: Unmistakable. Dark blue upperparts appear black in poor light; belly is snow-white.

Voice: A high-pitched, squeaky *chee-chee*.

Habits: Restricted to montane forest between 900 and 2,400 m. Often seen in favourite montane habitats around Gunung Kerinci, in Sumatra and Gunung Gede, in Java. This bird is always on the go, running in quick jerks up and down branches, often upside down, probing for tiny invertebrates. A certain fixture in montane bird waves, but quickly moves on out of sight.

Distribution: Sunda subregion. A locally common resident in montane parts of Sumatra and Java.

PAPUAN TREECREEPER

Cormobates placens 15 cm F: Climacteridae

Description: Note shape, posture and dark wings that contrast with streaked underparts. Photo shows female; male is duller and without red malar stripe.

Voice: An ascending series of whistling notes: *du du du du*.

Habits: Found only in montane forest between 1,200 and 2,600 m. Restricted to closed primary forest with tall trees, where it feeds by clinging vertically to the tree trunk, as shown in the photo. Often seen in resident pairs. This bird is quick and shy, so good views are difficult.

Distribution: New Guinea. A generally scarce resident in montane parts of West Papua.

FAN-TAILED BERRYPECKER
Melanocharis versteri 15 cm F: Dicaeidae

Description: Male shown in photo; female is a dark olive colour and has paler underparts. Distinguished from the lower montane Mid-mountain Berrypecker, *M. longicauda*, by its grey (not yellowish) underparts and longer tail. Placed in this heterogeneous family although very different from flowerpeckers.

Voice: A variety of harsh and squeaky notes.

Habits: Found in upper montane forest from 1,800 to 3,500 m. Occasionally occurs down to 1,400 m. May overlap locally with the Mid-mountain Berrypecker. Moves through the middle storey of moss forest in a characteristic fluttering and acrobatic manner, sometimes flying lower to pick up insects or small fruits.

Morten Strange

Distribution: New Guinea. A generally scarce resident in montane parts of West Papua.

YELLOW-BREASTED FLOWERPECKER
Prionochilus maculatus 10 cm F: Dicaeidae

Description: Note the diagnostic dark streaks on its yellow breast and its small orange crown. The sexes are similar.

Voice: Metallic clicks and a softer *tsweet-tsweet*.

Habits: Found in rainforest, from the lowlands into lower montane elevations; on Sumatra recorded at 1,500 m. Frequents primary forest, secondary forest and nearby scrub. Flits about quickly on flowering and fruiting trees and bushes, from the canopies down to eye-level. Often seen feeding with other flowerpeckers on mistletoe plants.

Morten Strange

Distribution: Sunda subregion. A locally fairly common resident in Kalimantan, but generally scarce there and on Sumatra.

CRIMSON-BREASTED FLOWERPECKER

Prionochilus percussus 10 cm F: Dicaeidae

Description: Look for diagnostic red patch on breast of male (see photo). The similar Yellow-rumped Flowerpecker, *P. xanthopygius*, endemic to Borneo, has a smaller patch and a yellow rump. The female is olive green with a yellow stripe down its belly.

Voice: Similar to the voice of other flowerpeckers.

Habits: Found in rainforest and along forest edges, mainly in the lowlands. Occurs on Sumatra to 1,000 m. A low-density forest bird, not really numerous anywhere within its range; little studied. Occasionally seen moving quickly through the middle storey, sometimes moving low near trails to feed on flowering or fruiting trees.

Distribution: Sunda subregion. A generally scarce resident on Sumatra; rare in Java and southern Kalimantan.

SCARLET-BREASTED FLOWERPECKER

Prionochilus thoracicus 10 cm F: Dicaeidae

Description: The male, shown in photo, is distinguished from other flowerpeckers by its black head and red patch on black breast. The female lacks black patterns, but has a reddish tinge on breast.

Voice: Metallic clicks, typical of the family.

Habits: This lowland rainforest bird can be found in primary as well as mature secondary forest. This low-density species prefers closed forest and does not visit trails and forest edges like some other members of this family. Occasionally spotted high in the middle or upper storeys, feeding mainly on small fruits, insects and some nectar.

Distribution: Sunda subregion. A rare resident on Sumatra; more numerous in Kalimantan, but generally few records.

GOLDEN-RUMPED FLOWERPECKER

Dicaeum annae 10 cm F: Dicaeidae

Description: Distinguished from the overlapping, rarer Thick-billed Flowerpecker, *D. agile*, occurring in the Oriental region by its yellowish (not white) underparts. Its yellow rump is difficult to see in the field.

Voice: A thin *seee*.

Habits: Found in a variety of wooded habitats, from sea level up to 1,800 m. Appears to be most numerous in elevated wet primary forest, but is also present in low deciduous woodlands and sometimes in nearby wooded cultivation. Moves quickly around the canopy and middle storey of large trees. Often seen feeding on small fruits in fig trees. Otherwise little is known about this species.

Morten Strange

Distribution: Indonesian endemic. A widespread and locally common resident on Sumbawa and Flores only.

YELLOW-VENTED FLOWERPECKER

Dicaeum chrysorrheum 9 cm F: Dicaeidae

Description: Note the distinctly streaked breast seen well from this angle. The yellow rump is also quite prominent from the side.

Voice: A short high-pitched *dzeep*.

Habits: This forest bird is found mainly along disturbed forest edges and around clearings near denser growth. Occurs from the lowlands up to 700 m on Sumatra and up to 1,400 m in Kalimantan. An active bird that feeds on flowers, small fruits and insects, both high in the trees and at eye level. Although present throughout western Indonesia, there have been few recent sightings. Does not appear to be numerous anywhere.

Distribution: Oriental region. A generally rare resident in Sumatra, Kalimantan, Java and Bali.

Morten Strange

ORANGE-BELLIED FLOWERPECKER

Dicaeum trigonostigma 9 cm F: Dicaeidae

Description: Male (bottom) is unmistakable. Note its bright orange underparts and bluish head and wings. The female (top) is a plain olive colour, with a yellow tinge on the lower belly.

Voice: A frequent metallic *chick*.

Habits: An adaptable forest bird found in dense wooded areas, often near lowland primary rainforest. Usually seen along disturbed edges of forest, logging trails and in nearby cultivation. Moves across the whole strata of the forest in a fast, jerky flight, feeding on small fruits and nectar. The nest is a tiny pouch with a side entrance, suspended from a twig in a tree.

Distribution: Oriental region. A locally fairly common resident in Sumatra, Kalimantan and Java; uncommon on Bali.

FLAME-BREASTED FLOWERPECKER

Dicaeum erythrothorax 9 cm F: Dicaeidae

Description: Unmistakable, the only flowerpecker within its range. Note red patch on grey breast; vent is pale yellow.

Voice: No information available.

Habits: Found in primary and secondary rainforest, along forest edges and in nearby cultivated areas. Moves high, flying quickly from tree to tree and so is not easy to see clearly. Seems to follow bird waves. Otherwise little is known about its feeding and nesting habits.

Distribution: Indonesian endemic. Reported as a common resident on Buru, but otherwise appears scarce within its range, which includes Halmahera, Bacan and Obi islands.

PAPUAN FLOWERPECKER

Dicaeum pectorale 9 cm   F: Dicaeidae

Description: Unmistakable, the only flowerpecker within its range. The male (top) has a red spot on its breast that is missing in the female (bottom).

Voice: Vocal; a weak, dry *buzz* and a frequent high-pitched note.

Habits: A forest bird found mainly in primary low-land and lower montane forest; often seen near forest edges and trails. Occurs occasionally to 2,400 m. Moves high in the tops of large trees, picking up small insects, spiders and fruits. Sometimes comes lower briefly, but good views of this restless bird are difficult to obtain.

Distribution: New Guinea. A widespread and generally fairly common resident all through West Papua and most adjacent islands.

BLACK-FRONTED FLOWERPECKER

Dicaeum igniferum 9 cm   F: Dicaeidae

Description: Unmistakable within its range, except on Flores where the montane Blood-breasted Flowerpecker might overlap above 1,100 m. Distinguished from that species by its red (not blue) crown. Photo shows male; female has white underparts.

Voice: A descending series of thin notes.

Habits: A fairly adaptable forest bird found in a variety of wooded habitats, from coastal deciduous woodlands and nearby cultivated areas, to wetter closed forest in the hills. Recorded to 1,200 m. Feeds actively in fruiting and flowering trees, often mixing with other species such as sunbirds, honeyeaters, white-eyes and parrots.

Distribution: Indonesian endemic. A locally fairly common resident on Sumbawa, Flores and the nearby smaller islands of Komodo, Lomblen, Besar, Pantar and Alor.

RED-CHESTED FLOWERPECKER

Dicaeum maugei 10 cm F: Dicaeidae

Morten Strange

Description: Unmistakable within its range, except on Timor where the montane Blood-breasted Flowerpecker might overlap above 1,000 m. Male (photo) has blue cap and back, and a red rump. The female has dusky upperparts and whitish underparts.

Voice: A high-pitched, whistled 2–3 notes.

Habits: Found in a variety of wooded habitats, from lowland coastal deciduous forest and nearby cultivation to wetter closed forest at 2,000 m on Lombok. Occurs to 1,200 m on Timor. Usually seen flying quickly about, high in the trees. Often feeds in flowering trees together with other nectar- and insect-eating birds.

Distribution: Indonesian endemic. A widespread and generally common resident on Lombok, Timor and some smaller nearby islands.

BLOOD-BREASTED FLOWERPECKER

Dicaeum sanguinolentum 9 cm F: Dicaeidae

B. Van Elegem

Description: Note bluish upperparts and distinctive breast pattern of the male shown in photo. The female looks much like the Buff-bellied Flowerpecker.

Voice: A series of 4–5 very high-pitched notes.

Habits: Much like the habits of other flowerpeckers. Found in primary forest and along forest edges. Restricted to the montane elevations between 1,000 and 2,400 m, except on Sumba where it faces less competition and also occurs down to sea level. Has also been reported from open woodland and nearby wooded cultivated areas.

Distribution: Indonesian endemic. A locally fairly common resident in montane parts of Java, Bali, Flores and Timor; on Sumba also occurs in the lowlands.

MISTLETOEBIRD

Dicaeum hirundinaceum 9 cm F: Dicaeidae

Description: Unmistakable; the only flowerpecker within its range. Photo shows a male; the female has brown upperparts and white underparts. Closely related to and possibly conspecific with the Blood-breasted and Buff-bellied Flowerpeckers.

Voice: A dry *tick* and a thin, high-pitched chatter.

Habits: Found in a variety of wooded habitats, from forest to nearby open woodlands and cultivated areas, as long as its favourite food source, mistletoe plants, are within easy reach. This busy, agile bird is often difficult to see in the canopy, where only its call might reveal its presence.

Distribution: Indonesian and Australia. A fairly common resident in Kai, Tanimbar and the Aru islands.

C. & D. Frith; Frithfoto

BUFF-BELLIED FLOWERPECKER

Dicaeum ignipectus 9 cm F: Dicaeidae

Description: Note the yellowish buff underparts and dark olive upperparts of the female (photo). The male is much like the Blood-breasted Flowerpecker, but with greenish (not bluish) upperparts.

Voice: Similar to that of other flowerpeckers.

Habits: A strictly montane member of this family; on Sumatra found between 800 and 2,200 m. Fairly regularly seen at Gunung Kerinci and other montane destinations, but occurs in low densities. Found in forest and along forest edges, feeding mainly on mistletoe plants high in the trees.

Distribution: Oriental region. In Indonesia, found only on Sumatra, where it is an uncommon resident.

Morten Strange

SCARLET-BACKED FLOWERPECKER

Dicaeum cruentatum 9 cm F: Dicaeidae

Description: Male (photo) distinguished from other flowerpeckers by its red crown and back. The female is a dull brown, with red vent only. On Java, Bali and Lombok, the Scarlet-headed Flowerpecker, *D. trochileum*, which has a full red head, takes over this niche.

Voice: A frequent metallic *tick*, often in flight.

Habits: Found along forest edges, in open woodlands, and cultivated areas and gardens. Flies from one treetop to the next, often feeding on mistletoe clusters. Difficult to spot, but its clicking call gives it away. An adaptable member of this mainly forest-based family.

Distribution: Oriental region. A widespread and locally fairly common resident in Sumatra and Kalimantan.

CRESTED BERRYPECKER

Paramythia montium 21 cm F: Dicaeidae

Description: Unmistakable, unlike any other bird. The only member of its genus.

Voice: A faint, squeaking note.

Habits: An upper montane forest specialist found in tall primary forest and in stunted alpine trees and low bushes at the highest elevations. Occurs from 2,500 m up to the tree line, but is usually seen at around 3,500 m. Feeds on fruits, small berries and seeds, usually in small active groups. This conspicuous and attractive bird is easy to observe in prime habitat.

Distribution: New Guinea. A fairly common resident in upper montane parts of central West Papua.

BROWN-THROATED SUNBIRD (Plain-throated Sunbird)
Anthreptes malacensis 14 cm F: Nectariniidae

Description: Male (left) distinguished from the following species by its brown throat and metallic-blue shoulder patch. The female (right) is distinguished with difficulty from other female sunbirds by its strong bill and uniformly olive-yellowish plumage.

Voice: A loud, monotonous *chiffchaff*.

Habits: An adaptable sunbird found along forest edges, in rural cultivated areas and mature gardens. Often seen near the coast and on offshore islands. Occurs inland on the larger islands to 1,000 m. Flies from flower to flower late in the morning, feeding on nectar and tiny insects. Visits the same bush day after day.

Distribution: Southeast Asia. A widespread and fairly common resident in the Sunda subregion, including most offshore islands and parts of Wallacea.

RED-THROATED SUNBIRD
Anthreptes rhodolaema 13 cm F: Nectariniidae

Description: Much like the previous species, but note the reddish throat and dull maroon wing patch of this male.

Voice: Typical sunbird-like chirps.

Habits: Found in closed lowland rainforest, mainly in primary forest, but also in nearby mature secondary growth, where it feeds high in the trees on orchid flowers. Reported in Sumatra from more open areas near forest. Occurs predominantly in the lowlands below 200 m; on Sumatra recorded at 1,000 m. Generally a low-density species often missed during surveys. More studies regarding habits and status are needed.

Distribution: Sunda subregion. A rare resident in Sumatra and Kalimantan.

RUBY-CHEEKED SUNBIRD

Anthreptes singalensis 10 cm F: Nectariniidae

Description: Note rufous throat of female (photo); male has metallic green cap and mantle.

Voice: A high-pitched *wee-eest*.

Habits: Found in a variety of habitats from primary rainforest to forest edges and nearby cultivation; recorded on Sumatra to 1,000 m. Occurs in small numbers only and does not appear to be numerous anywhere in Indonesia. Visits flowering and fruiting trees to feed on nectar and tiny fruits; sometimes a few birds are seen together, fluttering quickly around each other.

Distribution: Oriental region. A widespread but generally scarce resident in Sumatra, Kalimantan and Java.

PURPLE-THROATED SUNBIRD

Nectarinia sperata 10 cm F: Nectariniidae

Description: Note the bright purple throat and maroon belly of this male; wings are a dark metallic green; cap is a bright green; female is a uniformly dark olive.

Voice: A high-pitched series of chirps and whistles.

Habits: This sunbird is found in a variety of wooded terrains, from secondary rainforest and forest edges to plantations, especially coconut groves. For some reason it has not been able to capitalise on its adaptability and it is rather scarce. Only occurs in the coastal lowlands, and is not found above 200 m. This tiny, quick bird is always on the move, fluttering quickly about among flowers, high in the trees.

Distribution: Oriental region. A generally uncommon resident in Sumatra, Kalimantan and west Java.

BLACK SUNBIRD

Nectarinia aspasia 11 cm F: Nectariniidae

Description: Male (top) is all-black with metallic spots on shoulder and cap. The female (bottom) is distinguished from the female Olive-backed Sunbird by its grey head.

Voice: Shrill, sibilant notes.

Habits: The most common sunbird throughout much of eastern Indonesia. Found in primary forest, along forest edges, and in scrub and gardens. Moves around the outer canopies of large trees or low in ornamental flowers and bushes feeding on nectar and small insects. Sometimes seen together with the Olive-backed Sunbird. Quick and active, this bird moves constantly from flower to flower. Tame and attractive, a pleasure to watch.

Distribution: Indonesia east to Bismarck Islands. A locally common resident in Sulawesi, Maluku and West Papua.

Morten Strange

COPPER-THROATED SUNBIRD

Nectarinia calcostetha 14 cm F: Nectariniidae

Description: A fairly large, slender build. The male shown in the photo appears to be uniformly dark, but its green cap and purple breast and belly shine in good light. The female has a diagnostic greyish head and underparts; its upperparts are dark olive.

Voice: A characteristic long trill; also a rapid twitter.

Habits: A coastal specialist found exclusively in tidal mangrove forests and in the casuarinas and coconut groves just behind the coastline. Often difficult to find, then in the right habitat suddenly quite numerous. A conspicuous, vocal and active bird that is often seen flying from tree to tree, visiting flowers.

Morten Strange

Distribution: Southeast Asia. A generally uncommon resident in Sumatra, Kalimantan and Java.

OLIVE-BACKED SUNBIRD

Nectarinia jugularis 11 cm F: Nectariniidae

Description: Note diagnostic blue throat and breast of male (left) missing in female (right). The south Maluku subspecies has a black belly.

Voice: High-pitched chirps and chatters: *cheep, cheep, wheet.*

Habits: Found in all kinds of open woodlands and disturbed habitats. Abundant along the coast and on offshore islands, also numerous further inland. Occurs on some islands to 1,400 m. The most successful member of its family in Indonesia. Numerous in villages and gardens, and often visits ornamental flowers. Flutters nervously about, low in trees and bushes. Tame and easy to observe.

Distribution: Oriental region and east into northern Australia. A widespread and common resident throughout most of the Indonesian archipelago.

FLAME-BREASTED SUNBIRD

Nectarinia solaris 11 cm F: Nectariniidae

Description: Unmistakable on Timor, Roti and Wetar, where it is the only sunbird. On Sumbawa and Flores, the male (bottom) is distinguished from the previous species by its red belly. The female (top) has dull olive underparts. Sumba has a similar, single endemic species, the Apricot-breasted Sunbird, *N. buettikoferi*.

Voice: Similar to that of the previous species.

Habits: Found in primary forest as well as rural gardens. Occurs mainly in the lowlands and in hills up to 1,000 m. On Flores, where it overlaps with the previous species, it seems to prefer the elevated, forested habitats. This vocal and conspicuous sunbird feeds in flowering trees and bushes.

Distribution: Indonesian endemic. A widespread and locally common resident on Sumbawa, Flores, Timor and some smaller nearby islands.

WHITE-FLANKED SUNBIRD

Aethopyga eximia 13 cm F: Nectariniidae

Description: White flanks are diagnostic. Photo shows male; female is a dull olive colour, with white flanks.

Voice: High-pitched chatters: *tee-tee-tee.*

Habits: Inhabits montane forest from 1,200 m to alpine elevations above 3,000 m with small stunted trees. Gede-Pangrango National Park (summit: 3,019 m) is probably the best place to find this species. Can be locally numerous, but since it is shy and restless, good views like this are rare. Moves low in closed forest and sometimes in vegetation along trails and clearings, visiting flowers on trees, bushes and undergrowth.

B. Van Elegem

Distribution: Indonesian endemic. A locally fairly common resident in montane parts of Java only.

CRIMSON SUNBIRD

Aethopyga siparaja 11 cm F: Nectariniidae

Description: Male (top) is distinguished from the following species by its bluish-black (not red) tail. The female (bottom) has a reddish tinge on its throat.

Voice: A high-pitched chirp: *chit-chit-chew.*

Habits: Frequents rainforest, forest edges, secondary growth and nearby cultivated areas. Occurs on some islands at lower montane elevations; recorded on Sulawesi to 1,500 m elevation. Not easy to observe in Indonesia, since it is a low density-species and mainly visits flowers at canopy level. Sometimes seen on ornamental plants.

Morten Strange

Distribution: Oriental region. A widespread but generally scarce resident in Sumatra, Kalimantan, Java and Sulawesi.

SCARLET SUNBIRD (Temminck's Sunbird)

Aethopyga mystacalis (A. temminckii) 11 cm F: Nectariniidae

Description: The male (photo) is distinguished from the previous species by its red tail. The female is a drab olive, with a reddish tinge to its tail. The Javan sub-species has a purple tail and is treated by M&P (1993) as a full species, the Scarlet Sunbird, *A. mystacalis,* also, and more suitably called Javan Sunbird.

Voice: A high-pitched *cheet-cheet.*

Habits: Found in primary rainforest and mature secondary forest. Occurs on Sumatra and Kalimantan at lower montane elevations between 600 and 1,800 m and on Java from the lowlands to 1,600 m. Recorded on Sumatra to 2,300 m. Lives almost exclusively on nectar gathered from flowers in the upper storeys of the forest. Rarely seen in cultivated areas.

Distribution: Sunda subregion. An uncommon resident in Sumatra, Kalimantan and Java.

LITTLE SPIDERHUNTER

Arachnothera longirostra 16 cm F: Nectariniidae

Description: Distinguished from other spiderhunters by its small size, pale throat and bright yellow underparts.

Voice: A penetrating *chiit* in flight.

Habits: The most successful member of its genus. Found in primary forest, secondary growth and nearby cultivation. Occurs mainly in the lowlands, but also inhabits lower montane elevations. Reported on Sumatra to 2,000 m. Although fairly numerous, this bird is secretive and skulking, so is not easy to observe. Most often seen briefly as it darts across the trail, calling loudly. Flies quickly from flower to flower, feeding on nectar and small invertebrates.

Distribution: Oriental region. A locally fairly common resident in Sumatra, Kalimantan, Java and Bali.

SPECTACLED SPIDERHUNTER

Arachnothera flavigaster 21 cm F: Nectariniidae

Description: Note its yellow eye-ring and fairly short, thick bill.

Voice: A high-pitched *chit-chit*.

Habits: Found in primary and closed secondary forest. Occasionally ventures into nearby cultivation. Occurs from the lowlands into lower montane elevations. Recorded on Kalimantan to 1,000 m and on Sumatra to 1,500 m. Feeds in large flowering trees, usually high at canopy level, but sometimes lower. This appears to be a low-density species and is often missed by observers during surveys in Indonesia.

Morten Strange

Distribution: Sunda subregion; a generally uncommon resident in Sumatra and Kalimantan.

YELLOW-EARED SPIDERHUNTER

Arachnothera chrysogenys 18 cm F: Nectariniidae

Description: Distinguished from the previous species by the yellow tufts below its eye, smaller size and paler underparts.

Voice: A penetrating *chick*.

Habits: This fairly adaptable spiderhunter is found in primary rainforest, along disturbed edges and in nearby cultivation. Recorded to 1,400 m on Sumatra where it has also been reported breeding, however few recent sightings have been confirmed from Indonesia. Sometimes flies high over the forest, calling loudly. Feeds in flowering trees on nectar, seeds, small insects and spiders.

Distribution: Sunda subregion. A widespread but generally rare resident in Sumatra, Kalimantan and west Java.

Frank Lambert

GREY-BREASTED SPIDERHUNTER

Arachnothera affinis 18 cm F: Nectariniidae

Description: Distinguished from other spiderhunters by its dark greyish-olive plumage and faint streaks on breast.

Voice: A variety of high-pitched chatters.

Habits: Mainly a lowland rainforest species. Also found along forest edges and in nearby cultivation up to 900 m. Moves through the middle and upper storeys of the forest and occasionally lower down. A restless bird that flies quickly from tree to tree, searching for small insects and nectar in flowers. Often seen on wild bananas. The nest is a neat little cup fixed with spiders' webs under the shelter of a banana leaf, typical of the genus.

Distribution: Sunda subregion. A locally fairly common resident in Sumatra, Kalimantan and Java; rare on Bali.

ORIENTAL WHITE-EYE

Zosterops palpebrosus 11 cm F: Zosteropidae

Description: Note its all yellow underparts. Some subspecies (such as west Javan) have a grey belly with a yellow center stripe. The only lowland white-eye within its range in Indonesia, apart from the Yellow-spectacled White-eye and the Lemon-bellied White-eye, *Z. chloris*, confined to small offshore islands.

Voice: A frequent, high-pitched chatter.

Habits: Found in open woodlands, mangroves and cultivation. Also occurs in inland forest to 1,400 m (sometimes higher). Always seen in flocks, sometimes mixing with other small birds, moving restlessly through the trees, feeding on flowers, insects and small fruits.

Distribution: Oriental region. A widespread and fairly common resident on Sumatra, Java, Bali, Sumbawa and Flores.

BLACK-CAPPED WHITE-EYE

Zosterops atricapilla 11 cm F: Zosteropidae

Description: Unmistakable. Note its grey underparts and black forehead.

Voice: A soft chatter similar to that of other white-eyes.

Habits: A montane rainforest bird that occurs between 700 m and 3,000 m, especially at the higher end of this range. Locally abundant on some peaks such as Gunung Kerinci. An active and attractive bird that moves in small flocks through the trees of closed forest, constantly chattering and searching for insects and small berries.

Distribution: Borneo and Sumatra. A locally common resident in montane parts of Sumatra and Kalimantan.

MOUNTAIN WHITE-EYE

Zosterops montanus 12 cm F: Zosteropidae

Description: Usually the only white-eye with a grey belly within its range and elevation.

Voice: A high-pitched chatter: *peep-peet* and a light trill.

Habits: Found in primary forest, along forest edges and in nearby scrub at montane elevations. On Timor occurs down to 500 m, but is usually recorded from 1,200 m to the alpine habitat in the highest mountains at 3,500 m. At higher elevations it is locally numerous and the most common bird around. Feeds in restless small flocks, usually high in the canopies, but occasionally moves lower to pick small fruits.

Distribution: The Philippines and Indonesia. A locally common resident in montane parts of Sumatra, Java, Bali and parts of Wallacea.

YELLOW-SPECTACLED WHITE-EYE

Zonsterops wallacei 12 cm F: Zosteropidae

Morten Strange

Description: Unmistakable. Note its bright yellow head and lack of white eye-ring; a reddish tinge on forehead is sometimes visible.

Voice: A distinctive song with 10–14 thin, ascending and descending, warbling notes.

Habits: Found in primary forest, along forest edges and in nearby wooded cultivated areas, mainly in the lowlands and lower hills. Occurs on Flores to 1,000 m. Moves inside the canopies and lower in the middle storey. Also seen near the ground in scrub around roads and clearings. Frequents fruiting trees, often in the company of other species. Quick and skulking, but vocal and curious. Responds well to a mimic of its call.

Distribution: Indonesian endemic. A locally common resident on Sumbawa, Flores, Sumba and the smaller Komodo, Rinca, Besar and Lomblen islands nearby.

ASHY-BELLIED WHITE-EYE

Zosterops citrinellus 12 cm F: Zosteropidae

Morten Strange

Description: Unmistakable; the only grey-bellied white-eye within its range and elevation.

Voice: High-pitched, twittering notes.

Habits: Habits are typical of the family. Found in a variety of wooded habitats, from closed forest to dry coastal savanna woodlands and cultivated areas. Also visits gardens and scrub near forested areas. Occurs mainly at sea level and is often seen at the beach on small islands. On Timor recorded to 1,200 m. Sometimes congregates in flocks of up to 50 individuals in large flowering and fruiting trees.

Distribution: Indonesia into small islands off northern Australia, where it is scarce. A widespread and locally common resident on Sumba, Timor, Tanimbar and many smaller islands nearby.

CREAM-THROATED WHITE-EYE

Zosterops atriceps 12 cm F: Zosteropidae

Description: Unmistakable; the only white-eye within its range.

Voice: Thin, whistled notes.

Habits: Found in wooded habitat, from primary forest and forest edges to mangroves and nearby cultivated areas. Occurs locally to 700 m. Moves quietly through the outer branches of the trees, alone or in small groups, searching the foliage for invertebrates. Only recently discovered on Obi.

Distribution: Indonesian endemic. A locally fairly common resident in Halmahera, Bacan, Obi and the nearby Morotai islands.

BLACK-FRONTED WHITE-EYE

Zosterops atrifrons 12 cm F: Zosteropidae

Description: Photo shows a West Papuan individual; in Wallacea four subspecies have a distinct black forehead and white eye-ring.

Voice: A distinctive song of eight descending notes, like a squeaking wheel.

Habits: Frequents primary forest as well as degraded forest; also seen along roadsides and in nearby cultivated areas and scrub. Has a preference for forest on low hills; in Wallacea recorded between 100 and 1,500 m; in West Papua at altitudes from 400 to 1,500 m and occasionally lower. Moves restlessly in small flocks through the middle storey, stopping briefly to feed on small fruits and insects.

Distribution: Indonesia and Papua New Guinea. A widespread and locally fairly common resident in Sulawesi, Seram, West Papua and some smaller islands nearby.

WESTERN MOUNTAIN WHITE-EYE

Zosterops fuscicapilla 11 cm F: Zosteropidae

Description: Note the diagnostic uniformly dark olive plumage, including underparts.

Voice: A frequent *tyew* and some chipping notes.

Habits: Restricted to montane rainforest from 1,200 to 2,100 m. Moves from the forest into nearby roadsides, villages and cultivation. Travels in small groups through the canopy of large trees or moves lower at the edges to feed on small fruits and insects.

Distribution: New Guinea. A locally common resident in montane parts of West Papua.

NEW GUINEA WHITE-EYE

Zosterops novaeguineae 11 cm F: Zosteropidae

Description: Distinguished from the two previous species by a combination of grey belly and distinct white eye-ring.

Voice: A varied, high-pitched chatter and trills.

Habits: Has a somewhat discontinuous distribution, since it is montane on the Vogelkop Peninsula, but is replaced in the central mountains by the previous species. In the Trans-Fly region and on the Aru Islands, it occurs in hills from 750 to 2,600 m; rarely seen at sea level. Appears less numerous than the two previous species, but its habits are similar.

Distribution: New Guinea. A local and generally scarce resident in parts of West Papua.

YELLOW-BROWED DARKEYE (Yellow-browed White-eye)
Lophozosterops superciliaris 13 cm F: Zosteropidae

Description: Distinguished from the following species by a prominent pale eyebrow that contrasts with its grey face.

Voice: A series of bubbling, trilling notes.

Habits: Restricted to montane forest between 1,000 and 2,100 m. Can be quite numerous in closed forest at the right altitude, about 1,600 to 1,800 m. Moves through the middle storey of the forest or lower, usually in small groups. Sometimes these groups mix with other birds in moving flocks, presumably feeding on insects. Frequently visits fruiting trees and bushes. This skulking, restless bird does not respond well to a mimic of its call.

Distribution: Indonesian endemic. A locally common resident in montane parts of Sumbawa and Flores only.

CRESTED DARKEYE (Crested White-eye)
Lophozosterops dohertyi 12 cm F: Zosteropidae

Description: Note bright yellow underparts and prominent brown crown that contrasts with its pale face and throat.

Voice: A distinctive song of 14 clear, whistled notes; almost thrush-like.

Habits: Found in primary forest, in low hills from 300 to 1,400 m. Fairly predictable, but not really numerous anywhere. Does not seem to adapt well to forest disturbance. A skulking and inconspicuous bird that moves through the middle or lower storey, often near the following species and others. Does respond to a mimic of its characteristic call. This photograph was produced using this method.

Distribution: Indonesian endemic. A fairly common resident on Sumbawa and Flores, including nearby tiny Satonda island. Near-threatened with global extinction.

THICK-BILLED DARKEYE (Thick-billed White-eye)

Heleia crassirostris 13 cm F: Zosteropidae

Description: Unmistakable. Note its characteristic facial mask and pale underparts. Unique; the only member of its genus.

Voice: A loud and whistling song with trilling notes atypical of the family.

Habits: Occurs in closed forest, mainly in low hills from 100 m upwards. Recorded on Sumbawa to 1,200 m and on Flores to 1,800 m. Moves through the lower story inside cover, emerging only briefly along open edges of the forest. Often seen near other birds in waves. Locally fairly numerous but not easy to find. Responds instantly to a mimic of its call. Often this is the only way this shy and skulking species can be viewed.

Distribution: Indonesian endemic. A locally fairly common resident on Sumbawa and Flores only.

BLACKEYE (Mountain Blackeye)

Chlorocharis emiliae 14 cm F: Zosteropidae

Description: Unmistakable within its range; fairly large.

Voice: Has a melodious, thrush-like song; also a twittering contact call.

Habits: An upper montane specialist that occurs from 1,600 m, but occurs mainly at altitudes above 2,000 m to the tree limit. Note the typical upper montane moss-covered branches that this individual is resting on. Feeds mainly on insects gleaned from the foliage, while hopping through the stunted montane trees. Also takes some small fruits.

Distribution: Borneo endemic. A locally common resident in montane parts of Kalimantan.

DWARF HONEYEATER (Dwarf Longbill)

Oedistoma iliolophum 11 cm F: Meliphagidae

Description: Note drab brown plumage with paler underparts and narrow yellow eye-ring. Distinguished from the smaller sympatric Pygmy Honeyeater, *O. pygmaeum* (7 cm), by its longer bill and tail.

Voice: A series of weak staccato notes.

Habits: Occurs in primary forest, from the lowlands at 100 m to 1,800 m. Most observations seem to be from the hills and lower montane elevations. Prefers closed forest, seen less often at edges. Small, quick and restless. Difficult to observe since it feeds on nectar and small insects in tall, flowering trees. Sometimes it hovers and shifts location with lightning speed.

Morten Strange

Distribution: New Guinea. A generally scarce resident in West Papua and the nearby Waigeo and Yapen islands.

GREEN-BACKED HONEYEATER

Glycichaera fallax 11 cm F: Meliphagidae

Description: Note its small bill and nondescript olive plumage with paler, yellowish underparts. A monotypic genus.

Voice: A thin *peeep* and a warbling twitter.

Habits: Occurs in primary rainforest and along forest edges, mainly in the lowlands below 800 m. An inconspicuous, low-density species not often reported from Indonesia. Moves low inside closed forest or up into the middle storey, gleaning insects from the foliage. Often seen with other birds in bird waves. Seems more like a *Gerygone* warbler than a honeyeater.

Morten Strange

Distribution: New Guinea into Cape York Peninsula, northern Australia. A generally scarce resident in West Papua and most nearby islands.

SCALY-CROWNED HONEYEATER

Lichmera lombokia 14 cm F: Meliphagidae

Description: A nondescript, olive-brown honeyeater distinguished from the following species by the lack of yellow in plumage. The faint scales on forehead are not usually visible in field.

Voice: A nasal whistle and some chattering notes, not as clear and musical as those of a sunbird.

Habits: Found mainly in forest at montane elevations above 800 m. Occurs on Flores to 2,100 m. Has been recorded at sea level, but this is rare. An adaptable species that can live in both primary forest and disturbed re-growth; even seen in gardens. At the right elevation it can be quite numerous. Shy, restless and not easy to view well as it moves quickly through flowering trees and bushes.

Distribution: Indonesian endemic. A locally fairly common resident in montane parts of Lombok, Sumbawa and Flores only.

BROWN HONEYEATER

Lichmera indistincta 13 cm F: Meliphagidae

Description: Note the faint yellow mark behind the ear of this male; the female has a yellow throat. M&P (1993) treat the Bali/Nusa Tenggara subspecies shown here as a full species, the Indonesian Honeyeater, *L. limbata*.

Voice: A variety of loud chatters and whistling notes.

Habits: Found along forest edges, in open monsoon woodlands, and in nearby cultivated areas and gardens. Usually occurs from the lowlands to lower montane elevations, but has also been recorded at 2,600 m. This conspicuous and vocal bird feeds in small groups, mainly on nectar from ornamental flowers and flowering trees.

Distribution: Bali through Australasia into Australia. A locally fairly common resident in Bali, Nusa Tenggara and southern West Papua.

SCALY-BREASTED HONEYEATER (White-tufted Honeyeater)
Lichmera squamata 14 cm F: Meliphagidae

Description: Unmistakable within its range, where it is the only small honeyeater. Note the prominent scales on breast and brown crown.

Voice: A whistling *chirup* and a loud, descending trill.

Habits: An adaptable species that thrives in primary forest, dry coastal woodlands, mangroves, cultivated areas and at the edge of villages. Abundant and the most common bird on Tanimbar, Tayandu, Ree and probably other islands. This vocal and conspicuous bird moves fairly high, often feeding on coconut palms and other flowering trees. Also takes some insects.

Filip Verbelen

Distribution: Indonesian endemic. A widespread and common resident on Wetar, Leti, Moa, Babar, Tanimbar, Kai and many nearby islands.

YELLOW-EARED HONEYEATER
Lichmera flavicans 14 cm F: Meliphagidae

Description: Distinguished easily from the sympatric Streak-breasted Honeyeater by its yellowish-olive underparts that are spotted (not streaked) with black.

Voice: A soft call note *bzz* and a subdued, rapid, whistling song.

Habits: Found on Timor, in the drought deciduous forest typical of this rather arid island. Occurs from the lowlands into montane elevations at 2,000 m, mainly in low elevated hills. Prefers somewhat open woodland where it frequents flowering trees and bushes. Usually moves high in the canopies feeding on nectar. Rarely seen at eye-level. An attractive and active species that often mixes with sunbirds, flowerpeckers, orioles and other honeyeaters.

Morten Strange

Distribution: Indonesian endemic. A locally fairly common resident on Timor only.

DUSKY HONEYEATER (Dusky Myzomela)
Myzomela obscura 13 cm F: Meliphagidae

Description: A uniform, drab brown colour, sometimes with a faint reddish wash on throat and wings.

Voice: A soft, high-pitched *see-see*.

Habits: Frequents primary forest and forest edges; also found in gardens on West Papua. Restricted to lowlands below 100 m on West Papua; in Maluku also found in the hills; recorded at its highest elevation on Bacan at 1,200 m. A nondescript and inconspicuous nectar-eater, sometimes seen in flowering trees, moving from eye-level to the canopy, often with other nectarivorous birds.

Distribution: Australasia into northern Australia. A locally fairly common resident in parts of Maluku and West Papua.

SCARLET HONEYEATER
Myzomela sanguinolenta 10 cm F: Meliphagidae

Description: Unmistakable within its range; various subspecies. This individual is from Sulawesi; some populations have all-red underparts. The Indonesian population could be treated as one or more endemic species, but here follows Andrew (1992) and C&B (1997).

Voice: A descending trill and various high-pitched squeaks and twitters.

Habits: In Indonesia this is a forest bird found in primary and mature secondary forest. In Australia it also inhabits open woodlands. Occurs on the larger islands and is mainly montane, usually restricted to elevations between 700 and 2,400 m, although seen lower to sea level locally. Moves high in the canopies or on lower branches of large trees, feeding on flowers.

Distribution: Indonesia and eastern Australia. A locally fairly common resident on Sulawesi, Sula, Bacan, Buru, Seram, Babar, Tanimbar and some smaller nearby islands.

BLACK-CHESTED HONEYEATER (Red-rumped Myzomela)

Myzomela vulnerata 11 cm F: Meliphagidae

Description: Unmistakable within its range, with a red throat, crown and rump, and black chest and mantle. The sexes are similar. Its name follows C&B (1997).

Voice: A weak, but frequent, high-pitched chatter.

Habits: Found in primary forest, along forest edges and sometimes in nearby scrub. Occurs from sea level to 1,200 m. In open deciduous woodland with many flowering trees, it is locally abundant and more than 20 sometimes gather in one tree to feed. These vocal, energetic birds move quickly from flower to flower, extracting nectar and sometimes chasing each other and displaying.

Morten Strange

Distribution: Indonesian endemic. A widespread and locally common resident on Timor only.

RED-COLLARED MYZOMELA

Myzomela rosenbergii 11 cm F: Meliphagidae

Description: The male (photo) has a red breast and mantle. The sympatric but rarer Mountain Red-headed Myzomela, *M. adolphinae*, has the reverse colouring. The female is a sooty brown with a red throat.

Voice: A high-pitched *tss tss;* also a sibilant squeaky song.

Habits: Strictly montane, but an otherwise adaptable species found in tall primary rainforest, alpine scrub and lower montane cultivated areas. Occurs at altitudes from 1,500 to 4,000 m; recorded rarely down to 600 m. This vocal and active bird feeds in the canopies of large trees down to eye-level at forest edges and clearings.

Distribution: New Guinea. A widespread and common resident in montane parts of West Papua.

Morten Strange

STREAK-BREASTED HONEYEATER (Streak-breasted Meliphaga)

Meliphaga reticulata 16 cm F: Meliphagidae

Description: Note the diagnostic dark brown and white streaks on underparts.

Voice: A high-pitched *wik-wik-wik* and a series of 9–10 soft, whistling notes.

Habits: A fairly adaptable species found in open savanna forest, nearby cultivated areas and scrub right at the coast. Also occurs in closed forest, inland up to 1,200 m. Usually quite skulking and shy, but when attracted by flowering trees or bushes, it becomes bold and approachable.

Distribution: Indonesian endemic. A widespread and locally fairly common resident on Timor and nearby the smaller Semau island.

BLACK-THROATED HONEYEATER

Lichenostomus subfrenatus 20 cm F: Meliphagidae

Description: Distinguished with some difficulty from other honeyeaters by its black throat, dark olive breast and distinct facial pattern, seen well from this angle.

Voice: The call note is a soft *whik whik;* also has a loud, bubbling song.

Habits: In Indonesia this species is mainly reported from the high altitudes in the Snow Mountains, where it is quite predictable at the upper montane elevations near the tree limit. Recorded here at altitudes between 2,000 and 3,500 m; in other places occurs down to 1,400 m. Visits stunted trees and flowering bushes near alpine meadows, feeding on nectar, small berries and some insects.

Distribution: New Guinea. A generally scarce resident in upper montane parts of West Papua.

ORANGE-CHEEKED HONEYEATER

Oreornis chrysogenys 25 cm F: Meliphagidae

Description: Note large size, olive wings and distinct golden (not orange) patch behind eye. Unique, the only member of its genus.

Voice: A single, bubbling note, like a domestic chicken *clu-uck*.

Habits: This peculiar, specialised bird occupies a very narrow niche and only occurs in the interior of West Papua. It usually does not move out of the alpine terrain between 3,300 and 4,000 m, but has been recorded down to 2,600 m. Can be spotted flying from small trees at the tree limit, low into the alpine grass lands, to feed on berries, seeds and insects on or near the ground.

Morten Strange

Distribution: Indonesian endemic. A locally fairly common resident in upper montane parts of the Snow Mountains only.

WHITE-STREAKED FRIARBIRD

Melitograis gilolensis 23 cm F: Meliphagidae

Description: Unmistakable; the only member of its genus. The rarer, sympatric Dusky Friarbird, *Philemon fuscicapillus*, is much larger and lacks white streaks.

Voice: A single clear note; also a harsher call.

Habits: Found in forest, along forest edges, and in nearby disturbed and cultivated areas. Occurs from coastal mangroves to lower montane elevations. On Halmahera recorded to 960 m; on Bacan to 2,130 m. In spite of its unusual appearance, it can be quite inconspicuous as it feeds quietly in flowering trees. Flies heavily from flower to flower; often seen with parrots, sunbirds and other nectar-eating birds.

Morten Strange

Distribution: Indonesian endemic. A fairly common resident on Halmahera, Bacan and the nearby Morotai and Kasiruta islands.

HELMETED FRIARBIRD

Philemon buceroides 32 cm F: Meliphagidae

Description: Photo shows a female; male has uniform pale brown underparts contrasting with dark brown upperparts.

Voice: A noisy and harsh diagnostic bubbling call: *kowee ko keeyo.*

Habits: A lowland forest bird found in all kinds of wooded habitat, from primary forest to nearby disturbed areas and edges of villages. Occurs mainly below 700 m, although it has been recorded to 1,500 m on West Papua and some islands. Its loud call is often heard from the forest during the morning, but good views of this canopy skulker are difficult to obtain. Sometimes emerges in large flowering or fruiting trees.

Distribution: Australasia, from Lombok into northern Australia. A widespread and locally common resident in Nusa Tenggara and West Papua, including the Aru and Yapen islands.

NOISY FRIARBIRD

Philemon corniculatus 34 cm F: Meliphagidae

Description: Note the diagnostic bald head and fluffy white feathers around neck; underparts are pale brown.

Voice: A crow-like single call; also a harsh ringing song similar to that of the previous species, but weaker.

Habits: Prefers an open, park-like habitat such as dry savanna forest, coastal woodlands or nearby wooded cultivation. In Indonesia, the Trans-Fly region meets these requirements. This vocal bird flies actively about, perching high in the open in trees or near the ground.

Distribution: Southern New Guinea into eastern Australia. A locally fairly common resident in the Trans-Fly region of southern West Papua.

GREY-STREAKED HONEYEATER

Ptiloprora perstriata 20 cm F: Meliphagidae

Description: Distinguished by its heavily streaked (not plain grey) underparts from the sympatric Rufous-sided Honeyeater, *P. erythropleura*, which also occurs on the Vogelkop Peninsula.

Voice: A variety of soft, high, whistling notes: *deeyur whit, wee dyu*.

Habits: Found mainly in forest at the upper montane elevations, from 2,500 m to the tree limit around 3,600 m. Has been recorded down to 1,700 m. This quiet and inconspicuous mountain bird inhabits tall moss forest as well as vegetation near alpine grasslands, sometimes moving to lower elevations to feed on insects and flowers.

Distribution: New Guinea. A locally fairly common resident in upper montane parts of central West Papua.

SOOTY HONEYEATER

Melionyx fuscus 24 cm F: Meliphagidae

Description: Distinguished from the following species by its blue eye-skin, in an otherwise black plumage, and lack of a 'beard'.

Voice: A soft call: *schweep;* sometimes a high-pitched, whistling song: *see dee dee dee*.

Habits: Appears to be restricted to the upper montane forest habitat. Occurs from 3,000 m and above, into the alpine zone and to the edge of vegetation. Fairly inconspicuous and perhaps a low-density species. Feeds on small trees and bushes, extracting nectar from flowers and also taking some insects.

Distribution: New Guinea. A generally scarce resident in upper montane parts of central West Papua.

SHORT-BEARDED HONEYEATER

Melionyx nouhuysi 27 cm F: Meliphagidae

Description: Unmistakable; note prominent 'beard' of yellow elongated throat feathers. The similar Long-bearded Honeyeater, *M. princeps,* replaces this species in montane Papua New Guinea.

Voice: A buzzing alarm call: *chsh.*

Habits: Restricted to a small geographical range and only recorded at altitudes between 3,300 and 4,500 m. A locally fairly predictable bird found at the edge of the tree line and far into the alpine grassland zone above. Feeds in low trees, isolated clumps of bushes and on the ground, taking small fruits, berries, nectar and insects. Flies quickly from bush to bush, staying close to the ground.

Distribution: Indonesian endemic. A locally fairly common resident in the upper montane parts of the Snow Mountains of central West Papua only.

BELFORD'S HONEYEATER

Melidectes belfordi 27 cm F: Meliphagidae

Description: Distinguished from other honeyeaters by an olive streak in wing, a blue eye patch and whitish stripe in throat that contrasts with its blackish face.

Voice: A loud, gurgling and whistling song, sung from a high perch in early morning.

Habits: Found in a wide range of forest habitats, from 1,600 to 3,800 m; recorded down to 1,400 m. Usually moves high in the canopies of tall forest trees in primary forest and along edges near trails and villages. At higher elevations, moves lower in stunted upper montane trees and bushes at the edge of alpine grasslands. Numerous, vocal and conspicuous. Often visits flowering trees and flies low, in a characteristic flapping and gliding fashion.

Distribution: New Guinea. A widespread and common resident in montane parts of central West Papua.

ORNATE HONEYEATER

Melidectes torguatus 23 cm F: Meliphagidae

Description: Note the characteristic facial pattern, scaly mantle and pale belly speckled with black.

Voice: A loud, gurgling song performed from a hidden perch.

Habits: This lower montane specialist is restricted to forest in the zone from 1,100 to 1,750 m, where it seems to replace the previous species as the predominant member of its family. Found in primary forest as well as disturbed areas near villages and clearings. This somewhat skulking bird forages within the canopies of large trees or in dense undergrowth and is often attracted by flowering vegetation.

Distribution: New Guinea. A fairly common resident in lower montane parts of West Papua.

WESTERN SMOKY HONEYEATER (Arfak Honeyeater)

Melipotes gymnops 22 cm F: Meliphagidae

Description: Unmistakable within its range. A whitish belly distinguishes it from the following allospecies.

Voice: A frequent soft *wee wee wee.*

Habits: Found in a narrow montane range, from 1,200 to 2,700 m. Prefers tall primary moss forest, occurs less often near edges, and is locally numerous within this special habitat. The Arfak Mountains near Manokwari is a certain location for this restricted range species. Behaves like a bulbul in the Oriental region. Usually seen in fruiting trees where it moves high in the canopy or lower in hanging branches, often mixing with birds of paradise, bowerbirds and other frugivorous species.

Distribution: Indonesian endemic. A locally common resident in the mountains on the Vogelkop Peninsula of West Papua only.

COMMON SMOKY HONEYEATER

Melipotes fumigatus 22 cm F: Meliphagidae

Description: Note the distinct yellow facial skin and uniformly sooty-black plumage.

Voice: A weak *swit*.

Habits: Found in a wide altitudinal band, from 1,000 to 4,200 m. In Indonesia seems to be most numerous in tall moss forest between 1,800 and 2,500 m. This honeyeater is more lethargic than other honeyeaters and often sits quietly on a middle storey perch for long periods. Otherwise its habits are much like the previous closely-related species. Invariably attracted by fruiting trees and bushes.

Distribution: New Guinea. A locally common resident in montane parts of central West Papua.

MOUNTAIN FIRETAIL

Oreostruthus fuliginosus 13 cm F: Estrildidae

Description: Unmistakable. Juvenile (top). The adult (bottom) has red streaks on flanks. Sexes are similar, the female being duller. Its red rump is prominent from behind. A monotypic genus.

Voice: A soft *huwee* and a sharp *pit*.

Habits: A strictly upper montane forest bird found between 2,800 and 3,650 m; occasionally occurs down to 2,200 m. A low-density, uncommon species in Indonesia. Moves quietly, low in tall dense moss forest or in stunted growth near the alpine zone. Confiding but inconspicuous; sometimes emerges near trails and clearings, where it feeds largely on seeds.

Distribution: New Guinea. A local and generally scarce resident in the upper montane parts of central West Papua.

CRIMSON FINCH

Neochmia phaeton 13 cm F: Estrildidae

Description: Unmistakable. The photo shows a male; the female has a red face, grey breast and whitish belly.

Voice: A musical *pit,* a shrill *che-che-che* and a quiet, rasping song: *ra-ra-ra-reee.*

Habits: Frequents open country. Usually found near water, in reed beds, long grass areas and sugar cane fields. In Indonesia, the Wasur National Park near Merauke is a good place to find this bird, which moves about the grasslands in small flocks, sometimes mixing with munias. Feeds on grass seeds. The male sometimes sings softly from an open perch as shown in this photo.

Jon Hornbuckle

Distribution: New Guinea into northern Australia. A fairly common resident in the Trans-Fly region of West Papua.

ZEBRA FINCH

Taeniopygia guttata 10 cm F: Estrildidae

Description: Unmistakable. The male (top) has a distinct rufous cheek patch and grey breast. The female (bottom) is duller.

Voice: A soft but penetrating call note *teeaah;* the song is a nasal chatter.

Habits: Found in the dry drought deciduous savanna habitat typical of this part of Indonesia. Often seen in open grasslands with scattered trees, in fields near villages and along scrubby forest edges, but never in closed forest. Usually occurs in coastal lowlands, but on Timor also recorded inland to 2,300 m. Moves about in small to large dense flocks, flying fast and calling softly.

Morten Strange

Distribution: Indonesia and Australia. A widespread, common resident on Lombok, Sumbawa, Flores, Sumba, Timor and many smaller nearby islands in Nusa Tenggara; vagrant on Bali, Java and Kalimantan.

WHITE-RUMPED MUNIA

Lonchura striata 11 cm F: Estrildidae

Martin Hale

Description: Distinguished from the following species by its greyish (not pure white) belly, spotted upperparts and white rump. Distinguished from the rarer White-bellied Munia, *L. leucogastra*, of forest habitat, by its white rump.

Voice: A trilled *prrit*.

Habits: An open country munia found in cleared grasslands near forest, scrub and cultivated areas. Occurs mainly in the lowlands, but on Sumatra has been recorded to 1,500 m. Habits are similar to those of other munias. Can often be seen in mixed flocks, together with the Scaly-breasted and White-headed Munia, feeding on seeds in tall grasses and rice fields.

Distribution: Oriental region. In Indonesia found only on Sumatra, nearby Bangka Island and the Riau Archipelago, where it is a widespread and fairly common resident.

JAVAN MUNIA

Lonchura leucogastroides 11 cm F: Estrildidae

Morten Strange

Description: Unmistakable on Java and Bali. On Sumatra can be distinguished from the previous species by its bright white (not greyish) belly and dark (not white) rump.

Voice: A soft *chee-ee* and a shriller *pi-i*.

Habits: One of the most numerous birds in its range. This bird is found in all kinds of open country, grasslands, cultivated fields and gardens, from the beach up to 1,800 m. It is quite confiding. Spreads out to feed on seeds and insects in loose flocks during the morning and congregates in larger flocks at evening roosts in large trees. The nest is a large ball of vegetation with a side entrance, constructed deep inside a bush or tree.

Distribution: Indonesian endemic. A widespread and common resident on Java, Bali and Lombok; has also expanded into south Sumatra where it possibly has been introduced.

DUSKY MUNIA

Lonchura fuscans 11 cm F: Estrildidae

Description: Unmistakable; note its uniformly dark brown plumage, including belly.

Voice: Soft *teck teck* and a shriller *pee pee*.

Habits: Found in open country, often around cleared areas near forest, but also in wet grasslands and cultivated areas. Occurs mainly in the coastal lowlands, along riverbanks and inland up to 500 m. More skulking and secretive than other munias, it often clambers about in grasses or on the ground. When disturbed, it flies rapidly to another location, close to the ground, quickly dropping back into cover. The nest is usually built in a hole in a steep earth embankment, a hole in a tree, or high inside a dense tree canopy.

Billy Kon

Distribution: Bornean endemic. A widespread and fairly common resident in Kalimantan and nearby Natunas islands.

BLACK-FACED MUNIA

Lonchura molucca 11 cm F: Estrildidae

Description: Unmistakable; note its black face and breast, contrasting with a scaly belly.

Voice: A short *tri*.

Habits: Frequents forest clearings, open regrown areas, fields and plantations. Often found in tall grasses near roads and villages, its predominant habitat throughout Indonesia. Occurs from the coast into lower hills, and has been locally recorded at 1,200 m. Usually seen in pairs or small groups, feeding on grass seeds. Makes short flights into trees to rest. The nest is a woven ball of straw built in a low bush.

Morten Strange

Distribution: Indonesian endemic. A widespread and locally common resident throughout most of Wallacea.

SCALY-BREASTED MUNIA

Lonchura punctulata 11 cm F: Estrildidae

Description: Unmistakable; note its diagnostic scaly underparts.

Voice: A faint *kee-dee*.

Habits: An open country bird that frequents all kinds of open woodlands, fields, cultivation and gardens. Feeds in small flocks, often with other munias, picking up seeds from the ground or from grasses along roads and edges of fields. Can be quite confiding. Congregates in larger flocks at evening roosts in taller trees.

Distribution: Oriental region; introduced into Hawaii, Australia, Seychelles. A widespread and common resident on Sumatra, Java, Bali and parts of Wallacea.

STREAK-HEADED MUNIA (Streak-headed Mannikin)

Lonchura tristissima 10 cm F: Estrildidae

Description: A streaked head and mantle in combination with dark underparts are diagnostic. Its yellow rump flashes in flight. In the Trans-Fly region, this bird is replaced by the Black Munia, *L. stygia*.

Voice: A thin *tseed*.

Habits: Unlike most other munias, this species prefers scrub in forested areas and is seldom seen in open country proper. Found in lowland forest and lower montane elevations up to 1,400 m. Often seen moving low along forest edges and in bushes and grasses near clearings and roadsides. Good views of this skulking and quick bird are difficult to obtain. The nest is a suspended pouch.

Distribution: New Guinea. A local and generally uncommon resident in northern parts of West Papua.

FIVE-COLOURED MUNIA

Lonchura quinticolor 11 cm F: Estrildidae

Description: Look for a combination of white belly and chestnut upperparts. A fairly dull bird; the supposedly five colours are difficult to detect in field. Its yellow rump is distinct on takeoff.

Voice: A soft *geev-geev-geev* and a weak, chattering song.

Habits: Found in scrub and along edges of remnant forest patches and bamboo. Often flies into nearby open grasslands and paddy fields to feed, but does not appear really numerous anywhere. Occurs mainly in the lowlands, but recorded on Flores and Timor to 1,200 m. This fairly shy bird perches in low scrub or on the ground in open fields. Moves about in small flocks, feeding on grass seeds.

Distribution: Indonesian endemic. A widespread but scarce resident on Lombok, Sumbawa, Sumba, Flores, Timor, Tanimbar and some smaller nearby islands within Nusa Tenggara.

Filip Verbelen

CHESTNUT MUNIA

Lonchura malacca 11 cm F: Estrildidae

Description: Unmistakable. MacKinnon & Phillipps call this species the Black-headed Munia, *Lonchura malacca*. The Javan and Bali subspecies has a partly white head and is treated by M&P (1993) as a full species, the Chestnut Munia, *L. ferruginosa*.

Voice: A shrill *preeep*.

Habits: Found in open country, mainly in the lowlands. In Kalimantan occurs also at lower montane elevations; on Sulawesi to 800 m. Where abundant, this munia will form dense flocks during the day, swerving across grasslands and paddy fields before settling to feed. At night, birds disperse to roost inside individual pouch nests.

Distribution: Oriental region. A widespread and generally common resident in Kalimantan and Sulawesi; fairly common on Java and Bali; uncommon on Sumatra; the Halmahera population was probably introduced.

Morten Strange

WHITE-HEADED MUNIA

Lonchura maja 11 cm F: Estrildidae

Description: A white head contrasting with chestnut body is diagnostic.

Voice: A thin *peep*.

Habits: Similar to other munias. An open country bird often associated with coastal marshes, but also found in fields, cultivated areas and low scrub. Occurs on Sumatra up country to 1,500 m. Outside of breeding season, it forms dense flocks that roam across flat grasslands, often with other munia species. Picks up seeds from low straws or on the ground along grassy edges.

Distribution: Sunda subregion. A locally fairly common resident on Sumatra, Java and Bali.

BLACK-BREASTED MUNIA (Black-breasted Mannikin)

Lonchura teerinki 10 cm F: Estrildidae

Description: Unmistakable; the only munia within its range and elevation.

Voice: A soft *teu*.

Habits: Found in cleared grasslands in the lower montane zone, such as the Baliem Valley and other foothill areas around the taller peaks, from 1,200 to 2,200 m. Within this small world range it is locally abundant and one of the most common birds near villages and fields. Often seen in large flocks, flying conspicuously around tall grass areas, landing in bushes, on tall stems or on the ground to feed on seeds. This individual is picking up straws for a nest nearby.

Distribution: Indonesian endemic. A locally common resident in lower montane parts of the Snow Mountains of West Papua only.

SNOW MOUNTAIN MUNIA (Western Alpine Mannikin)

Lonchura montana 11 cm   F: Estrildidae

Description: Unmistakable; the only munia within its range and elevation. Its belly is white with black barring.

Voice: A thin *see see*.

Habits: Mainly restricted to the upper montane habitat, from 3,000 to 4,100 m, which is far above the tree limit. Has also been recorded down to 2,100 m. Moves about the open alpine grasslands, often near wet boggy patches with small, scattered trees. Large dense flocks have been reported locally, but it is mostly seen in smaller groups. Perches in low bushes and grasses, and drops to the ground to feed on seeds.

Morten Strange

Distribution: New Guinea. A locally fairly common resident in the upper montane parts of the Snow Mountains and Star Mountains only.

TIMOR SPARROW

Padda fuscata 13 cm   F: Estrildidae

Description: Distinguished quite easily from the Five-coloured Munia by its diagnostic white cheeks. Shares its own genus with the next species.

Voice: A short *tsip;* also a chipping song.

Habits: Found in open savanna woodlands, often in rural open country with scattered palm trees and grazing cattle. Occurs mainly in coastal lowlands, often at sea level, but has been recorded up to 700 m. Although this bird is adaptable, it is difficult to find in the wild and is not numerous anywhere. Moves about in pairs or small flocks, sometimes mixing with the more common Zebra Finch. Perches low in trees and drops down to the ground to feed on seeds.

Morten Strange

Distribution: Indonesian endemic. An uncommon resident on Timor and the nearby smaller Roti and Semau islands. Near-threatened with global extinction.

JAVA SPARROW

Padda oryzivora 16 cm   F: Estrildidae

Morten Strange

Distribution: Indonesian endemic. An uncommon resident on Java, Bali and the Kangean islands; introduced but generally scarce on Sumatra, Kalimantan, Lombok, Sumbawa, Sulawesi and some smaller islands.

Description: Unmistakable. This bird and the previous species are the only members of this genus. Captive photo.

Voice: A low churring *tup;* also a trilling song.

Habits: An open country species found in mangroves, open woodlands and often cultivated areas and villages. Occurs on the coast and inland up to 1,500 m. Previously abundant, but does take some rice and is hunted by farmers as a pest. Many are also captured for the bird trade. Escaped birds have established feral populations on other islands, even abroad. Now rarely seen in the wild and is regarded by BirdLife International as vulnerable to global extinction.

TREE SPARROW (Eurasian Tree-sparrow)

Passer montanus 15 cm   F: Ploceidae

Morten Strange

Distribution: Eurasia; introduced to other regions, e.g. Australia and the USA. A widespread and common resident in inhabited areas on many islands; expands east into Wallacea.

Description: Distinguished from other sparrows by its brown cap and streaked back, seen well from this angle.

Voice: A monotonous *chip-chip.*

Habits: The only Indonesian bird to be exclusively associated with humans. Surprisingly does not appear to occur in any truly wild habitats. Locally abundant in towns, villages and rural developments, where it feeds on grain and food scraps on the ground. During the breeding season it also takes many insects. Occurs mainly in coastal villages, but is also found inland up to 1,500 m. Its range has expanded, partly through the release of captive birds and ship stowaways. Nests in cavities, mainly in buildings.

STREAKED WEAVER

Ploceus manyar 14 cm F: Ploceidae

Description: The male is distinguished from the following species by faint dark streaks on chest. The female lacks yellow. The male shown in photo is not fully mature. The rare Asian Golden Weaver, *P. hypoxanthus* (see Strange (2000)), of west Java, has more yellow on neck and wings.

Voice: A low, chattering and whistling call.

Habits: Frequents open country, grassy areas and paddy fields, often near marshes. During breeding season settles in dense colonies. The nest is a rounded ball with a short entrance, placed low in grasses and bushes. The male attracts females by singing and displaying. Outside the breeding season, these weavers roam widely in loose flocks.

Distribution: Oriental region. In Indonesia, found only on Java and Bali, where it is a widespread and locally fairly common resident.

BAYA WEAVER

Ploceus philippinus 15 cm F: Ploceidae

Description: Best distinguished from the previous species by its nest, which is very different.

Voice: A sparrow-like *chip;* also a harsh, chattering song near nest.

Habits: Found in open country with some trees, usually near wetlands with long grass. Reported to be reduced in numbers, but recent reports indicate that large colonies still exist in prime locations. The carefully woven nest with a long entrance tube is suspended high in a tree near water. The photo shows a male putting finishing touches to an exceptionally large nest, before he entices a female in to occupy it.

Distribution: Oriental region. In Indonesia, found only on Sumatra and west Java, where it is locally fairly common.

SINGING STARLING

Aplonis cantoroides 20 cm F: Sturnidae

Description: Distinguished from the following species by its red eye; distinguished from the Metallic Starling by a stronger build and shorter tail.

Voice: A single *teyeww* and a clear, disyllabic whistle.

Habits: Found in open country and cleared areas, often near water such as the coast and inland river valleys; occurs to 1,500 m elevation. Sometimes seen near villages and towns, although urban wildlife in New Guinea is sparse due to the hunting tradition. Flies quickly about in flocks; perches high in trees, but also drops to the open ground to feed. The nest is built inside a cavity in a tree or a man-made structure.

Distribution: New Guinea. A widespread and fairly common resident in West Papua, including the nearby Waigeo, Misool and Aru Islands.

MOLUCCAN STARLING

Aplonis mysolensis 22 cm F: Sturnidae

Description: Distinguished from the Metallic Starling by its shorter tail and dark eye.

Voice: A slurred whistle; also some squealing notes.

Habits: Frequents disturbed forest edges, roads, cultivation and villages, from the lowlands up to 1,000 m. Always found in flocks, chattering and flying about high in the scattered trees; often congregates with other species in fruiting trees. Also gregarious during the breeding season, when it settles in colonies in large remnant forest trees, where each pair excavates a nest hole. As many as 200 individuals have been observed close together; usually the group numbers 15–50.

Distribution: Indonesian endemic. A widespread and fairly common resident in parts of Wallacea and islands off west West Papua.

SHORT-TAILED STARLING

Aplonis minor 19 cm F: Sturnidae

Description: On Java, Bali and Sulawesi, distinguished with difficulty from the following species by its bluish (not greenish) head and neck, and shorter bill and tail.

Voice: A metallic *chillanc* in flight; also a softer *seep*, and a short, whistling chatter.

Habits: Mainly a forest bird found in closed to somewhat open forest and along forest edges. Occasionally seen high in large trees near villages. Occurs from the lowlands to lower montane elevations; recorded on Flores to 1,600 m. Moves directly across the forest in fast-flying flocks, a behaviour typical of the genus. Congregates in fruiting trees. The nest is built in a cavity in a tree.

Morten Strange

Distribution: Indonesia north into Mindanao (Philippines). A generally uncommon resident in parts of Sulawesi and Nusa Tenggara; rare on Java and Bali.

ASIAN GLOSSY STARLING (Philippine Glossy Starling)

Aplonis panayensis 20 cm F: Sturnidae

Description: Distinguished from the previous species (which is sympatric on Java, Bali and Sulawesi) by the greenish (not bluish) metallic sheen on head and longer tail.

Voice: A ringing whistle in flight and a metallic *ink* when perched.

Habits: This open woodland bird is found along forest edges and roadsides, and in plantations and villages with large trees. For some reason it has not become abundant in Indonesia, as it has in other parts of its range. Often seen feeding high in fruiting trees or flying by in a fast and direct manner. Gregarious, even during the breeding season. Nests in cavities in trees.

Morten Strange

Distribution: Oriental region. A locally common resident in northern Sulawesi, but generally scarce throughout Sumatra, Kalimantan, Java and Bali.

METALLIC STARLING

Aplonis metallica 23 cm F: Sturnidae

Morten Strange

Description: Best distinguished from the sympatric Singing Starling by its long, graduated tail.

Voice: A short, nasal whistle; also twittering contact calls near nest.

Habits: Found along forest edges and roads, in logged-over forest and in cultivated areas. Also sometimes seen in villages and gardens. Occurs mainly in the lowlands. Recorded in Wallacea to 700 m and on West Papua seen rarely above 1,000 m. Does not nest in tree holes, rather in dense clusters of woven nests more resembling those of a weaver than a starling, which is unusual for this genus.

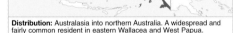

Distribution: Australasia into northern Australia. A widespread and fairly common resident in eastern Wallacea and West Papua.

ASIAN PIED STARLING

Sturnus contra 24 cm F: Sturnidae

David Tipling/Windrush Photos

Description: Easily distinguished from the following species by its black nape, neck and breast.

Voice: A noisy rattle.

Habits: An open country starling found in coastal savanna woodlands, rural areas and remote cultivation. Feeds mainly on the ground and congregates on evening roosts where food is plentiful. Indonesia constitutes the southern limit for this widespread species. Previously this bird was frequently reported, especially from dry open areas in east Java and Bali, but in later years it seems to have declined locally and is now uncommon, possibly rare.

Distribution: Oriental region. An uncommon resident on Java and Bali; vagrant in southern Sumatra.

BLACK-WINGED STARLING

Sturnus melanopterus 23 cm F: Sturnidae

Description: White body and black wings together are diagnostic. Captive photo.

Voice: Harsh whistles.

Habits: Found in open coastal woodlands and monsoon forest; also seen in nearby cultivated areas and on the edges of villages. Best site for this bird is the Baluran National Park in east Java, and the Bali Barat National Park in Bali. Perches in low trees and drops down to the ground to feed. Often seen flying in pairs across the savanna. Sings from an open perch, while nodding its head agitatedly. Builds its nest in a cavity in a tree or sometimes in a building.

Distribution: Indonesian endemic. A generally scarce resident on Java and Bali; vagrant on Lombok.

BALI STARLING (Bali Myna)

Leucopsar rothschildi 25 cm F: Sturnidae

Description: Unmistakable. Its snow-white plumage is distinctive; black wing tips flash in flight. The only member of its genus and the only vertebrate endemic to Bali. Captive photo.

Voice: A harsh, whistling chatter.

Habits: Historically confined to the monsoon deciduous coastal forest of northwest Bali. Found previously in flocks numbering hundreds, but in 1998 only 14 were left on the Prapat Agung Peninsula in the Bali Barat National Park, some reintroduced captive birds. Faces imminent extinction in the wild. Roosts in small flocks near the beach, foraging further inland during the day. Nests in tree holes. Possibly about 700 birds are held in captivity worldwide.

Distribution: Indonesian endemic. A rare resident along the northwest coast of Bali only. Critically endangered with global extinction.

COMMON MYNA

Acridotheres tristis 25 cm F: Sturnidae

Description: Unmistakable. Note chocolate body with black head and yellow facial skin.

Voice: A chattering and squeaky song.

Habits: An open country species largely associated with humans. Since 1982 has settled on the Riau islands and appears to be well established. Has possibly expanded from Singapore where abundant. Also reported from other localities in Sumatra, and occasionally from Kalimantan and Java, where feral populations do not seem to gain ground. This omnivorous and opportunistic species has been successful throughout its range.

Distribution: Oriental region. Introduced to New Zealand, Hawaii and South Africa. Has recently expanded into parts of Sumatra.

WHITE-VENTED MYNA (Javan Myna)

Acridotheres javanicus 25 cm F: Sturnidae

Description: Unmistakable in Indonesia. Has a shorter crest and less white on vent than the SE Asian subspecies; see Strange (2000).

Voice: A variety of harsh, chattering notes.

Habits: An open country species found along forest edges and in drier fields; often seen near rural villages. For some reason this starling has not settled in towns and cities and become abundant, as it has in other areas within its range. The proliferation of air guns and sling shots in Indonesia may be the cause. Feeds mainly on the ground and sometimes follows cattle during grazing.

Distribution: Oriental region. A widespread but generally scarce resident on Java and Bali; introduced on Sumatra, south Sulawesi, Flores and Sumba.

YELLOW-FACED MYNA

Mino dumontii 25 cm F: Sturnidae

Description: Distinguished by its black (not yellow) breast and neck from the sympatric but rarer Golden Myna, *M. anais*. Together they form their own genus. Otherwise unmistakable.

Voice: A characteristic loud croak: *twow*.

Habits: Found in forest, especially along forest edges and nearby cultivated areas with large trees. Occurs along the coast and inland up to 750 m; seen rarely to 1,500 m. Perches high, often calling loudly. Sometimes seen in groups with other frugivorous birds in fruiting trees.

Distribution: New Guinea east into Solomon Islands. A locally fairly common resident in West Papua.

SULAWESI CRESTED MYNA (Short-crested Myna)

Basilornis celebensis 23 cm F: Sturnidae

Description: Unmistakable. A similar species with a larger crest, the Helmeted Myna, *B. galeatus*, occurs on nearby Banggai and Sula islands. Captive photo.

Voice: A variety of whistling and nasal calls.

Habits: Found in primary forest, mature secondary forest and along forest edges. Rarely moves into nearby cultivation. Occurs from the coast to 900 m; occasionally recorded to 1,200 m. Usually moves high in the trees inside the canopies. Sometimes seen with other frugivorous birds in fruiting trees. Best viewed early in the morning and in late afternoon, when it perches on exposed branches.

Distribution: Indonesian endemic. A widespread and fairly common resident in Sulawesi.

WHITE-NECKED MYNA

Streptocitta albicollis 50 cm F: Sturnidae

Description: Unmistakable; note large size and prominent white collar. This species and the closely related Bare-eyed Myna, *S. albertinae*, endemic to nearby Sula Islands, form their own genus.

Voice: A variety of whistling calls, including a clear *towee*.

Habits: This unusual magpie-like starling is found in primary forest, along forest edges and in secondary growth, from the lowlands to 1,200 m. Sometimes spotted flying over open areas or perching prominently. Often seen in resident pairs.

Distribution: Indonesian endemic. A locally fairly common resident on Sulawesi, including the nearby smaller Muna and Butung islands.

HILL MYNA

Gracula religiosa 30 cm F: Sturnidae

Description: A large, powerful build. Note yellow wattles across neck, white spot in wing, and heavy flight silhouette.

Voice: A characteristic, penetrating whistle: *ti-ongg;* also chatters softly and mimics.

Habits: Mainly a forest bird found in closed primary forest and along forest edges. Also seen around coastal cultivated areas and often on offshore islands. Usually occurs in the lowlands below 500 m, locally at higher altitudes. On Sumatra recorded at 1,000 m. Perches high, often at the top of a dead branch near the forest's edge, calling loudly. Feeds in fruiting trees. Always seen in pairs, sometimes in larger groups. Much reduced in numbers.

Distribution: Oriental region. A widespread but generally scarce resident in Sumatra, Kalimantan, Java, Bali, Sumbawa, Flores and Alor; two records from Sumba likely to be escapees.

GROSBEAK STARLING (Finch-billed Myna)

Scissirostrum dubium 21 cm   F: Sturnidae

Description: Unmistakable. The only member of its genus. Its back and underparts are a dark grey colour.

Voice: Vocal; a frequent flight call *churip* and a nasal chatter.

Habits: Found in forest edges and open woodlands, from the coast inland to 1,000 m. Highly gregarious. Feeds in flocks in fruiting trees, often with other frugivorous species. Forms dense flocks in flight, swerving quickly before settling down to land. This species forms dense colonies when nesting, each pair excavating a nesting hole in a large, dead, free-standing tree trunk. Such a colony may house hundreds of noisy starlings.

Distribution: Indonesian endemic. A widespread and common resident on Sulawesi and some smaller nearby islands.

Margaret Kinnaird

DUSKY-BROWN ORIOLE (Dusky Oriole)

Oriolus phaeochromus 26 cm   F: Oriolidae

Description: Note its distinctive uniformly dark brown plumage. Distinguished from the Dusky Friarbird, *Philemon fuscicapillus,* by its shorter neck and smaller bill.

Voice: A liquid, two-note whistle.

Habits: Found in lowland primary rainforest and along forest edges, inland up to 450 m. Moves high in large trees and is usually located by call. This species has been little studied and this is the only known photograph of it. Feeds on fruits and spiders.

Distribution: Indonesian endemic. A scarce resident on Halmahera only; not recorded on nearby smaller islands.

Morten Strange

OLIVE-BROWN ORIOLE (Timor Oriole)

Oriolus melanotis 27 cm F: Oriolidae

Description: The only *Oriolus* within its range. The male (top) is unmistakable. The female (bottom) can be distinguished from the Helmeted Friarbird by its smaller size and lack of knob on bill.

Voice: Male performs a penetrating, fluty whistle *orry-orry-ole*.

Habits: Found in the drought deciduous open woodlands typical of these islands. Also occurs in denser savanna forest and nearby wooded cultivation. Mainly inhabits the coastal lowlands and lower hills at 300 m, possibly higher. Moves high inside the canopies of large trees, sometimes coming down into the lower middle storey.

Distribution: Indonesian endemic. A fairly common resident on Timor and the nearby smaller Roti, Semau and Wetar islands.

DARK-THROATED ORIOLE

Oriolus xanthonotus 20 cm F: Oriolidae

Description: Photo shows female; male has a yellow back, and black head and wings.

Voice: A characteristic fluty song, similar to that of the Black-naped Oriole, but somewhat weaker.

Habits: Found in lowland rainforest. On Sumatra recorded at 1,000 m, but this is rare. Frequents both primary forest and mature secondary growth with large trees. A low-density species, not numerous anywhere and difficult to observe. This vocal bird is usually located by its call. Moves high inside canopies, where it feeds on small fruits and insects. Flies quickly between trees.

Distribution: Sunda subregion. An uncommon resident in Sumatra, Kalimantan and Java.

BLACK-NAPED ORIOLE

Oriolus chinensis 27 cm F: Oriolidae

Description: Unmistakable; the female is somewhat duller than the male shown in photo.

Voice: A loud, fluty whistle; also a low, hissing sound.

Habits: This species varies in abundance. It is locally common on Sulawesi, Bali and other islands; on Sumatra and Java it appears to be less numerous; and for some reason it is virtually absent in Kalimantan. Occurs along forest edges and in open woodlands and nearby wooded cultivated areas. Often observed near the coast and inland at lower montane elevations. Takes fruits and insects in large trees. Can be seen clearly, flying high with a slow, undulating flight, usually in resident pairs.

Morten Strange

Distribution: Oriental region. A widespread and fairly common resident on Sumatra, Java, Bali and parts of Wallacea; vagrant in Kalimantan.

BLACK-AND-CRIMSON ORIOLE

Oriolus cruentus 22 cm F: Oriolidae

Description: Note bluish bill and red patch on breast of male in photo. Female has faint streaks of chestnut instead of red.

Voice: A short, melodious whistle; also a nasal mew.

Habits: A strictly montane species, mostly found in a narrow range between 1,200 and 1,800 m. Has been recorded between 500 and 2,400 m. Restricted to primary forest and does not come out near trails and disturbed areas. Moves inside the canopy, where it feeds mainly on caterpillars, often with other insectivorous species in bird waves.

Morten Strange

Distribution: Sunda subregion. A generally scarce resident in montane parts of Sumatra, Kalimantan and Java.

TIMOR FIGBIRD

Sphecotheres viridis 26 cm F: Oriolidae

Description: Look for distinctive olive-yellowish underparts and reddish mask on black head of male (top). Female (bottom) has heavy streaks on pale underparts. The nearby Wetar Island has a similar endemic species.

Voice: A characteristic, short, metallic whistle.

Habits: Found in primary monsoon deciduous forest and mature secondary growth; also observed in nearby forest remnants with large trees. Occurs from the coastal lowlands up to 200 m and probably higher. Numerous in prime habitat; small flocks will gather in fruiting fig trees. Moves high in large trees, but is conspicuous and easy to observe. The male calls from a top branch.

Distribution: Indonesian endemic. A generally common resident on Timor and the nearby smaller Roti and Semau islands.

BLACK DRONGO

Dicrurus macrocercus 29 cm F: Dicruridae

Description: Note its slender build and very long, deeply forked tail.

Voice: A variety of ringing calls.

Habits: The only member of this family found exclusively in open country. Frequents long grassy areas with scattered trees, cultivated fields and marshes. Sits on an open perch such as a fence pole, telephone wire or exposed branch. On Bali often seen riding on the backs of domestic cattle. Sallies out from there to catch insects in the air like a large flycatcher. Previously numerous, although now seen less often.

Distribution: Oriental region, East Asia; migratory. A widespread but generally scarce resident on Java and Bali; migratory birds from the north reach Sumatra as vagrants.

ASHY DRONGO

Dicrurus leucophaeus 29 cm F: Dicruridae

Description: Shaped much like the previous species. Note its somewhat shorter tail; plumage is an ashy grey colour.

Voice: A mewing call.

Habits: Found in a variety of wooded habitats, but mainly resident in montane forests between 600 and 2,400 m. Outside breeding season it roams widely and can be found locally down to sea level. This is a predictable bird in the right location, such as Gunung Kerinci on Sumatra and Gunung Gede on Java. Sits high on an open branch at the edge of the forest and flies out to catch insects in the air, returning to the same perch like a bee-eater or a flycatcher.

Distribution: Oriental region. A fairly common mainly montane resident in Sumatra, Kalimantan, Java, Bali and Lombok.

Morten Strange

CROW-BILLED DRONGO

Dicrurus annectans 27 cm F: Dicruridae

Description: Distinguished from other drongos by its stocky build and straight, slightly forked tail. The immature bird (photo) has white streaks in underparts plumage.

Voice: A typical drongo call, with loud whistles and harsh *churs*.

Habits: Indonesia constitutes the southern limit for the distribution of this species and only a few reach this country during the northern winter from October to April. In winter quarters it can turn up at any wooded location, from closed forest to coastal scrub. Usually seen sitting quietly alone in the middle storey.

Distribution: Oriental region; migratory. A rare winter visitor on Sumatra and west Java; a vagrant in Kalimantan.

Morten Strange

BRONZED DRONGO

Dicrurus aeneus 23 cm F: Dicruridae

Description: Its small size and glossy sheen in plumage are diagnostic.

Voice: A variety of clear whistles and harsh notes.

Habits: A forest bird found in closed forest, from the lowlands to lower montane elevations; on Sumatra has been recorded to 1,400 m. Prefers clearings near primary forest, where it sits high on an exposed branch, hawking for insects in the air. A vocal and conspicuous species; on occasions the resident pair flies acrobatically through the air, displaying and calling loudly.

Distribution: Oriental region. A locally fairly common resident in Sumatra and Kalimantan.

LESSER RACKET-TAILED DRONGO

Dicrurus remifer 25 cm + tail F: Dicruridae

Description: Note the diagnostic thin 'rackets' in tail.

Voice: Similar to that of other drongos; a variety of whistles, also mimics other birds' calls.

Habits: Strictly a montane species; on Sumatra recorded between 600 and 2,400 m elevation; most numerous in the 1,200 to 1,800 m range. Prefers the darker parts of primary forest; usually seen sitting passively in the middle storey, where it hawks for insects below the canopy. It also participates in bird waves.

Distribution: Oriental. A locally fairly common resident in montane parts of Sumatra and west Java.

SPANGLED DRONGO

Dicrurus bracteatus 31 cm F: Dicruridae

Description: A large drongo with a diagnostic backward-turned tip of tail. The only Dicruridae within its range except for the much smaller (20 cm), square-tailed Pygmy Drongo, *Chaetorhynchus papuensis* (Mountain Drongo; Beehler (1986)), of montane New Guinea.

Voice: A melodious, whistling call.

Habits: Found in forest and forest edges. Observed often near the coast and in the inland hills. Occurs in Maluku to 2,000 m on Bacan; recorded below 1,450 m in West Papua. Often seen in resident pairs, perching high in large trees. Selects an exposed branch and flies out from there to catch insects in the air. Also seen in fruiting or flowering trees.

Morten Strange

Distribution: Australasia, east into Australia. A fairly common resident in parts of Maluku and West Papua.

WALLACEAN DRONGO

Dicrurus densus 32 cm F: Dicruridae

Description: Unmistakable within its range; possibly conspecific with the previous species. Here follows Andrew (1992) and C&B (1997).

Voice: A harsh, whistling chatter.

Habits: Found in a variety of wooded habitats, from tall primary forest to disturbed areas and along roadsides with some large trees. Sometimes seen in nearby plantations. Occurs from sea level mangroves to interior lower montane forests; on Flores recorded to 1,600 m. This vocal and fairly conspicuous bird sits in the lower middle storey below the canopy, often in resident pairs. Flies out from there to catch insects. Seems to have a preference for flowering trees.

Morten Strange

Distribution: Indonesian endemic. A widespread and fairly common resident throughout Nusa Tenggara.

THE BIRDS OF INDONESIA **369**

HAIR-CRESTED DRONGO

Dicrurus hottentottus 31 cm F: Dicruridae

Description: Distinguished from other drongos by thin, hair-like feathers on crown.

Voice: Melodious whistles mixed with harsh calls, typical of the family.

Habits: A forest bird that prefers secondary forest, clearings and dense re-growth. Occurs from the lowlands up to 1,700 m on Sulawesi; in Kalimantan recorded mainly at lower montane elevations to 1,500 m. Hawks for insects from an open perch, but also searches tree trunks for insects and termites. This vocal and conspicuous bird also participates in bird waves and often follows monkeys around to catch insects that the monkeys disturb.

Distribution: Oriental region, East Asia. A fairly common resident in Kalimantan, east Java, Bali, Sulawesi and some smaller islands.

Morten Strange

GREATER RACKET-TAILED DRONGO

Dicrurus paradiseus 32 cm + tail F: Dicruridae

Morten Strange

Description: Distinguished from the Lesser Racket-tailed Drongo by its larger size and wider 'rackets' in elongated tail feathers.

Voice: A confusing variety of melodious and very harsh calls. Mimics other forest birds frustratingly well.

Habits: Can be found in a variety of wooded habitats, from closed primary forest to mangroves, forest edges and even nearby scrub with large trees. Although adaptable, this species seems to be in retreat in Indonesia. Still a predictable bird near good forest, especially in Kalimantan. Perches in the middle storey flying out to catch insects in the open space below the canopies.

Distribution: Oriental region. A generally scarce resident in Sumatra, Kalimantan, Java and Bali.

WHITE-BREASTED WOOD-SWALLOW

Artamus leucorhynchus 18 cm F: Artamidae

Description: On Sulawesi distinguished from the rarer endemic Ivory-backed Woodswallow, *A. monachus*, by its slaty-grey back. In West Papua distinguished from the montane Great Wood-swallow by its smaller size and coastal location.

Voice: A loud, harsh chatter.

Habits: Mainly a coastal species found in dry, open woodlands, often very near the beach. Also seen in cultivated areas, casuarinas and further inland along forest edges. Occurs locally to above 2,000 m on Sulawesi and Timor. On West Papua recorded to 800 m, where the larger species takes over. A conspicuous and social bird, enjoyable to observe.

Morten Strange

Distribution: Southeast Asia and Australasia into southern Australia. A locally fairly common resident throughout Indonesia; recorded from all the major islands.

GREAT WOOD-SWALLOW

Artamus maximus 20 cm F: Artamidae

Description: Much like the previous species. Has white underparts, but is significantly larger and darker. Note white rump seen well from this angle. All members of this small family belong to the same genus.

Voice: Much like that of the White-breasted Wood-swallow; often a soft, penetrating *cheep* during flight.

Habits: A montane forest bird found in tall primary moss forest from 800 to 2,800 m elevation. Sits very high in dead top branches of large trees, often near a clearing and sometimes in cultivated patches. Flies out to catch insects, flapping and gliding along the tree tops.

Brian J. Coates

Distribution: New Guinea. A locally fairly common resident in montane parts of West Papua.

BLACK-FACED WOOD-SWALLOW

Artamus cinereus 18 cm F: Artamidae

Description: Easily distinguished from the White-breasted Wood-swallow by its bluish-grey underparts and black mask.

Voice: A scratchy *chaf chaf;* also a chattering song with mimicry.

Habits: An open country bird found in arid coastal savanna forest and mangrove fringes. Also seen in paddy fields and cleared pastures with scattered coconut trees and scrub. Usually occurs at sea level, and sometimes inland to 300 m elevation. Hawks low over the grasslands for flying insects with the flapping, gliding flight pattern typical of its family. A vocal and conspicuous bird that often perches on fence posts, wires, hacked branches or palm leaves.

Morten Strange

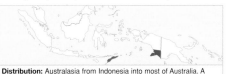

Distribution: Australasia from Indonesia into most of Australia. A generally uncommon resident on Timor and some smaller adjacent islands; Australian birds reach the Trans-Fly region in West Papua.

HOODED BUTCHERBIRD

Cracticus cassicus 32 cm F: Cracticidae

Morten Strange

Description: Unmistakable, apart from the Black-backed Butcherbird, *C. mentalis*, which overlaps in the Trans-Fly area. Distinguished from that species by its black (not white) throat and breast.

Voice: Vocal; a variety of noisy gurgles and clear, whistling notes; also mimics.

Habits: Found in tall primary rain-forest, often near clearings, roadsides and edges of cultivation. Occurs from the lowlands into hills reaching 1,400 m. Calls loudly from a high perch in a massive forest tree. Conspicuous and sociable, always two or more birds together. Flies low from tree to tree, feeding on invertebrates and fruits as shown in this photo.

Distribution: New Guinea. A generally fairly common resident in West Papua and most nearby islands.

BLACK BUTCHERBIRD
Cracticus quoyi 34 cm F: Cracticidae

Description: The only all-black butcherbird; distinguished from other black birds by the long, strong, greyish bill typical of this small Australasian family.

Voice: A loud, ringing *qua wen qua*.

Habits: A forest bird found in closed lowland and coastal mangroves. Occurs from sea level to 750 m; seen rarely to 1,400 m. Usually stays within the canopies, where it feeds on insects, small reptiles and fruits. Sometimes located by call, but rarely seen clearly. In Australia, where this photo was taken, it feeds in gardens, but this does not happen in Indonesia.

Bill Coster/Windrush Photos

Distribution: New Guinea into northern Australia. A generally scarce resident in West Papua and nearby Misool, Waigeo, Yapen and Aru islands.

VOGELKOP BOWERBIRD
Amblyornis inornatus 25 cm F: Ptilonorhynchidae

Description: A nondescript dull brown bird with a big head and strong bill. The sexes are similar (top). A characteristic bower is a cone-shaped hut decorated with coloured flowers, stones and plastic bits (bottom).

Voice: A metallic *chuck chuck*.

Habits: Found in primary rainforest at montane elevations between 1,000 and 2,000 m. The Arfak mountains is a certain location for this unusual species, locally called Burung Pinta (the skillful bird). It is worth the tough hike into these steep mountains to see the spectacular display ground with its carefully sorted collection of small treasures. This bowerbird is shy and skulking.

Morten Strange

Distribution: Indonesian endemic. A locally fairly common resident in mountains on the Vogelkop Peninsula in West Papua only.

MACGREGOR'S BOWERBIRD

Amblyornis macgregoriae 26 cm F: Ptilonorhynchidae

Description: The female is a uniform dull brown colour. The male (photo) is similar, but has a large crest with an orange streak, showing well in the photo.

Voice: A harsh *urschweet urschweet*.

Habits: Found in upper montane primary forest, from 1,600 to 3,300 m. Seen rarely at lower montane elevations around 1,200 m. The male displays at a bower of small twigs built up around a sapling on the forest floor. This bird is shy and skulking, so good views are difficult to obtain. Sometimes spotted in the canopy of a large forest tree, where it feeds on insects or small fruits.

C. & D. Frith; Frithfoto

Distribution: New Guinea. A generally scarce resident in upper montane parts of central West Papua.

MACGREGOR'S BIRD OF PARADISE

Macgregoria pulchra 39 cm F: Paradisaeidae

Description: Unmistakable; the only member of its genus and unlike any other bird. Its yellow primaries are barely visible when perched, but flash in flight.

Voice: A repeated *jeet jeet*.

Habits: This peculiar bird looks like a cross between a chicken and a crow, and is the only member of its family restricted to the upper montane zone between 3,200 and 3,500 m. Scarce but quite predictable and easy to find. Flies conspicuously between the low, stunted trees at the edge of the alpine zone with characteristic, rustling wing-beats. Sometimes feeds in bushes near the ground in the early morning hours and again in the late afternoon.

Morten Strange

Distribution: New Guinea. A very local and low-density resident in upper montane parts of central West Papua. Vulnerable to global extinction due to low numbers and hunting pressure.

PARADISE CROW

Lycocorax pyrrhopterus 42 cm F: Paradisaeidae

Description: Plumage appears all black, but it is in fact a very dark brown with somewhat paler wings. A unique bird, the only member of its genus.

Voice: An explosive and penetrating *wu-unk*.

Habits: Although this bird looks like a crow, it is in fact a bird of paradise, one of the two species to enter Wallacea. Little is known about its feeding and breeding habits since it is very shy and difficult to observe. Found in primary forest and forest edges; also ventures into nearby wooded cultivated areas. Occurs from the lowlands to 1,500 m. Flies through the forest among the canopies, often calling loudly. Has been observed in fruiting trees, but also takes some small prey.

Morten Strange

Distribution: Indonesian endemic. A generally scarce resident on Halmahera, Bacan, Obi and smaller adjacent islands.

TRUMPET MANUCODE

Manucodia keraudrenii 28 cm F: Paradisaeidae

Description: Distinguished with great difficulty from the three other all-black members of this genus in West Papua, by its glossy, shaggy mane of loose neck feathers.

Voice: A loud trumpet-like blast; also a weaker croak and a bell-like call.

Habits: Restricted to primary rainforest; occurs mainly in the hills and at lower montane elevations between 200 and 2,000 m. Looks somewhat like a gigantic *Aplonis* starling, but is shy and skulking. Like all manucodes, it is difficult to observe. Moves inside the upper or middle storeys of dense rainforest and is sometimes spotted flying quickly from one large tree to the next.

C. & D. Frith; Frithfoto

Distribution: New Guinea into Cape York Peninsula, Australia. A scarce resident on Vogelkop Peninsula and southern West Papua including the Aru Islands.

MAGNIFICENT RIFLEBIRD

Ptiloris magnificus 33 cm F: Paradisaeidae

Description: The female shown in the photo is similar to the female of the sympatric Twelve-wired Bird of Paradise, except for its brown cap and pale supercilium. Male is all-black, with a glossy blue breast. Captive photo.

Voice: A loud, liquid *woiieet-woit*.

Habits: Inhabits closed rainforest and sometimes forest edges, from the lowlands into lower hills; recorded to 1,400 m. Shy and skulking; usually moves within the canopies of large trees, but is also sometimes seen low and near the ground. Clambers about catching invertebrates, sometimes using its long bill as a chisel; also takes some fruits. Male calls and displays from a high perch, but good views are difficult in this habitat.

Distribution: New Guinea into Cape York Peninsula, Australia. A widespread but possibly fairly common resident in West Papua.

WALLACE'S STANDARDWING

Semioptera wallacei 27 cm F: Paradisaeidae

Description: Male (photo) is unmistakable. The female is plain brown and lacks elongated plumes on breast and back.

Voice: A variety of barking calls.

Habits: This forest bird usually stays within primary forest, but is sometimes also found in nearby closed secondary growth. Best seen in early morning at daybreak, when males perform spectacular displays to attract females into a large display tree in the forest. A local guide is required to find the location of these trees. During the day this bird is very shy and retiring, often heard but rarely seen. Moves high in the trees, feeding on fruits and invertebrates.

Distribution: Indonesian endemic. A locally fairly common resident on Halmahera, Bacan and Kasiruta.

TWELVE-WIRED BIRD OF PARADISE

Seleucidis melanoleuca 34 cm F: Paradisaeidae

Description: Photo shows an immature male during display; the mature male has a black breast, yellow belly and six wire-like feathers bending out from each side of tail. A monotypic genus.

Voice: A piercing, resonant *hahrr* and *koi koi koi*.

Habits: Restricted to primary rainforest in the extreme lowlands, such as flat alluvial swamp forest right at sea level. In Indonesia there are huge expanses of this special habitat, north and south of the Snow Mountains. Just before dawn the male displays prominently, calling loudly from a high, open perch while crawling around like a squirrel, but leaves abruptly at sun-up. During the day this species is difficult to find.

Distribution: New Guinea. A local and apparently low-density resident in extreme lowland parts of West Papua.

Morten Strange

SHORT-TAILED PARADIGALLA

Paradigalla brevicauda 23 cm F: Paradisaeidae

Description: Note the diagnostic greenish wattle on forehead. The sexes are similar. Distinguished from the rare Long-tailed Paradigalla, *P. carunculata*, from the Vogelkop and western Snow Mountains, by its smaller size and stubby tail.

Voice: A melodious *hoo ee* and a soft *churr churr churr*, which can be confused with the call of the sympatric Superb Bird of Paradise.

Habits: Occurs in primary forest and along forest edges at altitudes between 1,600 and 2,600 m. Shy and skulking, like all members of this family, and not often recorded in Indonesia. Sometimes spotted as it moves through the canopy and middle storey of moss forest.

Distribution: New Guinea. An uncommon resident in montane parts of central West Papua.

Morten Strange

BLACK SICKLEBILL

Epimachus fastuosus 110 cm F: Paradisaeidae

Morten Strange

Description: Photo shows female. Note its long tail and decurved bill. The male is uniformly black, with an even longer tail, the longest in the family.

Voice: A penetrating, liquid *quik quik*.

Habits: Occurs in tall primary rainforest between 1,300 and 2,100 m. Where it does not compete with next species extends to 2,500 m. The male calls and displays early in the morning, from a high perch deep inside the forest. Travelling and viewing conditions in this habitat are difficult, and getting to location early enough is a challenge. The female sometimes appears during the day, feeding in fruiting trees and mixing with honeyeaters and other birds of paradise.

Distribution: New Guinea. A generally scarce resident in montane parts of West Papua. Vulnerable to global extinction due to patchy distribution and hunting pressure.

BROWN SICKLEBILL

Epimachus meyeri 100 cm F: Paradisaeidae

Morten Strange

Description: Note the extremely long tail of the male (left and right photos); plumage is a sooty brown. Female is similar to the previous species, with a somewhat shorter tail and a diagnostic blue (not brown) iris.

Voice: A penetrating and explosive *ta-ta-ta-ta* that sounds remarkably like a rifle burst.

Habits: Found only in the upper montane zone, from 2,000 to 3,100 m. At higher elevations in the Snow Mountains, it seems to replace the previous species. Restricted to primary moss forest with large trees. The male calls loudly for about half an hour at dawn from some of the highest branches in the forest. Apart from that the bird is difficult to find.

Distribution: New Guinea. A generally scarce resident in upper montane parts of central West Papua.

SPLENDID ASTRAPIA

Astrapia splendidissima 46 cm F: Paradisaeidae

Description: Male (photo) is unmistakable; the female is duller and lacks the iridescent green colour. Brown underparts are barred with black.

Voice: A characteristic dry rattle: *greee*.

Habits: Found in primary montane moss forest between 1,800 and 3,500 m. A large and handsome bird of paradise that is frequently encountered at the right elevations. The male calls throughout the day from a hidden perch inside the canopy. Shy and skulking, it moves through the upper and middle storeys, flying briefly into the next tree. Gleans insects from the moss-covered trunks and thin branches. Also feeds in fruiting trees.

Morten Strange

Distribution: Indonesian endemic. A locally common resident in upper montane parts of Snow and Star mountains of West Papua.

SUPERB BIRD OF PARADISE

Lophorina superba 25 cm F: Paradisaeidae

Description: The male, shown in photo, is unmistakable. Note the spectacular, iridescent, permanently extended breast shield. The female is much like the following species, but is a smaller size, with a pale eyebrow.

Voice: A frequently heard harsh and penetrating 7–10 notes: *chee chee chee;* vocal throughout the day.

Habits: A shy, skulking forest bird found in primary forest at lower montane elevations. Occurs mainly between 1,500 and 1,800 m, but has been recorded from 1,200 to 2,300 m. This adaptable bird also moves into disturbed forest edges and isolated patches of scrub in cultivated areas. Probably the most numerous bird of paradise within its range.

Brian J. Coates

Distribution: New Guinea. A locally fairly common resident in the lower montane parts of West Papua.

WESTERN PAROTIA

Parotia sefilata 33 cm F: Paradisaeidae

Description: Male (top) is black with a greenish iridescent breast patch and elongated plumes on head, barely visible here. Female (bottom) is similar to the female of the previous species, but is larger and darker.

Voice: A harsh *gnaad gnaad*.

Habits: Occurs in a small geographical area and then only in the lower montane zone between 1,400 and 1,800 m. Seems to be quite numerous in primary rainforest within this small range. The male clears a display ground on the forest floor, much like that of the Magnificent and Wilson's Bird of Paradise. A local guide is required to find the location of the display.

Morten Strange

Distribution: Indonesian endemic. A locally fairly common resident in montane parts of the Vogelkop Peninsula of West Papua only.

KING OF SAXONY BIRD OF PARADISE

Pteridophora alberti 22 cm+head plumes F: Paradisaeidae

C. & D. Frith; Frithfoto

Description: The male (photo) has incredible 40-cm plumes extending from each side of its head. Note its yellow belly; upperparts are blackish. The female is a dull greyish colour, with scalloped underparts. A monotypic genus.

Voice: A short, insect-like, sputtering call.

Habits: Occurs in primary rainforest at altitudes between 1,500 and 2,800 m. This humid and rich habitat is dominated by very tall, moss-covered trees and tangled undergrowth. The male calls and displays high in a forest tree, as shown in the photo. This shy, low-density species is difficult to find in the dense vegetation on steep mountain slopes. However, a local guide can take you to the right location.

Distribution: New Guinea. A generally scarce resident in montane parts of central West Papua.

KING BIRD OF PARADISE

Cicinnurus regius 16 cm F: Paradisaeidae

Description: The male, shown in photo, is an unmistakable red bird with a white belly. Note two elongated tail feathers. The female is grey with finely barred underparts, brown wings and pale bill. A unique bird, here placed in its own genus.

Voice: A harsh, rolling call *kraan kraan kraan*.

Habits: Found in lowland rainforest, often in tall wet alluvial forest right at sea level. Also occurs in hills further inland at altitudes to 300 m; seen rarely to 850 m. The male of this species displays high in tangled vines and creepers in the middle storey, 15 to 20 m off the ground. Good views are often difficult in this dark environment, but its display is noisy, active, conspicuous and lasts all morning.

Morten Strange

Distribution: New Guinea. A generally scarce resident in West Papua and nearby Misool, Salawati, Yapen and Aru islands.

MAGNIFICENT BIRD OF PARADISE

Diphyllodes magnificus 18 cm F: Paradisaeidae

Description: Male (photo) is unmistakable. Note its orange wings and yellow neck feathers raised above the head during display. Female is distinguished with difficulty from other female birds of paradise by its bluish bill and patch behind the eye.

Voice: A variety of harsh and clearer notes near its display ground.

Habits: Prefers lower hills, from the coast to 1,500 m, although it avoids flat, alluvial swamp forest right at sea level. The male is best seen in early morning, performing at its display ground (lek) deep inside primary rainforest. Local people know where to find one. Feeds in fruiting trees during the day, often with other members of this unusual family.

Brian J. Coates

Distribution: New Guinea. A generally scarce resident in West Papua and the nearby Yapen and possibly Misool islands.

WILSON'S BIRD OF PARADISE

Diphyllodes respublica 17 cm F: Paradisaeidae

C. & D. Frith; Frithfoto

Description: Male (captive photo) is unmistakable within its range. Note its blue cap, red back and wings, and spiral tail feathers. The female is a greyish brown, with barred underparts and blue cap. This species and the previous similar species make up this monotypic genus.

Voice: Much like those of the previous species.

Habits: Similar to the previous species. The small Batanta Island, with access by boat from Sorong, is the most popular place to find this endemic. The rugged and expensive journey with a local guide, to the display ground inside the forest, culminates in an hour's uphill hike before dawn.

Distribution: Indonesian endemic. A generally scarce resident on the small islands of Waigeo and Batanta off mainland West Papua only.

GREATER BIRD OF PARADISE

Paradisaea apoda 44 cm F: Paradisaeidae

Morten Strange

Description: The male (photo) is distinguished from the following species by its dark (not pale brown) breast. The breeding male has yellowish plumes extending from under its wing. The female is a uniform brown. Captive photo.

Voice: A striking variety of deep and high-pitched raucous calls: *wauk-wauk* and *ki-ki*.

Habits: Usually found in primary forest; also occurs in disturbed secondary forest and nearby wooded cultivation, from sea level to 900 m. Best viewed at a large display tree where males gather in the morning. There is easy access to a display tree in Wasur National Park, close to Papua New Guinea. During the day, the birds disperse into the forest to feed on fruits and invertebrates.

Distribution: New Guinea. A locally fairly common resident in southern West Papua and the Aru islands

LESSER BIRD OF PARADISE

Paradisaea minor 32 cm F: Paradisaeidae

Description: Female (photo) distinguished from the previous species by its pale brown mantle and white breast and belly. The male is similar to the previous species, but is much smaller and has a paler breast. The two species apparently replace each other geographically.

Voice: Similar to that of the previous species, a loud series: *waik-waik* and *wok-wok*.

Habits: Found in primary rainforest, from sea level to lower hills inland at 1,000 m; rarely seen to 1,600 m. Also moves into forest edges and cultivated areas, to feed on fruits and insects. Females are seen much more often than mature males, which are seen best at the display site.

Distribution: New Guinea. A locally fairly common resident in northern and western West Papua, including the nearby Misool and Yapen islands.

Morten Strange

RED BIRD OF PARADISE

Paradisaea rubra 33 cm F: Paradisaeidae

Description: Unmistakable within its small range. The male (captive photo) has distinctive red tail plumes and long tail 'wires'. The female looks like the previous species, but has a black face and iris, and a yellowish breast.

Voice: A variety of deep, high-pitched, raucous calls: *wak-wak* and a higher *ka-ka*.

Habits: Found in primary lowland rainforest up to 600 m. There is a display tree near the village of Wai Lebed at the beach on Bantana Island that provides good views of this elusive species. This is the last of the three Indonesian members of the *Paradisaea* birds of paradise that exemplify this diverse family. In Papua New Guinea there are three additional species, plus a blue variety.

Morten Strange

Distribution: Indonesian endemic. A generally scarce resident on Waigeo, Bantana, Gemien and Saonek islands off mainland West Papua. Near-threatened with global extinction.

CRESTED JAY

Platylophus galericulatus 33 cm F: Corvidae

Description: Distinguished from the Black Magpie, *Platysmurus leucopterus* (of Sumatra and Kalimantan and with similar habitat, colour and behaviour), by its very long crest and white on neck. Together they form their own genus.

Voice: A loud, harsh rattle *tut-ut-ut-ut.*

Habits: A rainforest specialist usually found in primary forest. Occasionally seen near forest edges, but always inside cover. Occurs from the lowlands up to 1,000 m on Sumatra; in Kalimantan found to 1,100 m and possibly higher. Both of these forest Corvidae are noisy and rowdy, flying about in the dark middle storey below the forest canopy.

Distribution: Sunda subregion. A widespread but generally uncommon resident in Sumatra, Kalimantan and Java.

GREEN MAGPIE (Common Green Magpie)

Cissa chinensis 38 cm F: Corvidae

Description: Unmistakable in Indonesia. The Short-tailed Magpie, *C. thalassina*, is similar, but occurs rarely on Java only, see Strange (2000).

Voice: A peculiar variety of explosive whistles and chattering.

Habits: A mainly lower montane bird found between 700 and 2,100 m. Inhabits primary rainforest and edges, moving in the middle and lower storeys, often in pairs or as part of a bird wave. This shy and retiring bird only briefly emerges from cover. Otherwise it clambers about in the foliage, looking for large insects and small vertebrate prey. Best located by its call.

Distribution: Oriental region. A generally scarce resident in montane parts of Sumatra and Kalimantan.

SUNDA TREEPIE

Dendrocitta occipitalis 40 cm F: Corvidae

Description: Unmistakable. Photo shows the Borneo subspecies, treated by M&P (1993) as a separate species, *D. cinerascens*. Sumatran subspecies has a brown (not grey) back and white nape.

Voice: A clear, bell-like whistle and a rattling chattering.

Habits: A rainforest bird found in primary forest, along forest edges and occasionally in nearby cultivation. On Sumatra occurs from 800 to 2,300 m; rarely recorded down to 400 m. Gunung Kerenci is a good location for this species. This vocal and conspicuous bird moves through the canopies on the lookout for large insects; also takes small fruits.

Distribution: Borneo and Sumatra. A fairly common resident in montane parts of Sumatra and Kalimantan.

RACKET-TAILED TREEPIE

Crypsirina temia 35 cm F: Corvidae

Description: The combination of plumage, habitat and skulking behavior makes it unmistakable.

Voice: A soft mewing and a harsh *craak-craak*.

Habits: Found in forest edges and open woodland. Often occurs in mangroves and coastal scrub inland up to 1,500 m. Unlike the drongos, it does not hawk for insects and does not come to the ground like black crows. Creeps about in small trees like a malkoha (F: Cuculidae), and makes short flights to the next tree, the long tail dangling behind.

Distribution: Southeast Asia. In Indonesia found only on Java and Bali, where it is a generally scarce resident; a vagrant in south Kalimantan.

LONG-BILLED CROW

Corvus validus 49 cm F: Corvidae

Description: Distinguished from the sympatric Torresian Crow, *C. orru* (46 cm) of Maluku, east into Australia, by larger bill and long neck in flight.

Voice: A soft barking *ukk-ukk* call, less harsh than other crows'.

Habits: Mainly a forest bird found in primary forest, along edges and in nearby wooded cultivation, from the coast into lower montane hills. Quite conspicuous, often calls from an exposed perch high in the trees. Does not come to the ground like other members of this genus. Forages at canopy or middle storey level, but little information is available on preferred food or nesting habits.

Morten Strange

Distribution: Indonesian endemic. A widespread and fairly common resident on Halmahera, Bacan, Obi and some smaller adjacent islands.

LARGE-BILLED CROW

Corvus macrorhynchos 51 cm F: Corvidae

Description: Look for all-black plumage and large bill. The Slender-billed Crow, *C. enca* (of forests in the Sunda subregion and Sulawesi), has a narrow bill and shallow wing-beats.

Voice: A harsh *arr.*

Habits: Found in open country with large trees, often near coastal areas and villages. Also occurs inland at higher elevations, on Timor recorded at 2,000 m. Omnivorous; habitually scavenges and feeds on the ground, but flies into big trees to rest and nest. Seems to have declined in numbers in Indonesia and can no longer be classified as common.

Morten Strange

Distribution: Oriental region. A widespread but generally scarce resident on Sumatra, Java, Bali and parts of Nusa Tenggara; vagrant in Kalimantan.

GLOSSARY

Adult: mature plumage bird.

Allospecies: two closely related species replacing each other geographically.

Aquatic: water-living.

Arboreal: tree-living.

Australasia: a faunal region including Eastern Indonesia, New Guinea, Australia, New Zealand and the South-west Pacific.

BBNP: Bali Barat (= West Bali) National Park.

Bird wave: a mixed species flock feeding on invertebrates while moving through the forest.

Casque: an enlargement of the upper part of the bill on hornbills.

Conspecific: of the same species.

Coronal: along the edge of the crown.

Crepuscular: active in weak light at dusk and dawn.

Deciduous: leafless for part of the year (the cold or the dry season).

Diagnostic: a feature that establishes identification of a species.

Dimorphic: has two distinctive plumage types.

Dipterocarp: a hardwood tree of the Dipterocarpaceae family.

Diurnal: active by day.

Echolocate: to navigate in total darkness by sound.

Extinct: no longer present in area concerned.

Feral: domesticated population.

Frugivorous: feeding on fruits.

Genera: the plural of genus.

Genus: a division into which a bird family is divided.

Gregarious: congregates into social flocks.

Gunung: Indonesian for mountain.

Immature: used here to refer to any plumage stage older than juvenile and younger than adult.

Insectivorous: feeding on insects.

Juvenile: bird that has just fledged the nest.

Kelong: offshore fishing platform.

Local: unevenly distributed.

Migrant: a species that has moved temporarily away from its breeding area, usually to a warmer climate.

Monotypic: the sole representative of its species, genus or family.

Montane: pertaining to mountains; used here for areas above 900 metres elevation.

Nocturnal: active by night.

Nomadic: moves outside resident range when not breeding.

Non-breeding visitor: can be found at any time during the year, but no evidence of breeding.

Ocellus: an eye-like spot in the plumage; plural is ocelli.

Oriental: a faunal region including south and Southeast Asia.

Paddy: wet rice field.

Palearctic: a faunal region covering Europe, north Africa and northern Asia and south to the Yangtze River; here used synonymously with Eurasia.

Passerine: a perching bird of the order Passeriformes including all families from Broadbills to the end of sequence.

Pelagic: ocean-living.

Pied: patterned in black and white.

Plume: an elongated (display) feather.

Primary forest: original, virgin forest.

Race: synonymous with subspecies.

Raptor: a popular term for a bird of prey from the order Falconiformes, e.g. the Accipitridae or Falconidae family.

Resident: a species breeding or believed to be breeding in that area.

Secondary forest: logged or otherwise disturbed forest.

Sedentary: present in its breeding area all year; antonym for migratory.

Shorebird: long-legged water bird of the suborder Charadii, i.e. primarily the Charadriidae or Scolopacidae family.

Stenotopic: confined to only one type of habitat.

Storey: a level in the forest.

Straggler: a bird found outside its usual geographical range.

Streamer: a greatly elongated tail feather.

Subspecies: a population visibly distinguishable from other populations of the same species (sometimes only in the hand).

Sunda: a faunal subregion covering the Malay Peninsula, Borneo, Sumatra, Java and Bali.

Supercilium: eye-stripe.

Sympatric: same distribution.

Terrestrial: ground-living.

Vagrant: very rare, irregular and accidental in occurrence.

Wader: popular term for shorebird.

Wallacea: a faunal subregion covering Sulawesi, Maluku and Nusa Tenggara.

Wattle: a patch of coloured skin hanging from the head or neck.

SELECTED BIBLIOGRAPHY

The following is a list of works used in the preparation of this book. Additional information was extracted and compiled from articles in *Kukila*, Volumes 1–10, published by the Ornithological Society of Indonesia, and in the *OBC Bulletin* and the *Forktail*, published by the Oriental Bird Club.

Andrew, P. (1992), *The Birds of Indonesia: A Checklist (Peter's Sequence)*, Indonesian Ornithological Society, Jakarta.

Beehler, B.M., Pratt, T.K. & Zimmerman, D.A. (1986), *Birds of New Guinea*, Princeton University Press, New Jersey.

Coates, B.J., Bishop, K.D. & Gardner, D. (1997), *A Guide to the Birds of Wallacea*, Dove Publications, Queensland.

Collar, N.J., Crosby, M.J. & Stattersfield, A.J. (1994), *Birds to Watch 2; The World List of Threatened Birds*, BirdLife International, Cambridge.

del Hoyo, J., Elliott, A. & Sargatal, J. (eds.) (1992-97), *Handbook of the Birds of the World*, Vol. 1–4, Lynx Editions, Barcelona.

Flegg, J. & Madge, S. (1995), *Photographic Field Guide—Birds of Australia*, New Holland, London.

Gibbs, D. (1990), 'Wallacea: A site guide for birdwatchers', Private trip-report.

Gibbs, D. (1993), 'Irian Jaya 1991: A site guide for birdwatchers', Private trip-report.

Gosler, C. (1991), *The Photographic Guide to Birds of the World*, Reed International Books Limited, London.

Hornbuckle, J. (1988), 'Birding in Indonesia—Spring 1988', Private trip-report.

Howard, R. & Moore, A. (1991), *A Complete Checklist of Birds of the World*, Academic Press Limited, England.

Inskipp, T., Lindsey, N. & Duckworth, W. (1996), *An annotated Checklist of the Birds of the Oriental Region*, Oriental Bird Club, England.

Jepson, P. & Ounsted, R. (eds.) (1997), *Birding Indonesia*, Periplus Editions (HK) Ltd, Singapore.

King, B., Woodcock, M.W. & Dickinson, E.C. (1975), *A Field Guide to the Birds of South-East Asia*, Collins, London.

Kinnaird, M. (1995), *North Sulawesi: A Natural History Guide*, Wallacea Development Institute, Jakarta.

Lekagul, B. & Round, P.D. (1991), *A Guide to the Birds of Thailand*, Sah Kharn Bhaet Co., Bangkok.

Lewis, A., Morris, P. & Higgins, N. (1989), 'Thailand and Malaysia Dec 1988–Aug 1989', Higgins, Lewis and Morris, England.

Lim, K. S. & Gardner, D. (1997), *Birds: An Illustrated Field Guide to the Birds of Singapore*, Sun Tree Publishing, Singapore.

MacKinnon, J. & Phillipps, K. (1993), *A Field Guide to the Birds of Borneo, Sumatra, Java and Bali*, Oxford University Press, London.

Marle, J.G. van & Voous, K. H. (1988), *The Birds of Sumatra: An annotated check-list*, British Ornithologists' Union, London.

Mason, V. & Javis, F. (1989), *Birds of Bali*, Periplus Editions (HK) Ltd, Singapore.

Oosterzee, P. van (1997), *Where Worlds Collide; The Wallace Line*, Cornell University Press, New York.

Periplus Editions (1998), *Indonesia Travel Atlas*, Periplus Editions (HK) Ltd, Singapore.

Poonswad, P. & Kemp, A.C. (eds.) (1993), *Manual to the Conservation of Asian Hornbills*, Hornbill Project, Thailand.

Prieme, A & Heegaard, M. (1987), *Birdwatching in the Far East 86*, Danish Ornithological Society, Copenhagen.

Sibley, C.G. & Monroe, B.L. (1990), *Distribution and Taxonomy of Birds of the World*, Yale University Press, New Haven & London.

Smythies, B.E. (1981), *The Birds of Borneo*, The Malayan Nature Society, Kuala Lumpur.

Stone, D. (1994), *Tanah Air: Indonesia's Biodiversity*, Archipelago Press, Singapore.

Strange, M. (1998), *Birds of South-east Asia*, New Holland, London.

Strange, M. (1998), *Tropical Birds of Southeast Asia*, Periplus Editions (HK) Ltd, Singapore.

Strange, M. (2000), *A Photographic Guide to the Birds of Southeast Asia, including the Philippines and Borneo*, Periplus Editions (HK) Ltd., Singapore.

Strange, M. & Jeyarajasingam, A. (1993), *Birds: A Photographic Guide to the Birds of Peninsular Malaysia and Singapore*, Sun Tree Publishing, Singapore.

Tho, L.W. (1957), *A Company of Birds*, London.

Turner, K. & Smith, S. (1992). 'Birding in Irian Jaya', Private trip-report.

Verbelen, F. (1996), 'Birding in Sumba and Timor', Private trip-report.

Verbelen, F. (1996), 'Birding in Seram, Kai and Tanimbar', Private trip-report.

Wheatley, N. (1996), *Where to Watch Birds in Asia*, Christopher Helm, London.

White, C.M.N. & Bruce, M.D. (1986), *The Birds of Wallacea: An annotated check-list*, British Ornithologists' Union, London.

Whitmore, T. C. (1981), *Wallace's Line and Plate Tectonics*, Clarendon Press, Oxford.

Most of these titles include more extensive lists of relevant books and papers. Unpublished trip reports produced by travelling birdwatchers are often another valuable source of current and first-hand information. Eight such reports are listed here. These and more are available from the Oriental Bird Club.

The following three societies continuously publish news on Indonesian birds and will be able to provide specialized information:

Oriental Bird Club
The Lodge
Sandy
Bedfordshire SG19 2DL
U.K.
Web site: http://www.orientalbirdclub.org/

Ornithological Society of Indonesia
P.O. Box 310
Bogor 16003
West Java
Indonesia

BirdLife International Indonesia Programme
Jl. Jend. A. Yani 11
Bogor 16161
P.O. Box 310/Boo
Bogor 16003
Tel: 62-251-333234/371394
Fax: 62-251-357961
E-mail: birdlife@indo.net.id

Since new titles on Indonesian birdlife appear almost every year, it is recommended to check for the latest issues with:

Nature's Niche Pte. Ltd.
Botanic Garden Shop
1 Cluny Road
Singapore 259569
Tel: 65-4752319
Fax: 65-4751597
E-mail: nniche@singnet.com.sg

INDEX OF COMMON NAMES

INDEX OF SCIENTIFIC NAMES